The Philosophy Student Writer's Manual

Anthony J. Graybosch
California State University, Chico

Gregory M. Scott
University of Central Oklahoma

Stephen M. Garrison
University of Central Oklahoma

SECOND EDITION

Prentice Hall
Upper Saddle River, New Jersey 0745

Library of Congress Cataloging-in-Publication Data

Graybosch, Anthony.
     The philosophy student writer's manual / Anthony J. Graybosch,
Gregory M. Scott, Stephen M. Garrison.— 2nd ed.
          p. cm.
     Includes index.
     ISBN 0-13-099166-X
     1. Philosophy—Authorship.   2. Philosophy—Study and teaching.
I. Scott, Gregory M.   II. Garrison, Stephen M.   III. Title.
B52.7 .G73 2003
808'.0661—dc21

2002011445

*To
Divna
Jeremy
Melissa*

VP/Editorial Director: Charlyce Jones-Owen
Senior Acquisitions Editor: Ross Miller
Executive Managing Editor: Jan Stephan
Production Liaison: Joanne Hakim
Editorial/Production Supervision: Bruce Hobart (Pine Tree Composition)
Prepress and Manufacturing Buyer: Brian Mackey
Art Director: Jayne Conte
Cover Designer: Bruce Kenselaar
Marketing Manager: Chris Ruel
Copy Editor: Carol Lallier

This book was set in 10/12 New Baskerville by Pine Tree Composition, Inc.,
and was printed and bound by Hamilton Printing Company.
The cover was printed by Coral Graphics.

© 2003, 1998 by Pearson Education, Inc.
Upper Saddle River, New Jersey 07458

Printed in the United States of America
10   9   8   7   6   5   4   3   2   1

ISBN: 0-13-099166-X

Pearson Education LTD., *London*
Pearson Education Australia PTY, Limited, *Sydney*
Pearson Education Singapore, Pte. Ltd
Pearson Education North Asia Ltd, *Hong Kong*
Pearson Education, Canada, Ltd., *Toronto*
Pearson Educación de Mexico, S.A. de C.V.
Pearson Education—Japan, *Tokyo*
Pearson Education Malaysia, Pte. Ltd
Pearson Education, *Upper Saddle River, New Jersey*

Contents

Preface   x

I   An Introduction to the Discipline of Philosophy   1
I.1   Philosophy Is Nothing New   1
I.2   Are You Dreaming?   2
I.3   What Is Philosophy?   8
I.4   What Does Philosophy Accomplish?   11

PART ONE A Handbook of Style for Philosophy   15

1   Writing as Communication   17
1.1   Writing to Learn   17
    1.1.1   Challenge Yourself   20
    1.1.2   The Nature of the Writing Process   22
    1.1.3   Maintaining Self-Confidence   22
1.2   Organizing Your Writing   23
    1.2.1   The Nature of the Process   23
    1.2.2   Selecting a Topic   24
    1.2.3   Narrowing Your Topic   24
    1.2.4   Defining a Purpose   25
    1.2.5   Finding a Thesis   28
    1.2.6   The Thesis Sentence   30
    1.2.7   Defining Your Audience   32
1.3   Invention Strategies   33
    1.3.1   Free Writing   33
    1.3.2   Brainstorming   34
    1.3.3   Asking Questions   35
    1.3.4   Outlining   36
        1.3.4.1   Outlining for Yourself   36

iii

1.3.4.2   Outlining for Your Reader   37
1.3.4.3   Formal Outline Papers   37
1.3.5   Organizing Your Thoughts   38
1.4   The Rough Draft   38
1.4.1   Language Choices   39
1.4.1.1   Level of Formality   40
1.4.1.2   Descriptive Language   40
1.5   Revising Your Writing   42
1.5.1   Editing   44
1.5.2   Catching Mistakes   45
1.5.3   Miscues   45
1.5.4   Proofreading   46

2 *Writing Competently* 49

2.1   General Rules of Grammar and Style   49
2.1.1   Competent Writing   49
2.1.1.1   Consider Your Audience   50
2.1.1.2   Aim for Consistency   51
2.1.1.3   Have Confidence in What You Know   51
2.1.1.4   Eliminate Chronic Errors   51
2.2   Sentence Structure   52
2.2.1   Fused Sentences   52
2.2.2   Sentence Fragments   53
2.2.3   Dangling Modifiers   54
2.2.4   Parallelism   54
2.3   Pronoun Errors   56
2.3.1   *Its* Versus *It's*   56
2.3.2   Vague Pronoun References   56
2.3.3   Pronoun Agreement   57
2.3.4   Shift in Person   57
2.4   Punctuation   58
2.4.1   Apostrophes   58
2.4.2   Capitalization   59
2.4.2.1   When to Capitalize   59
2.4.2.2   When Not to Capitalize   60
2.4.3   Colons   61
2.4.4   Commas   61
2.4.4.1   The Comma Splice   61
2.4.4.2   Commas in a Compound Sentence   62
2.4.4.3   Commas in a Series   62
2.4.4.4   Commas with Restrictive and Nonrestrictive Elements   63
2.4.5   Quotation Marks   63
2.4.5.1   When to Use Quotation Marks   64

2.4.5.2 Quotation Marks in Relation
to Other Punctuation 65
2.4.6 Semicolons 65
2.5 Spelling 66
2.5.1 Commonly Confused Words 66
2.5.2 Commonly Misspelled Words 67
2.6 Technical and Ordinary Usage of Philosophical Terms 69

PART TWO *Conducting Research in Philosophy* **71**

3 *Organizing the Research Process* 73

3.1 Gaining Control of the Research Process 73
3.2 Effective Research Methods 77
3.3 Ethical Use of Source Material 83

4 *Information in Your Library and Similar Places* 87

4.1 Information Resources in Your College Library 87
4.1.1 Directories 87
4.1.2 Dictionaries 91
4.1.3 Periodicals 91
4.1.4 Periodical Indexes 93
4.2 Research Institutes 94

5 *Philosophy and Cyberspace* 95

5.1 Narrow Sources of Information 96
5.2 General Sources of Information 98
5.2.1 Four Major Directories 98
5.2.2 Encyclopedias 99
5.2.3 Directories of Texts 99
5.2.4 Advice on How to Write a Philosophy Paper 99
5.2.5 Internet Resources for Writing Well 99
5.3 Advice for Distance Learners 100

6 *Formats for Philosophy Papers* 104

6.1 Getting Started 104
6.2 General Page Format 105

6.3   Title Page   106
6.4   Abstract   107
6.5   Table of Contents   107
6.6   Lists of Tables and Figures   108
6.7   Text   109
6.8   Chapter Headings   109
6.9   Illustrations and Figures   109
6.10 Reference Page   110
6.11 Appendixes   110

7 Citing Sources   111
7.1   Preliminary Decisions   111
      7.1.1   What to Document   112
      7.1.2   Which Citation System to Use   112
      7.1.3   The Importance of Consistency   112
      7.1.4   Using the Style Manual   113
7.2   Documentary-Note System: Numbered References   113
      7.2.1   General Format Rules   113
              7.2.1.1   Numbering System   113
              7.2.1.2   Placement of Superscript Numerals   113
              7.2.1.3   Multiple Notes   114
      7.2.2   Models for Documentary Notes
              and Bibliographical Citations   114
              7.2.2.1   Differences Between Endnotes
                        and Bibliography   114
              7.2.2.2   Books   114
              7.2.2.3   Periodicals   119
              7.2.2.4   Public Documents   121
              7.2.2.5   Electronic Sources   123
              7.2.2.6   Interviews   126
              7.2.2.7   Unpublished Sources   127
              7.2.2.8   Subsequent or Shortened References
                        in Notes   128

PART THREE How to Think and Write Like a Philosopher   131

8 Principles of Argument   133
8.1   The Throws of Argument   133
8.2   The Definition of an Argument   135
8.3   The Two Basic Types of Argument   136
8.4   Validity and Soundness   137

       8.4.1   Deductive Validity   137
       8.4.2   Nondeductive Validity   137
       8.4.3   Cogency   139
  8.5 Patterns of Reasoning   139
  8.6 Valid Forms of Argument   140
       8.6.1   Tautologies   141
       8.6.2   Modus Ponens   142
       8.6.3   Hypothetical Syllogisms   142
       8.6.4   Modus Tollens   144
       8.6.5   Dilemmas   145
       8.6.6   Indirect Proof or Reductio
              ad Absurdum   145
       8.6.7   Contradictions   146
       8.6.8   Analogies   146
       8.6.9   Induction by Elimination   147
       8.6.10 Induction by Enumeration   147
       8.6.11 Inference to the Best Explanation   148
       8.6.12 The Hypothetical-Deductive Method   148
  8.7 Applications   149
  8.8 A Map of How to Arrange a Philosophy Paper   150

9   *Avoiding Fallacies*   *152*

  9.1 Formal Fallacies   152
       9.1.1   Denying the Antecedent   152
       9.1.2   Affirming the Consequent   153
       9.1.3   The Exclusive Fallacy   153
  9.2 Informal Fallacies   154
       9.2.1   Susceptibility to Fallacies   154
       9.2.2   Invalid Appeal to Authority   155
       9.2.3   Straw Person   156
       9.2.4   Inconsistency   156
       9.2.5   False Dilemma   156
       9.2.6   Complex Question   157
       9.2.7   Begging the Question   157
       9.2.8   Suppressed Evidence   157
       9.2.9   Lack of Proportion   158
       9.2.10 Appeal to Unknowable Statistics   158
       9.2.11 Ad Hominem   158
       9.2.12 Guilt by Association   158
       9.2.13 Two Wrongs Make a Right   158
       9.2.14 Equivocation   159
       9.2.15 Appeal to Ignorance   159
       9.2.16 Composition   159
       9.2.17 Division   159

9.2.18   Hasty Conclusion   159
9.2.19   Questionable Cause   160
9.2.20   Questionable Analogy   160
9.2.21   Appeal to Pity   161
9.2.22   Appeal to the Stick   161
9.2.23   Appeal to Loyalty   161
9.2.24   Provincialism   161
9.2.25   Popularity   162
9.2.26   Double Standard   162
9.2.27   Invincible Ignorance   162
9.3   Identifying Fallacies   162
9.4   Calculating Probabilities   163
9.5   Emotive Language   164

10 Writing Sound Arguments   167
10.1   What Is a Position Paper?   167
10.2   The Steps to Writing a Position Paper   168
10.2.1   Selecting a Topic   168
10.2.2   Conducting Research   169
10.2.3   Selecting a Position   170
10.2.4   Defining Premises   170
10.2.5   Constructing an Outline   171
10.2.6   Checking for Fallacies   173
10.2.7   Writing the Argument   174
10.2.8   Testing the Argument   174
10.2.9   Revising the Argument   175
10.3   The Format of a Position Paper   175

11 History of Philosophy Papers   176
11.1   A Very Short History of the Great Philosophers   176
11.2   How to Write a History of Philosophy Paper   180
11.3   Hints on Writing History of Philosophy Papers   181
11.4   The Contents of a History of Philosophy Paper   183

12 Writing Applied Ethics Papers   184
12.1   What Is Ethics?   185
12.2   The Distinction Between Fact and Value   187
12.3   Approaches to Ethics   188
12.3.1   Consequentialism   188
12.3.2   Deontology: Kant   192

12.3.3   Other Ethical Theories   196
12.4   Perennial Issues for Political Ethics: Justice and Rights   198
12.5   Applying Ethical Theories and Political Philosophy   202
12.6   Professional Codes of Ethics   204
12.7   Analyzing a Professional Code of Ethics   206

13   Writing a Personal Ethics Statement   208
13.1   Examples of Famous Statements of Ethics   209
    13.1.1   Kindergarten Wisdom   209
    13.1.2   Ten Commandments   209
    13.1.3   Man is Born in Tao   210
    13.1.4   Declaration of Independence   211
    13.1.5   Humanist Manifesto II   211
    13.1.6   Thus Spoke Zarathustra   212
    13.1.7   The Unabomber Manifesto   213
13.2   Writing Your Own Personal Code of Ethics   213
    13.2.1   Situation 1   214
    13.2.2   Situation 2   214
    13.2.3   Situation 3   214
    13.2.4   Situation 4   215
13.3   The Contents of a Personal Ethics Statement   215
13.4   Two Sample Student Ethics Statements   215
    13.4.1   Jeremy Scott's Essay   215
    13.4.2   Chris Allen's Essay   219
13.5   Writing a Critique of a Brief Ethics Statement   223
    13.5.1   Target Statement Selection   224
    13.5.2   Target Statement Analysis   224
    13.5.3   System Definition   224
    13.5.4   Criteria Definition   225
    13.5.5   Verify Identification   225
    13.5.6   Error Identification   225
    13.5.7   Conclusion   225

14   Sample Student Papers   226
14.1   A Paper from Personal Values: *The Matrix*   226
14.2   A Paper from Biomedical Ethics: *Stem Cell Research*   232
14.3   A Group Paper from Moral Issues in Parenting: *Should We Be Raising Altruists?*   237

Glossary   247

Index   255

Preface

TO THE STUDENT

One of the most frustrating tasks students face is mastering the requirements of the different disciplines they encounter in their college careers. Philosophy presents a particularly difficult challenge, since most students do not study philosophy in a formal manner until they reach college. I know I find myself sitting all by my lonesome self in the auditorium during summer orientation for incoming students who have declared interest in particular majors. My colleagues in other disciplines are swamped, but I have time for reading. So before I describe how this book is going to benefit you, let me make the following unpaid commercial announcement: Philosophy majors score significantly higher than all other humanities and social science majors on standardized tests for admission to graduate and professional study. This includes tests for business, medical, and law school. Majoring in philosophy is one of the wisest investments you can make in your education.

Philosophy is an un-American discipline. As Americans, we are entitled to believe anything we want to believe. But philosophy actually challenges your entitlement to a view. It is impolite. It asks for reasons for even our most cherished and "private" beliefs, such as those about religion. Perhaps this is because philosophers do not believe that there are any views that are truly private. Or perhaps the philosopher you encounter in your first class is devoted more to the validity of the process by which you arrive at a belief than to the truth of the belief itself. I wish philosophy were taught at an earlier age, in elementary school and high school. But there is significant opposition to including religion in public schools, let alone the critics of religion. In any case, beginning philosophy students are puzzled at being asked to express a view on a controversial topic. And then further dismay is occasioned when simply stating an opinion is not enough. The instructor expects not only a personal view but a reasoned defense in addition!

Many students take courses in college that encourage them to describe their feelings. In one of the first undergraduate courses I taught, a student wrote in the first person about the morality of abortion. She told me that she had been impregnated by a man who was not her boyfriend, that it was difficult for her current boyfriend to accept her pregnancy, and that she had considered abortion and rejected the option as not right for her. However, she was concerned that other women have a right to abort. Her paper went on for several pages. I kept reading, looking for an argument that never appeared, and ended up feeling that I had inadvertently invaded her privacy. And any grade I would be tempted to put on her papers could be a negative evaluation of her life.

In philosophy, we are not really interested in people, but in arguments. I did not want to validate or condemn the author of the abortion paper. I was interested, and left uninformed, as to why she felt her boyfriend had a right to an opinion on her abortion, what reasons had played a significant part in her decision, and why the reasons that were not good enough for her might be good enough for those other women whose choice she was inclined to protect. In other words, I would never want to tell her that her decision was wrong; but perhaps I would say that she had no right to her decision.

If you have just come from a class in which expression of feelings and exposition of life history and your inner voice were emphasized, then you may be frustrated by different expectations. Expectations in philosophy are different than they are in some other disciplines. But rest assured, if you learn how to write good argumentative essays, this skill will assist you in many other courses, your professional career, and your life as a citizen. You will not be an easy mark for the various hucksters whom we face in our daily life.

The Philosophy Student Writer's Manual contains all the material you need to write successful philosophy papers. The introduction is a brief discussion of skepticism meant to illustrate the nature of philosophy for those taking their first philosophy course. Chapters 1 through 9 focus on the basics of good writing, research, and philosophical argument. The lists of sources in Chapter 4 provide descriptions of major reference works, such as the *Encyclopedia of Philosophy,* as well as specialized reference encyclopedias such as those devoted to bioethics and philosophy of religion. Chapter 5 presents sources available through the Internet, such as discussion lines, and the American Philosophical Association's home page on the World Wide Web. Chapter 6 discusses the format expected by philosophy journals, and so should be of particular interest to those preparing for a career in philosophy. Chapter 7 offers a comprehensive description of source citation and bibliographical formatting procedures for research papers.

Chapters 10 through 13 are, for the most part, devoted to specific types of philosophy papers. Philosophy is such a broad field that it is impossible to include chapters on every philosophy course you might encounter. Some attention has been paid to writing for the most popular undergraduate courses. But the chapters on philosophical argument and ethics should provide guidance even if your particular course is missing. New to this edition, Chapter 14 includes samples of student writing from introductory courses to use as models for your writing.

A glossary is also provided, and I recommend that you scan it for the occurrence of terms you feel you already understand. One difficulty philosophy presents is that it uses terms from ordinary language and other disciplines in a technical manner. It is not uncommon for terms like *idealism, pragmatism,* and *utilitarian* to be bandied back and forth between class participants without any communication going on at all. I have included a section in Chapter 2 on the most common equivocal terms.

TO THE TEACHER

I dread correcting the first writing assignment of the semester. There are always a few students who have shown interest in philosophy and have made good contributions to class discussion who demonstrate that they have serious trouble with the written word. Perhaps your students are consistently better prepared than mine. But you probably find it difficult to justify the class time it takes to explain the different expectations they face in philosophical writing from the more exegetical approaches of other disciplines. Or you may teach courses in professional and applied ethics that have no prerequisites. I do. I teach ethics and criminal justice. Students come in ready to discuss questions like police use of deadly force, corruption, discretion, and undercover work. But it is quite likely that they have little or no background in ethical theory or argumentative writing. If any real philosophical thinking is going to occur in the course, we must first spend considerable time on the basics of ethical theory. And the expectation that a paper or essay go beyond regurgitation leads many students to feel frustrated.

In *The Philosophy Student Writer's Manual* your students will find the necessary tools—background in philosophy, helpful writing strategies, research tips, and format instructions—for philosophical writing. This text should allow you to spend more time on content and also allow you greater flexibility in selecting course readings. With the writer's manual, you can construct a reader tailored to your course with exactly the material you desire instead of adopting an anthology that will always be an imperfect fit. This manual will also be helpful in distance learning courses, again allowing you to spend more time answering content questions than answering questions about format or research.

If you are teaching business ethics, you can direct your students to material that explains basic ethical theories, references to business ethics journals, explanations of common logical fallacies, suggestions on drawing up an outline, basic guidance on using electronic research tools, and a glossary of philosophical terms. This manual allows you to spend more class time on your subject and less time giving instruction on the basics of writing or philosophy.

Your comments and corrections are most welcome. I hope that you will place models of good student writing on your own homepage to supplement the few I have included in the manual. And I would certainly like to include links to such items on my homepage. My email address currently is agraybosch@csuchico.edu, and the homepage is http://www. csuchico.edu/~graybosc.

Thanks to the editorial staff at Prentice Hall, especially Ross Miller and Carla Worner for their interest and advice on this edition and to Bruce Hobart, the production editor at Pine Tree Composition. I would like to extend a special thanks to the Prentice Hall reviewers, especially Charles L. Reid, Youngstown State University, for their invaluable comments and suggestions. And thanks to my colleagues at Chico—Marcel Daguerre, Ron Hirschbein, and Becky White—for the samples of student work they suggested for this edition.

Anthony J. Graybosch

An Introduction to the Discipline of Philosophy

In the distribution of functions, the scholar is the delegated intellect. In the right state, he is, Man Thinking. *In the degenerate state, when the victim of society, he tends to become a mere thinker, or, still worse, the parrot of other men's thinking.*

—Ralph Waldo Emerson, *The American Scholar,* 1837

Nothing comes to sleepers but a dream.

—Lowell Fulson

I.1   PHILOSOPHY IS NOTHING NEW

Even if this is your first philosophy class, you have been doing philosophy all your life. All of us have thought and even argued about the big questions of philosophy: free will, the existence of God, and the nature of knowledge. If you are partial to literature or film, especially science fiction, you have considered such questions as these: Can there be a thinking machine? If so, does it have a soul? *Do Androids Dream of Electric Sheep?* asks the title of a novel by science fiction writer Philip K. Dick. But you don't have to be a moviegoer or a science fiction buff to "do" philosophy; it permeates all aspects of our lives.

Like any good philosopher, children are always asking embarrassing questions. Perhaps it is this embarrassment that causes us to teach our children, as they grow, to avoid philosophy. We prefer to sidestep conflict, and we still follow the old adage "Don't discuss religion or politics." But to reject this advice, to embrace the conflict that always attends a worthwhile argument, is to begin to practice philosophy.

What you learn in this book about constructing arguments and writing critically will serve you well in other disciplines. Your psychology course, for example, may have different writing standards, especially regarding footnoting and bibliographical formats, which in a psychology paper will probably correspond to the guidelines prevalent in the social sciences and not the humanities. But good argumentative writing in psychology shares fundamental characteristics with good argumentative writing in philosophy, and the same is true for the writing you will do in your history class, your economics class, or your class in American literature. Since the fundamentals of argumentative writing are always the same, why not learn them from the originators and the experts—in other words, from philosophers?

The purpose of this book is to introduce you to the basics of philosophical writing. We will be concerned with how you should, and should not, engage in doing and writing philosophy. Along the way we will do quite a lot of philosophy. Studying philosophy without actually philosophizing would be like taking a course in aesthetics without ever listening to a piece of music or reading a poem or a short story. In fact, even before we move on to Chapter 1, we are going to explore a standard philosophical question in order to give you a feel for philosophical argumentation.

I.2   ARE YOU DREAMING?

How do we know that we are not dreaming? This question, once raised by the French philosopher René Descartes (1596–1650), always sparks a variety of answers on day one of my Introduction to Philosophy class. One student will say that we can determine we are not dreaming by pinching ourselves. Sometimes another student reports that she does not dream in color, so if she is having visual presentations—in other words, if she is seeing something—in color, then she is not dreaming. There is always one student who says that he would ask someone else. And then, after a little discussion, someone says it is a stupid question.

These commonsense responses are so natural that they must be valid in some context. What I mean is that, in a rough-and-ready manner, the type of knowledge they illustrate and support is, in most situations, good enough. Someone asks you if the New York Jets will be in the Super Bowl next year. You reply, "No." If the person then asks, "How do you know?" your first response is not to assume that he is asking you the question "How do we know anything?" which is a question about the foundation of knowledge. Rather, you ask your interrogator if perhaps he would like to make a wager on whether the Jets will be playing in the Super Bowl this January or watching the game on television.

"Are you dreaming?" is, in most contexts, like the question "Are you paying attention?" asked by a teacher. The proper response to your teacher is to sit up straight and reply, "Yes, ma'am, I was just thinking about the Pythagorean theorem," or whatever else the teacher is trying to teach you. In ordinary contexts, these two questions are not taken literally. The former is really a challenge to your seriousness about whatever topic is being discussed. The latter is a request for a promise that you will begin paying attention, or at least look like you are.

But despite its oddness when taken literally, the question "Are you dreaming?" raises some serious questions. It is not enough to offer the replies given by students in my intro class. Some of us do dream in color, or at least report that we do. And even if we had visual presentations at different times of two types, colored and shades of gray, we could not justify, simply on the basis of the variety of pigments, saying that one was an experience of reality and the other was not.

Nor is the idea of pinching ourselves to see if we can experience pain a good reply to the question. I have had dreams in which I experienced a great deal of pain. When I woke up I was very pleased to realize that I still had my arms and legs. But while the dream was going on, I "felt" like I was in pain. So when I pinch myself now and do feel pain, I have to realize that I might just be dreaming and, in the dream, dreaming that I feel pain. After all, when I am dreaming and am pinched, I do dream that I feel pain.

As to asking someone if I am now dreaming, that will not help at all. People in dreams are no more reliable than people in real life. The person I ask may be a liar, or the dream person I ask may be dreamt as a liar. And in any case, what person could be reliable enough to know if I am dreaming if I cannot know it myself?

All you biology and psychology majors out there are dying to tell me that someone else could tell whether I was dreaming by looking for REMs (rapid eye movements). You might not be able to tell me while I am dreaming that I am dreaming, but you certainly could tell me when I woke up. We could imagine a lab in which someone is asleep. The lab instructor—let's call him Professor Skinner—says to psychology student Freud, "Mr. Freud, go determine if Jung is dreaming." Freud goes over and peeks under Jung's eyelids, discovers REMs, and reports back to Professor Skinner, "Yes, Jung is dreaming." So Skinner says, "Remember to tell him he was dreaming when he wakes up. Now, Mr. Freud, look at the next patient, Mr. Adler, over there on the other slab."

This lab scene we have invented is similar to commonsense contexts. The lab instructor and his student Mr. Freud have a tacit agreement as to what counts as grounds for saying that a patient is dreaming: the presence of REMs. Our lab inhabitants are no different, really, from the commonsense reasoners that I get in my classes, those advocating pinching or some other proof. The lab just has its own set of rules for being justified in saying that so-and-so is dreaming. Does this mean that a good answer to the question of dreaming in your perceptual psychology class may not be a good answer in your philosophy class? Yes, it does. It also suggests that the philosopher is asking a different question, or at least emphasizing an aspect of a question that is usually taken for granted elsewhere.

I probably have no need to point this out, but our Mr. Freud has no way of knowing that he is actually in a lab performing an experiment. He cannot ask Professor Skinner. Skinner might be just a dream. And Jung, he is asleep. And Adler, he does not dream, so the question makes no sense to him.

So what is the philosophical question that Descartes was asking when he raised this dream issue? Locating the question is an important task in reading philosophy. And once you determine what the question is, stop and give your own preliminary answer. This will help you organize the material and develop a critical stance on the topic. Printed below is what he said. But before you read Descartes, try to answer the following questions to your own satisfaction:

- How do you know at this moment that you are not dreaming?
- Does it make sense to look for a proof of your own existence?
- Do other people have minds, feelings, dreams? How do you know?
- When Kasparov lost his chess match to Deep Blue, should you have concluded that either the program or the machine had ideas?
- What is the philosophical question, or questions, that the dream argument raises?

It is now some years since I detected how many were the false beliefs that I had from my earliest youth admitted as true, and how doubtful was everything I had since constructed on this basis; and from that time I was convinced that I must once for all seriously undertake to rid myself of all the opinions which I had formerly accepted, and commence to build anew from the foundation, if I wanted to establish any firm and permanent structure in the sciences. . . .

Now for this object it is not necessary that I should show that all of these are false—I shall perhaps never arrive at this end. But inasmuch as reason already persuades me that I ought no less carefully withhold my assent from matters which are not entirely certain and indubitable than from those which appear to me manifestly to be false, if I am able to find in each one some reason to doubt, this will suffice to justify my rejecting the whole. . . . [F]or owing to the fact that the destruction of the foundations of necessity brings with it the downfall of the rest of the edifice, I shall only in the first place attack those principles upon which all my former opinions rested.

All that up to the present time I have accepted as most true and certain I have learned from the senses or through the senses; but it is sometimes proved to me that these senses are deceptive, and it is wiser not to trust entirely to any thing by which we have once been deceived. . . .

I must remember that I am a man, and that consequently I am in the habit of sleeping, and in my dreams representing to myself the same things or sometimes even less probable things, than those who are insane in their waking moments.

. . . At this moment it does indeed seem to me that it is with eyes awake that I am looking at this paper; that this head which I move is not asleep, that it is deliberately and of set purpose that I extend my hand and perceive it; what happens in sleep does not appear so clear nor so distinct as does all this. But in thinking over this I remind myself that on many occasions I have in sleep been deceived by similar illusions, and in dwelling carefully on this reflection I see so manifestly that there are no certain indications by which we may clearly distinguish wakefulness from sleep that I am lost in astonishment. And my astonishment is such that it is almost capable of persuading me that I now dream. (*The Philosophical Works of Descartes*. Vol. 1. Ed. Elizabeth S. Haldane and G. R. T. Ross. New York: Cambridge University Press, 1911. 144–146.)

Much of this passage is written in the first person. First person writing is normally avoided in philosophy and most academic writing, but Descartes is hoping that his confession will strike a chord of recognition in his readers. He is hoping that they, too, will say that they have had a similar experience. Descartes is searching for agreement to several important premises he needs to launch his dream argument and asking the reader to reason along with him.

A premise is a claim that is used to support a further claim. Philosophers would like all their premises to be supported by good arguments, to be borne out as conclusions of good arguments. But no matter how supportive a premise can be to a particular claim, there is always the question of what supports the premise. In other words, no matter how far we go in any investigation, we philosophers tend to feel a need to find support for each new piece of evidence.

Descartes' problem of the justification of ultimate premises has led many philosophers to embrace the view that there are some ultimate premises that do not depend on other premises for their justification. Such philosophers are generally called foundationalists. Descartes is a foundationalist. Foundationalists believe that some true or warranted premises are given; foundationalists do differ on what special mark these givens possess and whether the knowledge of the given is reiterative. That is, foundationalists disagree over whether being in a state of basic knowledge guarantees that a person knows that she is in such a state.

But Descartes is a foundationalist with a mission: He wants to make sure that the ultimate premises he believes in are error-free. Although he does not explicitly state it, in the first paragraph of his meditation he accepts a tacit premise that it is very hard to discover all possible sources of error. So although he may have become aware of some false premises he accepted in his youth and is now suspicious of anything else he learned from the same sources, he simply may not remember where all his youthful premises came from, and so he knows that he may still discover further false beliefs. The only way he can be sure that his knowledge, which he compares to a building with a foundation, is reliable is to tear it down and begin again with a new foundation. This leaves him with the problem of how to build a new, error-free foundation of knowledge. What tools should he use? What sorts of "knowledge" should he discard?

In his second paragraph Descartes asks us to withhold belief not only from false premises but also from those that we have any reason to doubt. Then he moves on to consider how trustworthy his senses are as tools for discovering trustworthy beliefs. He knows that he cannot investigate each individual premise we have come to accept through our sensory experience of the world of trees and automobiles. That would be an impossible task to complete. But if there is some reason to doubt the reliability of the source of all these empirical beliefs, then we should doubt the whole class.

Descartes is not arguing that sense always gives us false beliefs. Rather, he argues that because sense is sometimes confused with dreaming, we cannot sort out those contexts in which we are being given false sensory beliefs in dreams from those contexts in which we are being given reliable sensory beliefs by our actual, waking senses. The fact that we cannot determine when we are dreaming rather than sensing throws doubt on the fact that we are sensing, not dreaming, now and in each context in the past when we thought we were sensing.

At this point in the argument, Descartes' "reasonable" premise about when we should withhold belief seems to suggest that we should believe nothing that is based on the senses. Sure enough, it is possible to come up with situations in which the senses don't seem completely trustworthy. For example, your senses may tell you the first line below is longer than the second. When you measure them, however, they turn out to be equal.

But do such examples really mean that you must doubt all the data supplied by the senses (including the measuring)? Not necessarily. This is not a knockout argument against the senses because, odd as it may sound, you must accept the reliability of the senses (your ability to make a measurement) in order to cast doubt upon them. Descartes cannot, after all, call the senses into question unless, at least in some contexts, they are beyond question.

So far, Descartes' question about dreaming has led him to question some of our most basic assumptions about life, such as the validity of cherished ideas and the trustworthiness of our senses. His argument about dreaming goes on, becoming more complex, implicating still other assertions that we commonly make about life. Ultimately, Descartes cannot claim with certainty that he knows whether he is dreaming or not. But what was his point in entertaining this rather odd question in the first place? Remember that we began looking at the dream argument in an attempt to see the philosophical—not psychological—issue animating it. What a philosopher wants to discover by considering dreaming is different from what a psychologist is interested in determining. Descartes has not undertaken his question in order to establish a laboratory definition of states of consciousness. He is looking, ultimately, for a way to determine those premises that belong in the foundation of knowledge. He is looking for an acid test of certainty. He is trying to preserve a particular picture of knowledge, the foundationalist picture.

The criterion for this test is not a psychological one. Imagine you receive a call from Wal-Mart saying your mom has been picked up for shoplifting. My response would be "Not my mom! You have the wrong number or the wrong Graybosch." And if security showed me a videotape of my mom putting Star Wars figures into her purse, I would think the tape had been doctored. I am psychologically incapable of thinking that my mom would steal anything. And I hope you have that type of certainty, also. But psychological certainty is not what Descartes is looking for. By doubting everything, Descartes is looking for premises there can be no reason to doubt. Those premises, if they exist, are the ones that will provide the foundations for the sciences—the ultimate premises. He is looking for evidential, not psychological, certainty. (Eventually, Descartes came to believe that he had established a class of "clear and distinct" premises that are safe from doubt.)

So, in a sense, the dream argument is not really about dreaming. It is an example of an argument that allows us to enter into a philosophical discussion of the nature and possibility of human knowledge. Philosophers often approach questions very indirectly. We begin with a common question that embodies or provokes a philosophical discussion.

Used by permission of Benjamin Graybosch.

Within the discipline of philosophy, you will find philosophical activities classified according to how they are carried out today or how they were accomplished in different times and places. You will become familiar with the names of philosophical movements, such as pragmatism and idealism, and even movements associated with particular eras and geographic locations, such as Anglo-American (analytic) philosophy and continental philosophy. One basic contrast you will run into in much philosophical talk is a distinction between Western and non-Western or Eastern philosophy based in prevailing conceptions of reason. I hasten to add that there are representatives of so-called Western philosophy in non-Western philosophy and vice versa.

Many non-Western philosophers have been interested in the nature of dreams and dreaming. But a common concern with a phenomenon, even one as familiar as dreaming, does not guarantee a common interpretation or perception of its nature. Chuang Tzu, a Taoist philosopher who lived in China sometime between 400 and 295 BCE, used dreams to raise important metaphysical and moral questions. Here is a passage from Chuang Tzu's "The Equality of Things," in which Tzu conceives of the relationship between dreaming and reality in a way different from Descartes' conception.

> Once I, Chuang Tzu, dreamed that I was a butterfly and was happy as a butterfly. I was conscious that I was quite pleased with myself, but I did not know that I was Tzu. Suddenly I awoke, and there I was, visibly Tzu. I do not know whether it was Tzu dreaming that he was a butterfly or the butterfly dreaming that it was Tzu. (*A Sourcebook in Chinese Philosophy*. Ed. Wing-tsit Chan. Princeton: Princeton

University Press, 1963. 189–190. I have profited from the discussion of this passage in Gary Kessler. *Voices of Wisdom.* Belmont, CA: Wadsworth Publishing Co., 1991. 1–3.)

For Chuang Tzu, the experience of dreaming leaves him unable to tell what kind of existence is properly his own. Is he ultimately a butterfly or a man? But what is important is that whether he is a man or a butterfly, Chuang Tzu still undergoes both experiences. There is a fundamental underlying unity that holds the two together. Chuang Tzu does not take the road Descartes travels. He does not try to distinguish reality by separating illusion from truth. Instead, Chuang Tzu accepts all experience as equally real. The common experiences of being a different entity yet the same person, of being unable to distinguish dream from waking life, lead him to seek a view of reality in which conflicting claims are reconciled in a deeper unity. And if this unity exists within the self, the microcosm, then it will exist for reality as a whole, the macrocosm.

Descartes and Chuang Tzu use dreaming as a launch pad for a larger argument about the nature of reality, but their approaches and their conclusions are different. You may not want to accept Chuang Tzu's conclusion about reality. Perhaps you are more inclined to Descartes's view of reality, which holds that reality can be comprehended in separate, discrete parts. But this brief exposure to Chang Tzu's view of dreams should provoke you to wonder what place Descartes assigns to dreams in a person's psychic life as well as how each philosopher approaches the question of self-identity.

Let's stop here and do a little philosophy. Answer the following questions:

- Should Chuang Tzu's story of the butterfly be taken seriously? Literally?
- Does it make sense to compare our ordinary relationships to dreams? Are some of our email relationships akin to dreams?
- Isn't Chuang Tzu's attempt to reconcile conflicting perspectives by asserting an underlying unity a case of circular, and therefore flawed, reasoning?
- Are philosophical questions worthless because they are incapable of being answered once and for all? Does philosophy ever make any progress?
- From what you have read so far, do you feel that philosophy is hostile to religious belief?

I.3 WHAT IS PHILOSOPHY?

Philosophy is both a discipline—an area of study—and an internalized mode of doing something. Philosophers are guided by the principle that nothing should be allowed to stand in the way of inquiry. Since many of the ideas worth inquiring about are the ones that people feel a great deal of attachment to, philosophers often seem either silly or irreverent. They question beliefs that many of us take for granted, such as the existence of an external world. And they want to discuss questions that our culture has labeled private and immune to polite challenge, such as the existence of God or the definition of terrorism.

One concept of philosophy is that it is a discipline committed to a reasoned investigation of any significant area of existence. It tries to uncover presuppositions of cherished beliefs and subject them to further discussion. Consider the following exchange between Socrates and the theologian Euthyphro, in which the concept of piety, or reverence shown toward a deity, is given a philosophical workout. When we join the discussion, Socrates and Euthyphro have already agreed to distinguish between what subjectively pleases the gods (and so might be identified by a list of examples) and what objectively makes an action worthy of being appreciated by the gods (and so could be used to recognize all examples of piety independently of a list.).

Socrates: [I] can only ask again, what is the pious, and what is piety? Do you mean that they are a science of praying and sacrificing?

Euthyphro: Yes, I do.

Socrates: Then piety, Euthyphro, is an art which gods and men have of doing business with one another? . . . I wish, however, that you would tell me what benefit accrues to the gods from our gifts. . . . If they give everything and we give nothing, that must be an affair of business in which we have greatly the advantage of them.

Euthyphro: And do you imagine, Socrates, that any benefit accrues to the gods from our gifts?

Socrates: But if not, Euthyphro, what is the meaning of the gifts which are conferred by us upon the gods?

Euthyphro: What else, but tributes of honor; and, as I was just now saying, what pleases them?

Socrates: Piety, then, is pleasing to the gods, not beneficial or dear to them?

Euthyphro: I should say nothing could be dearer. . . .

Socrates: Were we not saying that the holy or pious was not the same with that which is loved of the gods? . . . And are you not saying that what is loved of the gods is holy; and is not this the same as what is dear to them—do you see?

Euthyphro: True.

Socrates: Then we were either wrong in our former assertion; or, if we were right then, we are wrong now. (*The Dialogues of Plato.* "Euthyphro." Trans. Benjamin Jowett. Vol. 1. New York: Random House, 1937. 13a–16a.)

The question is, Where does piety fit? And this question suggests the larger one of why humans should bother to pray. No topic is immune from philosophical investigation.

Notice that Socrates and Euthyphro agree on at least one claim: The gods are not the sort of creatures who need human assistance. They could still have discussed piety without this agreement, but their difficulty in arriving at an answer to the question of the nature of piety partially depends on this agreement. After all, if the gods did need human assistance, then—as Socrates and Euthyphro obviously realize—the gods would not be the gods! You may not be able to settle on a particular definition of piety, but you can come to see that if you believe something about the nature of the gods, you will be committed to other specific views on issues such as the nature of piety, the existence of human free will, and the possibility of divine foreknowledge of our choices. Certain beliefs logically require you to hold other beliefs, which in turn saddle you with still others.

The dialogue between Socrates and Euthyphro demonstrates that Wilfred Sellars was right when he defined philosophy as the study of the ways things in general hang together. How is that for a clear and concise definition of philosophy? But Socrates and Plato would prefer that we notice that the dialectic method is applied in the interest of determining whether a definition commits us to an inconsistency. That is the dilemma Socrates raises for Euthyphro at the end of the selection and the reason he offers for renewing the inquiry.

Socrates and his student Plato, who wrote the dialogues in which Socrates is the primary speaker, have their own concept of philosophic inquiry called the Socratic method. You have just seen it in action in the above passage from the dialogue "Euthyphro." The Socratic method requires the philosopher or teacher to ask the other participant in the dialogue question after question, basing each new question on the participant's responses. Often a participant is required to offer a definition, as Euthyphro does for piety, and then to answer questions about it. The questions are aimed at clarifying the reasoning behind the beliefs of the participant, who sometimes, in the course of the dialogue, discovers errors in his beliefs. Sometimes the Socratic method leads to no particular conclusion, as in the above discussion of piety. But that's all right. The point of the Socratic method is not to assert the superiority of the philosopher's position at all costs, but to clarify positions and to reveal error in order to arrive, if possible, at truth.

In this case Euthyphro clearly does not want to say prayer or sacrifice benefit the gods. That would be inconsistent with the notion of the gods as self-sufficient. So he claims that the gods are merely pleased by displays of honor. Socrates is testing his definition of piety to see if it leads to an inconsistency, which Euthyphro avoids by retreating from benefit to appreciation. Socrates then reminds him of an earlier agreement that being pleasing to the gods was an accidental, a contingent, aspect of the pious and not its essence. The invitation with which the selection closes is to revisit the argument that led to the earlier conclusion inconsistent with the present definition. And the dialogue ends with a comical representation of a theologian who is too busy to continue a discussion of piety. What could be more important for Euthyphro?

Can we put all our attempts at definition together and come up with a coherent notion of what philosophy is? We might be able to do so if we stayed within the Western philosophical tradition. But even then we would fall short by making very minimal claims. For instance, some people think that Socrates was not trying to get us to reach any philosophical truths. These people treat him as a skeptic who perhaps believed that happiness came from realizing that he knew nothing. Socrates himself supposedly remarked that he was the wisest of all men because others thought they knew something and he knew that he knew nothing. The inconsistency inherent in claiming that one knows that one knows nothing is just too obvious for it not to be a Socratic flourish.

But if I have to point to the core of philosophy, I would have to say that it is a discipline in which one is always on the road to a conclusion. As Stanley Cavell said, philosophers are indeed the hoboes of thought. Philosophers consider arguing with people to be a sign of respect and believe that the unexamined life is not worth living. Some philosophers even believe that philosophy is the only road to a happy life. I would like to think that any good philosopher appreciates the process of seeking answers to questions that cannot be answered finally, and that this appreciation translates into both rigorous investigation and also a sense of humor informed by the human condition.

I.4   WHAT DOES PHILOSOPHY ACCOMPLISH?

Some philosophers, like Descartes, might tell you that philosophy's job is to provide the foundations of the natural and social sciences. Others might say that it tries to dissolve what we call philosophical questions by showing that they are based in category mistakes or outworn metaphors. Perhaps philosophy is just an attack on traditional religious and political beliefs. Or it may be the natural development of religious thought that moves from a narrative phase appropriate to a popular uneducated audience to a reasoned one appropriate for the more sophisticated elite. And there are even philosophers who would hold that philosophy has established some truths.

But perhaps the one goal of philosophy most often agreed upon is to help people lead a better life. Socrates understood this goal. His attachment to philosophy had made him a thoughtful person who would not embark upon a rash course of action. He was also a person who was interested in important issues and not trivial gossip or worldly success. I will not be rash enough to claim that a wider appreciation of philosophy would lead to a better society. But it does seem that philosophical inquiry allows you to form your own opinions about crucial issues in a manner appropriate to a free adult.

This goal of helping people live better has always been important in philosophy. Ancient philosophers worked to arrive at a concept of wisdom that would serve them in the effective pursuit of a truly happy life, and philosophers today pursue the same goal with growing interest, whether they are concerned with the philosophy of technology, professional ethics, or even the theory of knowledge. The notion that philosophy is concerned with human happiness is important to both Western and non-Western philosophic traditions, though with certain differences of approach.

As they invented Western philosophic thought, the Greeks generated a wide variety of rational constructions of the good life. By rational, I mean that Western philosophers have always sought to answer these questions on the basis of evidence that has withstood reasoned criticism. This is the response of Western philosophy to the narrative, often mystical answers given by the great religious traditions: The Western philosopher responds to creation stories with the question, Who made God? In the dialogue on piety sampled above, both Socrates and Euthyphro are concerned with the nature of the deity and the way humans should regard the divine.

Non-Western philosophy, however, often gives more credence to narratives and appeals to emotions and intuitions than Western philosophy does. Non-Western philosophy also has a greater tendency to respect the mystical and see unanswerable questions as occasions for intellectual and spiritual insight and growth. Consider the style of argument in the following selection from Chuang-Tzu:

> When an archer is shooting for nothing
> He has all his skill.
> If he shoots for a brass buckle
> He is already nervous.
> If he shoots for a prize of gold
> He goes blind
> Or sees two targets—
> He is out of his mind!
> His skill has not changed. But the prize
> Divides him. He cares.
> He thinks more of winning
> Than of shooting—
> And the need to win
> Drains him of his power. (*The Way of Chuang Tzu*. Trans. Thomas Merton.
>   New York: New Directions Press, 1965. 107.)

What conclusion does Chuang-Tzu want you to accept? What evidence does he offer? What is the source of the persuasive power of the "argument?"

The skeptic Sextus Empiricus (c. 200 CE) tells us that he began the study of philosophy in order to arrive at knowledge so that he could lead a good life. And, like the painter who wanted to depict foam at the mouth of a horse and only succeeded when he became frustrated and threw a sponge at the painting, Sextus arrived at happiness by accident. By coming to the view that he did not know if knowledge were even possible, he fell into a condition he calls *ataraxia*, which he tells us is freedom from belief—and in that freedom, he found happiness. So even a skepticism that suspects that knowledge is not possible for humans led to a vision of the good life.

PART ONE

A Handbook of Style for Philosophy

1

Writing as Communication

I will not have in my writing any elegance or effect or originality to hang in the way between me and the rest like curtains. I will have nothing hang in the way, not the richest curtains. What I tell I tell for precisely what it is.

—Walt Whitman, *Leaves of Grass*, 1855

To speak truly, few adult persons can see nature.

—Ralph Waldo Emerson, *Nature*, 1836

1.1 WRITING TO LEARN

Good writing is a way of ordering your experience. No matter what you are writing—it may be a paper for your class, a short story, a limerick, a grocery list— you are putting pieces of your world together in new ways and making yourself freshly conscious of these pieces. This is one of the reasons writing is so hard. From the infinite welter of data that your mind continually processes, you are selecting only certain items significant to the task at hand, relating them to other items, and phrasing them in a new coherence. You are mapping a part of your universe that has hitherto been unknown territory. You are gaining a little more control over the processes by which you interact with the world around you.

This is why the act of writing, no matter what it leads to, is never insignificant. It is always communication, if not with another human being, then with yourself. You may, for example, have consulted your notes on the night before the big exam and wondered, "Now what could I have possibly meant by that?" Writing is an attempt to order your world creatively and critically. It can also be a way of entering the world of others, communicating your own views. And when you fail to communicate, when you cannot understand your own notes, writing can indicate the areas of your world that need to be reexamined.

In graduate school I had a professor who advised me to write philosophy as if I were writing for the travel section of a newspaper. His explanation was that if I wrote about a place I had seen for an audience who may never get to visit it in person, I would be less likely to overlook needed details and would provide the transitions necessary for comprehension. Often students conceive their audience to be their instructor or other students in a class. You will do better to write for someone who has never visited the places you have been. A roommate or friend who has not taken the class or read the material can be a good test of whether you can communicate your ideas effectively or need to rework them in some way. And if you have a paper due, it is important to write the first draft a few days ahead of time. Sometimes, as in the case where we take notes we later cannot comprehend, we think we understand what we mean. If we write a paper and allow it to sit for a week and then revisit it, our lack of comprehension of our own past thoughts can point us in the directions we need to go to improve our work.

Writing, therefore, is also one of the best ways to learn. This statement at first may sound odd. If you are an unpracticed writer, you may share a common notion that the only purpose writing can have is to express what you already know or think. According to this view, any learning that you as a writer might do has already been accomplished by the time your pen meets the paper; your task is to inform or even surprise the reader. But if you are a practiced writer, you know that at any moment as you write, you are capable of surprising yourself. And it is surprise that you look for: the shock of seeing what happens in your own mind when you drop an old, established opinion into a batch of new facts or bump into an unquestioned belief from a different angle. Euthyphro has a hint that if he continues his discussion with Socrates, he will experience a shock. And so he withdraws.

Writing synthesizes new understanding for the writer. E. M. Forster's famous question "How do I know what I think until I see what I say?" is one that all of us could ask. We make meaning as we write, jolting ourselves by little, surprising discoveries into a larger and more interesting universe. We think much better when we use our pencils or keyboards than we do when we use just our brains.

The help that writing gives us with learning and with controlling what we learn is one of the major reasons why your instructors will require a great deal of writing from you. To write is to believe in something, and to know what we believe in is the product of successful writing. One of the things that all Americans have in common is the belief that they have a right to believe anything they want. Our private beliefs are like our homes, supposedly immune from invasion. John Stuart Mill thought that if all of society except for one person were in agreement on an issue, it would be wrong for society to silence the one dissenter. The dissenter can be of the greatest value to society by correcting a false belief or engaging the society in producing better arguments for its views. You can make little progress in doing philosophy, in learning how to argue your point of view or an as-yet unfixed new conclusion, unless you commit your ideas to dialogue with others. And one of the most effective ways of engaging in dialogue with others and with yourself is by committing your views to paper, disk, or an online discussion group.

Philosophy may require commitment to a variety of professions. If you are interested in the philosophy of science or law, then you will have to maintain an acquaintance with those fields also. You will also need to master enough of the history of philosophy to partake in the discussions that occur in your classes and with fellow students. There is also the technical side of philosophy, a field with its own specialized terms that, unfortunately, overlap with common expressions in a way that is not always illuminating. The term metaphysics, for example, means something different to your philosophy instructor than to the proprietor of an occult bookstore.

Writing is the entryway into philosophy and into public life as well. Virtually everything that happens in public life happens on paper first. Documents are wrestled into shape before their contents can affect the public. Great speeches are written before they are spoken. The last forty years have seen philosophers becoming increasingly involved in public life, at least indirectly. A great number of philosophy courses are applied courses. Philosophers are interested in the professional ethics of disciplines such as law and medicine. Feminist philosophers are major influences on your local and federal laws governing abortion and pornography. Philosophers participate in political life by writing and teaching on topics such as ethics in government, criminal justice, and nuclear war.

The written word has helped bring slaves to freedom, end wars, and shape the values of nations. Take Frederick Douglas's 5 July 1852 speech "What to the Slave Is the Fourth of July?" in which Douglas attacked the conscience of northern whites and helped fuel the New England opposition to slavery:

> What, to the American slave, is your 4th of July? I answer: a day that reveals to him, more than all other days of the year, the gross injustice and cruelty to which he is the constant victim. To him, your celebration is a sham; your boasted liberty, an unholy license. . . . ("What to the Slave is the Fourth of July?" 22 January 2001 *http://afgen.com/douglas.html*)

Douglas points out the inconsistency of a nation committed to equality and liberty that tolerates slaves while welcoming oppressed European immigrants to its shores.

Often gaining recognition for our ideas and ourselves depends less upon what we say than upon how we say it. While accurate and persuasive writing is absolutely vital to the philosopher, honesty is the primary virtue. We do not hide our premises in order to become more persuasive. How often do you read a newspaper editorial and find the writer telling you right off the bat what premises are the basis of the argument you are about to encounter and how the argument will proceed from premises to the conclusion? This is typical procedure for a philosopher.

1.1.1   Challenge Yourself

There is no way around it: Writing is a struggle. Writing is hard for everybody, great writers included. Bringing order to our thoughts about the world is never easy. The rewards of the writing struggle may include delight as well as understanding. The careful craftsmanship that went into the famous passage below, from Henry David Thoreau's *Walden*, is obvious. Think of what delight he must have felt at the completion of this argument. Notice how Thoreau first grasps his reader's attention with vivid images that reduce the life of labor to the ridiculous, flatters the audience with reference to the founding of Rome, marshals the Bible to support his praise of idleness, and then finally brings his point home by comparing the life of the so-called free person to that of a slave. Also apparent in the energy of the passage and the charm of its images is the joy that all writers experience when they have connected with a subject that matters to them and are finding their way through it with confidence.

I see young men, my townsmen, whose misfortune it is to have inherited farms, houses, barns, cattle, and farming tools; for these are more easily acquired than got rid of. Better if they had been born in the open pasture and suckled by a wolf, that they might have seen with clearer eyes what field they were called to labor in. Who made them serfs of the soil? Why should they eat their sixty acres, when man is condemned to eat only his peck of dirt? Why should they begin digging their graves as soon as they are born? They have got to live a man's life, pushing all these things before them, and get on as well as they can. How many a poor immortal soul have I met well nigh crushed and smothered under its load, creeping down the road of life, pushing before it a barn seventy-five feet by forty. . . . The portion less, who struggle with no such unnecessary inherited encumbrances, find it labor enough to subdue and cultivate a few cubic feet of flesh.

But men labor under a mistake. The better part of the man is soon ploughed into the soil for compost. By a seeming fate, commonly called necessity, they are employed, as it says in an old book, laying up treasures which moth and rust will corrupt and thieves break through and steal. It is a fool's life, as they will find when they get to the end of it, if not before. . . .

Most men, even in this comparatively free country, through mere ignorance and mistake, are so occupied with the factitious cares and superfluously coarse labors of life that its finer fruits cannot be plucked by them. . . .

I sometimes wonder that we can be so frivolous, I may almost say, as to attend to the gross but somewhat foreign form of servitude called Negro Slavery, there are so many keen and subtle masters that enslave both north and south. It is hard to have a southern overseer; it is worse to have a northern one; but worst of all when you are the slave-driver of yourself. (*Walden, or Life in the Woods.* New York: Library of America, 1985. 326–328.)

Even though we may not have Thoreau's talents, the writing process makes use of skills we all have. The ability to write, in other words, is not some magical competence bestowed on the rare, fortunate individual. We are all capable of phrasing thoughts clearly and in a well-organized fashion. But learning how to do so takes practice. The one sure way to improve your writing is to write.

One of the toughest but most important jobs in writing is to maintain enthusiasm for your writing project. Commitment may sometimes be hard to come by, given the difficulties inherent in composition—difficulties that can be made worse when the project assigned is unappealing at first glance. How, for example, can you be enthusiastic about having to write a paper analyzing Thomas Hobbes's theory of the social contract when you have never once thought about the justification of government and look upon the very process of providing such justification as the rationalizations of an oppressor?

One of the worst mistakes that unpracticed student writers sometimes make is to fail to assume responsibility for keeping themselves interested in their writing. No matter how hard it may seem at first to drum up interest in your topic, you have to do it—that is, if you want to write a paper you can be proud of, one that contributes useful material and a fresh point of view to the topic. If you are bored with your writing, your reader will be too. So what can you do to keep your interest and energy level high? Challenge yourself. Think of the paper not as an assignment for a grade, but as a piece of writing that has a point to make. To get this point across persuasively is the real reason why you are writing, not the simple fact that a teacher has assigned you a project. If someone were to ask you why you are writing your paper, what would you answer? If your immediate, unthinking response is, "Because I've been given a writing assignment," or "Because I want a good grade," or some other non-answer along these lines, your paper may be in trouble. If, on the other hand, your first impulse is to explain the challenge of your main point— "I'm writing to show that Thoreau's devaluation of ordinary labor illustrates a major fault in the transcendentalism he borrowed from Emerson that can be contrasted fruitfully with the attitude toward work developed by Karl Marx"—then you are thinking usefully about your topic.

1.1.2   The Nature of the Writing Process

As you engage in the writing process, you are doing many different things at once. While planning, you are no doubt defining the audience for your paper at the same time that you are thinking about the paper's purpose. As you draft the paper, you may organize your next sentence while revising the one you have just written. Different parts of the writing process overlap, and much of the difficulty of writing is that so many things happen at once. Through practice—in other words, through writing—it is possible to learn how to control those parts of the process that can be controlled and to encourage those mysterious, less controllable activities. No two people go about writing in exactly the same way. It is important for you to recognize routines, modes of thought as well as individual exercises, that help you negotiate the process successfully. When I write, I like to change my environment, writing one day at home, the next day outside, sometimes in the auto repair shop's waiting room, and especially while traveling.

The Georgian poet Vladimir Mayakovsky was, for a time, a committed socialist. When another poet, Sergey Esenin, committed suicide, Mayakovsky saw Esenin's despair as an attack on the ideals of the Soviet system. Mayakovsky resolved to defuse the force of Esenin's beautiful suicide poem by constructing a poem of his own that would both speak to Esenin and replace the beauty of death with the beauty of a committed social struggle. Ironically, Mayakovsky himself committed suicide four years later, leaving behind perhaps the most beautiful suicide poem ever written, "Past One O'clock." Here is how Mayakovsky described the process of writing "To Sergey Esenin."

> For about three months I came back day after day to my subject and could think of nothing sensible. . . . The same hotel rooms, the same water-pipes, the same enforced solitude. These surroundings wound me into themselves, they wouldn't let me escape, they refused me the feelings and words I needed in order to brand and negate, they gave me no material from which I could educe sane and healthy impulses.
>
> Whence comes what is almost a rule: to do anything poetic you positively need a change of place or of time. . . . In order to write about the tenderness of love, take bus No. 7 from Lubyansky Square to Nogin Square. The appalling jolting will serve to throw into relief for you, better than anything else, the charm of a life transformed. A shake-up is essential, for the purpose of comparison. (*How Verses Are Made.* London: Grossman Publishers, 1970. 30–33.)

It is also important to give yourself as much time as possible to complete the process. Procrastination is one of the writer's greatest enemies. It saps confidence, undermines energy, destroys concentration. Working regularly, keeping as close as possible to a well-thought-out schedule, often makes the difference between a successful paper and an embarrassment.

1.1.3   Maintaining Self-Confidence

Having a sense of confidence in your ability to write well about your topic is essential for good writing. This does not mean that you will always know what the end result of a particular writing activity will be. In fact, you have to cultivate your ability to tolerate a high degree of uncertainty while weighing evidence, testing hypotheses, and experimenting with organizational strategies and wording. Be ready for temporary confusion, for seeming dead ends, and remember that every writer faces them. It is from your struggle to combine fact with fact, to connect fact and value judgments, to buttress conjecture with evidence, that order arises.

Do not be intimidated by the amount and quality of work already done in your field of inquiry. The array of opinion and evidence that confronts you in the published literature can be confusing. But remember that no important topic is ever exhausted. There are always gaps, questions that have not yet been satisfactorily explored either in the published research on a subject or in the prevailing popular opinion. For example, new technologies such as in vitro fertilization are causing us to re-examine our views on issues such as abortion. It is in these gaps that you establish your own authority, your own sense of control. And it is through confronting hard cases on the borderline of your established moral distinctions that you establish your own self and values.

Remember that the various stages of the writing process reinforce each other. Establishing a solid motivation strengthens your sense of confidence about the project, which in turn influences how successfully you organize and write. If you start out well, using good work habits, and give yourself ample time for the various activities to gel, you should produce a paper that will reflect your best work, one that your audience will find both readable and useful.

1.2   ORGANIZING YOUR WRITING

As in other disciplines, philosophy will require you to write specific types of papers, with structures that may seem governed as much by blind tradition as by the characteristics of the subject. When rigid external controls are placed on their writing, some writers tend to feel stifled, their creativity impeded by a "paint-by-numbers" approach to structure. It is vital to the success of your writing that you never allow yourself to be overwhelmed by the pattern rules of a particular type of paper. Remember that such controls are in place not to limit your creativity but to make the paper immediately and easily useful to its intended audience.

1.2.1   The Nature of the Process

Although the various parts of the writing process are interwoven, there is naturally a general order to the work of writing. You have to start somewhere! What follows is a description of the various stages of the writing process—planning, drafting, revising, editing, proof reading—along with suggestions on how to approach each most successfully. Planning includes all activities that lead up to the writing of the first draft. These activities differ from person to person. Some writers, for instance, prefer to compile a formal outline before writing that draft. Some writers perform brief writing exercises to jump-start their imaginations. Some draw diagrams; some doodle. Later on we'll look at a few individual starting strategies, and you can determine which may be of help to you. Right now, however, let us discuss some early choices that all writers must make about their writing during the planning stage.

1.2.2   Selecting a Topic

No matter how restrictive an assignment may seem to be, there is no reason to feel trapped by it. Within any assigned subject, you can find a range of topics to explore. What you are looking for is a topic that engages your own interest. Let curiosity be your guide. If, for example, you have been assigned the subject of evaluating utilitarian and deontological theories (now is a good time to check the glossary), then find some issue common to both of these forms of ethical theory that will allow you to illustrate, refine, and compare them. Perhaps you are an aeronautical engineering major. How much risk is morally acceptable in aircraft design according to utilitarianism?

Any good topic comes with a set of questions; you may well find that your interest increases if you simply begin asking questions. Ask and answer your questions on paper. Like most other mental activities, the process of exploring your way through a topic is transformed when you write down your thoughts as they come instead of letting them fly through your mind unrecorded. It is not egotistical to keep a notebook. Remember the old adage from Louis Agassiz, "A pen is often the best of eyes" (*A Scientist of Two Worlds: Louis Agassiz.* Ed. Catherine Owens Pearce. Philadelphia: Lippincott, 1958. 106).

While it is vital to be interested in your topic, you do not have to know much about it at the outset of your investigation. In fact, having too heartfelt a commitment to a topic can be an impediment to writing about it; emotions can get in the way of a reflective perspective.

1.2.3   Narrowing Your Topic

The task of narrowing your topic offers you a tremendous opportunity to establish a measure of control over the writing project. It is up to you to hone your topic to just the right shape and size to suit both your own interests and the requirements of the assignment. Do a good job of it, and you will go a long way toward guaranteeing yourself sufficient motivation and confidence for the tasks ahead of you. Do it wrong, and somewhere along the way you may find yourself without direction and out of energy.

Generally, the first topics that come to your mind will be too large to handle in your research paper. Beginning philosophy students often submit topic proposals such as "Nature or Nurture?" or my favorite, "Humans: Good or Evil?" Both topics, in addition to being, perhaps, false dilemmas, are obviously too large for a lifetime, let alone a five-page paper. But even advanced students attempt to evaluate all of Western philosophy or maybe just Plato in ten pages. Instead of trying to find an answer for an overwhelming dilemma, it would be more practical for you to address only a part of the question. Rather than trying to determine if abortion is always bad or always good, you might compare accepted practices of disposing of frozen embryos. Or instead of addressing the nature of truth, how about discussing how Descartes and Sextus Empiricus handle the problem of finding a criterion of truth?

The problem with most topics is not that they are too narrow or too completely explored; it is that they are too rich. There are so many useful ways to address the topic that choosing the best focus is often difficult. Take some time on the job of narrowing the topic. Think through the possibilities that occur to you, and, as always, jot down your thoughts. Remember that it is all right to say explicitly that you cannot handle aspects of a topic in the space and time provided. For instance, you may wish to postpone for another time the question of whether eating meat is moral and concentrate your paper on a comparison of two practices—eating meat acquired at the supermarket versus meat from hunting. Just make sure you let your reader know early on what the scope and focus of your paper are.

Often it can be helpful to jot down your immediate ideas and associations for a particular topic. This should tell you what, if anything, you have to say about the issue. For instance, I find that many students, given a choice of essay topics, select the one they want to write about. But that topic is often the one that they know the least about or possess the strongest feelings about. Either situation can lead to problems. The former can lead to a poorly substantiated thesis if sufficient extra research is not conducted. The latter can lead to an inefficient reasoning process that blinds us to the worth of arguments on the other side. When confronted with alternative topics for a paper or an exam, do a quick outline, and then chose the one you are best prepared to handle in the time available on paper, whether or not it is the topic you most wish to explore.

1.2.4   Defining a Purpose

There are many ways to classify the purposes of writing, but in general, most writing is undertaken either to inform or to persuade an audience. The goal of informative or expository writing is simply to impart information about a particular subject, while the aim of persuasive writing is to convince your reader of your point of view on an issue. The distinction between expository and persuasive writing is not hard and fast. Most writing has elements of both exposition and persuasion. Most effective writing, however, has a clearly chosen focus of either exposition or persuasion. In philosophy, expository writing is really preparatory for persuasive writing.

It is common for instructors to assign expository papers, especially for beginning students. These papers can vary in length. Some teachers assign frequent, short, expository papers to reinforce learning; others assign less frequent, more extensive papers to provide an opportunity for comparing and contrasting positions. Some assign both. Obviously, the extent of depth in your essay will be affected by the space allowed to you.

But philosophy instructors generally desire to move you at some point in the course to persuasive papers. The views of free will advocated by Spinoza and

William James are interesting in themselves, but your involvement in the processes of philosophy deepens not just when you make them argue with each other in an expository paper but when you have to arrive at a tentative position of your own in response to their arguments. In my Criminal Justice Ethics class I am happy if students recognize on the first exam the ethical values behind various positions on whistle-blowing in the police force (pun intended). By the final exam, however, I want them to write policy statements on deadly force or prisoners' rights, using major ethical theories as the explicit foundation of their views. You will encounter similar expectations of philosophical growth over a semester from your instructors, so it is important to master the various types of philosophical papers.

EXERCISE: To Explain or to Persuade

Can you tell from the titles of these two papers, both written on the same topic, which is an expository and which a persuasive paper?

1. *Roe v. Wade* and the New Reproductive Technology
2. *Roe v. Wade*: A Bad Decision

The first title probably led most of you to say that it is an expository paper. Your task in such a paper would be to describe the *Roe v. Wade* decision, and in particular the role of reproductive technology in that decision, in as coherent and impartial a manner as possible. If you feel strongly about this issue, it may be very difficult to refrain from evaluative comments on the decision. But that would be acceptable as long as your feelings do not produce static that interferes with your rendering of the details of the decision relevant to your topic. As you develop your topic you will come to the question of the role of new technologies in effectively moving the point of viability (the moment when independently viable life begins) earlier than the six-month cutoff accepted by the Supreme Court. In an expository paper you would ordinarily stop at that point. But I am sure you perceive the moral relevance of an earlier point of viability established by medical technology to a decision made when that technology was not available. Expository papers can and should, as long as facts are relevant to moral decision-making, lead into moral discussions.

So your expository paper might describe in a coherent and impartial way the *Roe v. Wade* decision, the state of medical technology at the time of the decision, and recent relevant improvements that bear on the question of viability. In an expository paper you should also indicate the moral relevance of the improved technology—what sort of moral questions does it suggest for review?

If you are trying to persuade your reader that there should be more stringent regulation of the time when abortions may be performed, your strategy may be different because you are now writing to influence the opinions of the audience toward the subject. This strategy should show up in your opening paragraphs, where you tell your reader how you are going to use both facts and values to arrive at an evaluative decision. But in philosophy we like to encourage persuasive writers to use only rationally sound and not emotive or fallacious reasoning to establish a position, no matter how much more effective nonrational means are. If argument is wrestling or war, it still does not follow that we should fight without rules. Using rational means of persuasion theoretically widens the audience you may reach and ethically shows respect for other persons. It also prevents you from gaining agreement without proper reasons. It makes you convince yourself fairly as you seek to convince others.

Writing assignments break down the distinction between expository and persuasive writing in a number of ways. You may be called upon to analyze sociopolitical situations, such as the proper response to the World Trade Center attack, or to evaluate government programs aimed to increase air travel security that impact privacy. You may have to speculate on directions in social policy, such as regulating police use of force, or to identify or define problems within a field or range of fields. In any of these papers, your instructor may expect you to suggest solutions and rehearse moral considerations. For instance, an expository assignment might be to explain the utilitarian and deontological positions on the relative moral importance of privacy and security.

By the time of your final draft, you must have a very sound notion of the point you wish to argue or the position you wish to support. If, during the writing of that final draft, someone were to ask you to state your thesis, you should be able to give a satisfactory answer with a minimum of delay and no prompting. If, on the other hand, you have to hedge your answer because you cannot easily form a notion of your thesis in your own mind, you may not yet have arrived at a final draft.

Two writers have been asked what point they wish to make in their papers. Which of the writers has a better grip on her writing task?

Writer 1: "My paper is about whether someone in the reserves should be called to serve in a police action in another country."

Writer 2: "My paper argues that although we have a volunteer military, it is unfair to call these volunteers to fight in areas where the United States lacks a well-defined interest, a just cause, and the ability to protect its own troops without violating the international rules of engagement."

The first writer knows what her general area of concern is: whether volunteering for the military transfers to the government the absolute right to decide where and whether you will keep the peace. But the second writer has a more developed sense of how she is going to approach this issue. Note that the second writer has narrowed the field of information she is going to consult to establish her point. Her topic statement, for instance, does not require her to look at the details of the enlistment contract but does require her to make reference to international law and the moral notion of just cause. It may be that you will have to write a draft or two or engage in one or two of the prewriting activities described below in order to arrive at a secure understanding of your task.

Watch out for bias! No matter how hard you may try to produce an objective paper, the fact is that every choice you make as you write is influenced to some extent by your personal beliefs and opinions. What you tell your readers is colored—sometimes without your knowing—by a multitude of factors. The influence such factors produce can be very subtle, and it is something you must work to identify in your own writing as well as in the writing of others in order not to mislead or be misled. Responsible writers keep an eye on their own biases and are honest with their readers about them. One of the most responsible things you can do for your readers is to speak clearly on those matters that you have strong beliefs about and let them have a chance to correct for bias. Also, remember that it is one thing to admit that your race or gender may influence your beliefs and quite another to claim that someone else's background makes his or her views false or irrelevant.

1.2.5   Finding a Thesis

No matter what type of paper you are assigned, you will be expected to produce a clearly labeled and appropriately narrowed thesis statement. It should occur at the outset of your paper. And, of course, any thesis you assert will require the support of reasons. You can easily see, however, that if every assertion requires a reason, you will never finish the paper. When have you given enough support to a claim? One answer is when your reasons are uncontested or generally accepted. But the most reliable gauge is the extent of support required for assertions by your instructor in class and the readings for the course.

As you plan, be on the lookout for an idea that would serve as your major thesis. I say *major* because any thesis worth arguing about will be the result of a great number of subsidiary arguments that you will produce and evaluate along the way to your major conclusion. A thesis is not a statement that can be immediately proven by recourse to recorded information; it is, instead, a hypothesis worth discussing. Your thesis sentence should reveal to your reader not only the argument you have chosen but also your orientation toward it, the conclusion that your paper will attempt to prove, and how you will go about establishing it.

In looking for a thesis, you are doing four jobs at once:

1. You are limiting the amount and kind of material that you must cover, making it manageable.
2. You are increasing your own interest in the narrowing field of study.

3. You are working to establish your paper's purpose, the reason why you are writing about your topic. (If the only reason you can see for writing is to earn a good grade, then you probably won't.)
4. You are establishing your notion of who your audience is and what sort of approach to the subject might best catch their interest.

In short, you are gaining control over your writing context. For this reason, it is a good idea to come up with a thesis early on, a working thesis, which will very probably change as your thinking deepens but which will allow you to establish a measure of order in the planning stage.

EXERCISE: Find the Major Thesis

Here is an excerpt from a short article by Dino Corbin, general manager of television station KHSL in Chico, California. See if you can find his major thesis, and develop a narrowed thesis of your own that you would use to respond to his argument.

On October 20 [1995], I canceled talk show *Jenny Jones* from KHSL-TV. I canceled the program and breached the contract because the show seriously stepped outside of the guidelines of decency that KHSL has stood for in this community since 1953. . . . America has rejected the idea that these shows are representative of this country. They are representative of the worst of this country. Your response has also caused our industry to stop and take note of its impact and obligations to our society. In short, it is obvious that the American people expect and demand more from the greatest medium on earth.

As broadcasting grew, it became quickly apparent it possessed a unique power and impact on society. Because of this unique dynamic and in an effort to insure the spirit of the First Amendment, the government issued a license to broadcast, which is ultimately granted by the people of the community served by the broadcast license. The owner or general manager became obligated as the gatekeeper: someone held locally responsible for the proper operation of the station. It is set forth in law, a broadcaster shall operate in the best interest of his or her community. A simple, straightforward approach that has worked for over 45 years. Unfortunately, a dictate so simple it is easily forgotten by those of us in the day-to-day battle for ratings and dollars.

I have heard the excuse that the media just reflects society. That is true to some extent. It does not have to be the norm, however. Today our society is not as healthy as in the past. Unfortunately, a cycle develops that continues to feed upon itself. From our movies to the video games our children play, violence and unacceptable behavior begin to take on the image of normalcy. Add to this equation the corrosion of the American family, throw in a dose of government, and you have a recipe for disaster.

It is apparent that the most powerful factor here is the media. Then, cannot the media take a position toward correcting the problem? People in my position need to accept the notion that we have an obligation first and foremost to the communities we serve. (*Chico Enterprise-Record,* 3 December 1995.)

Here is a second extended argument found in an opinion piece written by Richard Dawkins, Professor of the Public Understanding of Science at Oxford. Once again, isolate the major thesis and write one of your own that you would use in a reply. But this time, try to isolate several other subtheses that Dawkins offers.

The problem with the human guidance system is precisely this. Unlike the pigeon version, it knows that a successful mission culminates in its own destruction. Could we develop a biological guidance system with the compliance and dispensability of a pigeon but with a man's resourcefulness and ability to infiltrate plausibly? What we need, in a nutshell, is a human who doesn't mind being blown up. He'd make the perfect on-board guidance system. But suicide enthusiasts are hard to find. Even terminal cancer patients might lose their nerve when the crash was actually looming.

Could we get some otherwise normal humans and somehow persuade them that they are not going to die as a consequence of flying a plane smack into a skyscraper? If only! Nobody is that stupid, but how about this—it's a long shot, but it just might work. Given that they are certainly going to die, couldn't we sucker them into believing that they are going to come to life again afterwards? Don't be daft! No, listen, it might work. Offer them a fast track to a Great Oasis in the Sky, cooled by everlasting fountains. Harps and wings wouldn't appeal to the sort of young men we need, so tell them there's a special martyr's reward of 72 virgin brides, guaranteed eager and exclusive.

It's a tall story, but worth a try. You'd have to get them young, though. Feed them a complete and self-consistent background mythology to make the big lie sound plausible when it comes. Give them a holy book and make them learn it by heart. Do you know, I really think it might work. As luck would have it, we have just the thing . . .: a ready-made system of mind-control which has been honed over centuries, handed down through generations. Millions of people have been brought up in it. It is called religion and, for reasons which one day we may understand, most people fall for it (nowhere more so than America itself, though the irony passes unnoticed). Now all we need is to round up a few of these faith-heads and give them flying lessons.

. . . I am trying to call attention to the elephant in the room that everybody is too polite—or too devout—to notice: religion, and specifically the devaluing effect that religion has on human life. I don't mean devaluing the life of others (though it can do that too), but devaluing one's own life. Religion teaches the dangerous nonsense that death is not the end. (Richard Dawkins. "Religion's Misguided Missiles." *The Guardian*, 15 September 2001.)

1.2.6   The Thesis Sentence

The introduction of your paper will contain a sentence that summarizes the task that your paper intends to accomplish. This thesis sentence communicates your main idea, the one you are going to prove or defend or illustrate. The thesis sets up an expectation in the reader's mind that is your job to satisfy. But a thesis sentence is more than just the statement that informs your reader of your goal. In the planning stage, the thesis is a valuable tool to help you narrow your focus and confirm in your own mind your paper's purpose.

Imagine that you are taking a course on the philosophy of war and your initial topic is information warfare. You may be drawn to discuss the military's increased reliance on information warfare by promotional literature from a branch of the military. Your thesis might be that information warfare should be carried out during peacetime because it deters war and limits risk to both military and civilians during war. But perhaps you will come across a remark by an official in an information-poor society to the effect that the only option to combat information warfare is to use nuclear weapons. So, your eventual thesis might focus on the question of whether voluntary adoption of limits on information warfare by information-rich governments is a morally superior alternative even though it embraces increased risk when hostilities breakout.

Note that your thesis develops in two ways. First, in your research you go beyond the assumptions presented as fact in the media and promotional literature. You need to also read the relevant documents produced by information warfare advocates in order to find the relevant arguments and weigh their plausibility. The second way you develop your thesis is by asking questions of value. What is the relative value of deterring war versus the responsibility to advance a nation's international policy by nonviolent means? You have just begun to untangle the thesis by consulting past fact and clashing values. And the process can go on further, perhaps leading you to investigate political philosophy on just cause and just means during war. Your duty is to refine the thesis into a manageable proposition that confronts the real aspects of a real problem and not an imagined scenario.

In a course on the history of philosophy you might be drawn to Descartes' proof of his existence. Perhaps you will begin with his discussion framed in terms of the famous, or infamous, *Cogito ergo sum*, Latin for "I think, therefore I am." No doubt you will soon discover that Descartes subsequently reworked his position as "*Sum* is true each and every time I say it." A paper could address why Descartes altered his view. Or you might investigate the extent of influence St. Augustine's similar proof of existence had on Descartes' view. Or again, you might do a paper on whether Descartes was adequately responding to Sextus Empiricus' argument that there is no knowledge of conscious states or the self. Such a paper, whether expository or persuasive, must include an adequate exposition of the philosophers' arguments. It would also have a factual component directed at exhibiting conscious links between Descartes and Augustine. Can we, for instance, ascertain on textual evidence or indirect evidence, such as typical reading of the period, whether Descartes was likely to have read Augustine? But whether the answer is yes or no, another portion of the paper will argue that the perspective of St. Augustine is relevant to Descartes' argument, perhaps supplementing it by addressing issues Descartes overlooked. So again, there are at least two important types of exposition involved.

At some time during your preliminary thinking on a topic, you should consult the library to see how much published work has already been done. This search is beneficial in at least two ways. It acquaints you with a body of writing that will become very important in the research phase of the paper, and it gives you a sense of how your topic is generally addressed by the community of scholars you are joining.

Is the topic as important as you think it is? Has there already been so much research on the topic as to make your inquiry, in its present formulation, irrelevant? These questions can be answered by turning to the literature. Unfortunately, many libraries have fallen behind the march of scholarship. If the items in your bibliography (and your syllabus) are all from a previous decade or your parents' college years, you may want to consult the latest electronic research tools to find more recent sources.

As you go about determining your topic, remember that one goal of writing philosophy is to enhance your reasoning abilities. Do not be afraid of the conclusions your reasoning leads you to accept on paper. You need not act on your conclusions at this moment in time. You can always postpone action to consider more argument. But allow yourself to participate in what Plato called the healing power of the argument. Your philosophy papers are just first, tentative steps toward forming your own views on the important issues of your life, and your philosophy instructors will not be sending copies of your papers home to your parents to evaluate.

1.2.7   Defining Your Audience

In any class that requires writing from you, it may sometimes be difficult to remember that the point of your writing is not simply to jump through the technical hoops imposed by the assignment. The point is communication, the transmission of your knowledge, your conclusions, to the reader in a way that suits you. Your task is to pass to your reader the spark of your own enthusiasm for your topic. Readers who were indifferent to your topic should look at it in a new way after reading your paper.

It is tempting to think that most writing problems would be solved if the writer could view his or her writing as if another person had produced it. The ego barrier between writer and audience is the single greatest impediment to accurate communication. In order to reduce the discrepancy between your understanding and that of your audience, you must learn to consider the audience's needs. By the time you begin drafting, most, if not all, of your ideas have begun to attain coherent shape in your mind, so virtually any words in which you try to phrase those ideas will reflect your thought accurately—to you. Your readers, however, do not already have in mind the conclusions that you have so painstakingly achieved. If you leave out of your writing material that is necessary to complete your readers' understanding of your argument, they may well not be able to supply that information themselves.

The potential for misunderstanding is present for any audience, whether it is made up of general readers, experts in the field, or your professor, who is reading, in part, to see how well you have mastered the constraints that govern the relationship between writer and reader. Make your presentation as complete as possible, writing always as if to an audience whose previous knowledge of your topic is limited to information easily available to the general public. Do not write for your professor. Suppose you find yourself wondering whether you should include something and conclude you do not need to because "the professor knows that already." Include it. The professor wants to know what you have mastered, not what you think the professor already knows. It also helps to remember that your paper may not be read by the professor, but by a teaching assistant.

1.3   INVENTION STRATEGIES

In this chapter we have discussed methods of selecting and narrowing the topic of a paper. As your focus on a specific topic sharpens, you naturally begin to think about the kinds of information that will go into the paper. In the case of papers that do not require formal research, material comes largely from your own recollections. Indeed, one of the reasons instructors assign such papers is to convince you of the incredible richness of your memory, the vastness and variety of the "database" that you have accumulated and that, moment by moment, you continue to build.

So vast is your horde of information that it can sometimes be difficult to find within it the material that would best suit your paper. In other words, finding out what you already know about a topic is not always easy. Invention, a term borrowed from classical rhetoric, refers to the task of discovering, or recovering from memory, information about your topic. As we write, all of us go through some sort of invention procedure that helps us explore our topic. Some writers seem to have little problem coming up with material; others need more help. Over the centuries writers have devised different exercises that can help locate useful material housed in memory. We shall look at a few of these briefly.

1.3.1   Free Writing

Free writing is an activity that forces you to get something down on paper. There is no waiting around for inspiration. Instead, you set yourself a time limit— three minutes, five minutes—and write for that length of time without stopping, not even to lift the pen from the paper or your hands from the keyboard. You can free write on a typewriter or a computer. Focus on the topic, and don't let the difficulty of finding relevant material stop you from writing. If necessary, you may begin by writing, over and over, some seemingly useless phrase, like "I cannot think of anything to write about," or perhaps the name of your topic. Eventually, something else will occur to you. (It is surprising how long a three-minute free writing can seem to take!)

At the end of the free writing, look over what you have produced for anything of use. Granted, much of the writing will be unusable, but there may be an insight or two that you did not know you possessed.

In addition to its ability to recover usable material for your paper, free writing has a couple of other benefits attached to it. First, it takes little time to do, which means you may repeat the exercise as often as you like within a relatively short span of time. Second, it breaks down some of the resistance that stands between you and the act of writing. There is no initial struggle to find something to say; you just write.

EXERCISE: Freewriting

Here are some sample topics from various philosophy classes. Surely you are in a class where at least one of these topics is relevant. Try free writing on a topic or two and then apply it later when you are working on a paper assignment. It would be especially helpful to have a classmate perform the exercise also and exchange papers for comments. When you comment, do not be overly kind, but avoid hurtful expressions. In other words, do not write comments such as "great idea" or "this is stupid." Ideally, a third classmate should then comment on the original free writing and on the other reader's comments.

1. Is God's knowledge of the future compatible with human free will?
2. Should citizens serve as members of police review boards that investigate police use of force?
3. Should a nonfamily member have the power to veto a living will?
4. Do real estate brokers have a moral responsibility to tell clients that they are obliged to represent the interests of the seller, not the buyer?
5. Was the attempt of World Trade Organization (WTO) protestors to overwhelm the Internet information site for the WTO meeting in Seattle a justified form of nonviolent civil disobedience?
6. Should agricultural conglomerates be allowed to patent genetically engineered strains of wheat?

1.3.2 Brainstorming

Brainstorming is simply making a list of ideas about a topic. It can be done quickly and, at first, without any need to order items into a coherent pattern. The point is to write down everything that occurs to you, as quickly and briefly as possible, in individual words or short phrases. Once you have a good-sized list of items, you can group the items according to relationships that you see among them. Brainstorming, then, allows you to uncover both ideas stored in your memory and useful associations among those ideas.

EXERCISE: Brainstorming

In my criminal justice ethics class I asked students to brainstorm on police use of deadly force. Here is one student's list of responses.

Los Angeles, Rodney King, flight is a danger to the community, cops get shot too, body mass, the death penalty, my career, my family, due process, punishment, fellow officers.

The student quickly realized that some of his associations fell into natural topic categories:

- The role of the police: apprehend offenders, protect the community, due process, police apprehend but do not punish.
- Conflicting personal duties: to the community, to my family and partner, to the suspect.
- Questions of justice: whether deadly force is disproportionately applied to minorities; whether it should be applied to people fleeing crimes that would not result in the death penalty.

This student decided to write on the third topic: whether there is reason to believe that police forces apply deadly force in a racially biased manner. Which of the remaining items in the original list would be helpful in developing this paper? Why?

1.3.3   Asking Questions

It is always possible to ask most or all of the following questions about any topic: Who? What? When? Where? Why? How? These questions force you to approach the topic in something like the way a journalist does, setting the topic within different perspectives that can then be compared to discover resonance within the material.

EXERCISE: Asking Questions

For a class in bioethics, a professor asked her class to write a paper describing the impact of living wills on the medical process. Here are some questions that a student in the class might logically ask to begin thinking toward a thesis.

- Who are the candidates for mercy killing? (May parents write such wills for children?)
- What are the qualifications for monitoring and overseeing the carrying out of a living will?
- What, exactly, will be allowed in such a will? (Will doctors merely order the removal of life-sustaining technology, or will they also terminate feeding or administer terminal doses of drugs to end suffering?)
- When during the course of an illness is a patient no longer competent to write such a will?
- Where will living wills be carried out? (Is there a good reason not to allow such practices in a hospital, the home, or a nursing home?)
- How are the wills to be written, filed, and stored?
- Why do some people have living wills? Why would someone need to terminate life-supporting treatment?
- When does the state or another social institution such as a religious hospital have a right to interfere in the application of a living will?

Can you think of other questions that would make for useful inquiry?

As you engage in invention strategies, you are also doing other work. You are still narrowing your topic, for example, as well as making decisions that will affect your choice of tone or audience. You move forward on all fronts, each decision you make affecting the others. This means you must be flexible enough in your understanding of the paper's development to allow for slight course adjustments, alterations in your understanding of your goal. Never be so determined to prove a particular theory that you fail to notice when your own understanding of it changes. Seek out people who disagree with you. They are actually your best guides to refining your own views and attempting to approach something like objectivity.

1.3.4 Outlining

A paper that has all the facts but gives them to the reader in an ineffective order will confuse rather than inform or persuade. While there are various methods of grouping ideas, none is potentially more effective than outlining. Unfortunately, no organizing process is more often misunderstood.

1.3.4.1 Outlining for Yourself

There are really two jobs that outlining can do. First, it can serve as a means of forcing you, the writer, to gain a better understanding of your ideas by arranging them according to their interrelationships. There is one primary rule of outlining: Ideas of equal weight are placed on the same level within the outline. This rule requires you to determine the relative importance of your ideas. You have to decide which ideas are of the same type or order and into which subtopic each idea best fits.

If, in the planning stage, you arrange your ideas with care in a coherent outline, your grasp of your topic will be greatly enhanced. You will have linked your ideas logically together and given a skeleton to the body of the paper. This sort of subordinating and coordinating activity is difficult, however, and as a result, inexperienced writers sometimes fail to pay the necessary attention to the outline and begin to write their first draft without an effective outline, hoping for the best. That hope is usually disappointed, especially in complex papers involving research.

1.3.4.2 Outlining for Your Reader

The second job that an outline does is aimed not at the writer's understanding, but at the reader's. An outline accompanying your paper can serve the reader as a blueprint to the paper, a summary of the paper's points and their interrelationships. Let the reader determine that your paper is worth reading by allowing a quick grasp of your paper's goal and the argument you have used to promote it by consulting your outline. This accompanying outline, then, is very important, since its clarity and coherence help to determine how much attention your audience will give to your ideas.

1.3.4.3 Formal Outline Pattern

Following the pattern below during the planning stage of your paper helps to guarantee that your ideas are placed logically.

Thesis sentence (prefaces the organized outline)
I. First main idea
    A First subordinate idea
        1. Reason, example, or illustration
        2. Reason, example, or illustration
            a. Detail supporting reason #2
            b. Detail supporting reason #2
    B Second subordinate idea
II. Second main idea

Notice that each level of the paper must have more than one entry; for every A there must be at least a B (and, if required, a C, D, and so on); for every 1 there must be a 2. This arrangement forces you to compare ideas, looking carefully at each one to determine its place among the others. The insistence on assigning relative values to your ideas is what makes your outline an effective organizing tool.

1.3.5   Organizing Your Thoughts

Kareem, a student in an information ethics class, attended a Metallica concert. He has a friend who works with the sound crew, and the friend gave Kareem the tape from the mixing board as a souvenir. Kareem knows that his friend did not own the tape and that Metallica is not friendly to the unauthorized release of tapes of live performances. Yet Kareem also knows that the tape would be enjoyed by many people and feels it would be selfish to keep it just for himself. And he cannot bear to destroy it, since the performance was a good one and he has the best available tape.

Since he is studying information ethics, Kareem knows about copyright laws as well as the moral arguments that advocates of copyright protection for artists such as the Recording Industry Association of Artists (RIAA) use to justify these laws. He is familiar with the issue of artistic control, for instance. Yet he knows that if he does not duplicate this tape, it will never be issued, and many Metallica fans will be deprived of a wonderful experience. The greater social good seems to be to begin duplicating the tape. But the artists' property rights and right to control distribution of their creations suggest that putting the performance up on the online file sharer Audiogalaxy is wrong.

I do not know what Kareem did with the tape, but his paper addressed the duty of artists to make a reasonable return to the cultural commons that inspired their creations. He addressed the issue in terms of rights to compensation—both the artists' and the culture's. This approach provided a useful framework for his moral conflict.

Do you think that Kareem made the correct logical grouping? Or are there other categories that he overlooked that would provide a better organization for approaching this moral issue?

EXERCISE: Formulate a Thesis

As an exercise, formulate a thesis about the morality of digital music file sharing via Napster or Audiogalaxy described above. Can you fill in the outline sketch above with your own ideas? Can you produce a more extensive outline? It might help you to free write before attempting the outline.

1.4   THE ROUGH DRAFT

Sometime toward the end of the planning comes the writing of the first draft. Using your thesis and outline as direction markers, you must now weave your amalgam of ideas, data, and persuasion strategies into logically ordered sentences and paragraphs. Though adequate prewriting may make the drafting easier than it might have been, still it will not be easy. Writers establish their own individual methods of encouraging themselves to forge ahead with the draft, but here are some tips to bear in mind.

Remember that this first effort at writing is a rough draft, not the final draft. At this stage, it is not necessary that every word you write be the best possible word. Do not put that sort of pressure on yourself; you must not allow anything to slow you down now. Writing is not like sculpting, where every chip is permanent; you can always go back to your draft later and add, delete, reword, and rearrange. No matter how much effort you have put into planning, you cannot be sure how much of this first draft you will eventually keep. It may take several drafts to get one that you find satisfactory.

Give yourself sufficient time to write. Don't delay the first draft by telling yourself there is still more research to do. You cannot uncover all the material there is to know on a particular subject, so don't fool yourself into trying. Remember that writing is a process of discovery. You may have to begin writing before you can see exactly what sort of final research you need to do. Remember that there are other tasks waiting for you after the first draft is finished, so allow for them as you determine your writing schedule.

This matter of giving yourself time is very important for another reason. The more time that passes after you write a draft, the better your ability to view it with greater objectivity. It is very difficult to evaluate your writing accurately soon after you complete it. You need to cool down, to recover from the effort of putting all those words together. The "colder" you get on your writing, the better able you are to read it as if it were written by someone else. Thus, the better able you will be to acknowledge the changes you will need to make to strengthen the paper.

Stay sharp. Keep in mind the plan you created for yourself as you narrowed your topic, composed a thesis sentence, and outlined the material. But if as you write you feel a strong need to change the plan a bit, do not be afraid to do so. Be ready for surprises dealt you by your own growing understanding of your topic. Your goal is to render your best thinking on the subject as accurately as possible.

1.4.1 Language Choices

To be convincing, your writing has to be authoritative. That is, you have to sound as if you have complete confidence in your ability to convey your ideas in words. Sentences that sound stilted, that suffer from weak phrasing or the use of clichés, are not going to win supporters for the aims that you express in your paper. So, a major question becomes: How can I sound confident? Here are some points to consider as you work to convey to your readers that necessary sense of authority.

1.4.1.1 Level of Formality

Tone is one of the primary methods by which you signal to your readers who you are and what your attitude is toward them and toward your topic. The major choice you make has to do with the level of language formality that you feel is most appropriate to your audience. The informal tone you would use in a letter to a friend might well be out of place in a paper on "The Argument from Design as a Proof of the Existence of God." Remember that tone is only part of the overall decision that you make about how to present your information. Formality is, to some extent, a function of individual word choices and phrasing. Is it appropriate to use contractions like "isn't" or "they'll"? Would the strategic use of a sentence fragment for effect be out of place? The use of informal language, the personal "I," and the second person "you" is traditionally forbidden—for better or worse—in certain kinds of writing. Often, part of the challenge of writing a formal paper is simply how to give your prose bite while staying within the conventions.

1.4.1.2 Descriptive Language

Language that appeals to the reader's senses will always engage his interest more fully than language that is abstract. This is especially important for writing in disciplines that tend to deal in abstracts, such as philosophy. The typical paper, with its discussions of abstract principles, is usually in danger of floating off on a cloud of abstractions, drifting further away in each paragraph from the felt life of the reader. Whenever appropriate, appeal to your reader's sense of sight, hearing, taste, touch, or smell. How much attention does Richard Dawkins buy from his audience with his equation of pigeons and human beings?

Jargon

One way to lose readers quickly is to overwhelm them with jargon—phrases that have a special, usually technical meaning within your discipline but are unfamiliar to the average reader. The very occasional use of jargon may add an effective touch of atmosphere, but anything more than that will severely dampen a reader's enthusiasm for the paper. Often, a reason for jargon is the writer's desire to impress the reader by sounding lofty or knowledgeable. Unfortunately, all jargon usually does is make for confusion. In fact, the use of jargon is often an index of the writer's lack of connection to the audience.

Philosophical writing is a minefield of jargon. For better or worse, philosophers have borrowed many technical terms from ordinary usage, such as *utilitarian* and *idealism*, and given them special technical meanings. Be careful: You may think you understand a philosophical term when you do not. How do you know when to check a glossary like the one at the back of this book? You could scan it now and see which terms are familiar. Read those terms and see if they have meaning different from what you associate with them. (What is metaphysics, anyway?) Or use the rule that if a term recurs several times in a philosopher's work, you had better check it.

Jargon also occurs when writers do not commonly address nonspecialists and believe their readers are all completely attuned to their terminology. It may be that these writers occasionally hope to obscure damaging information or potentially unpopular ideas in confusing language. Or the problem could simply be fuzzy thinking on the writer's part. Unfortunately, not all the great philosophers were great writers. Whatever the reason, do not imitate the style of writers, no matter how great they are as philosophers, if they engage in jargon and obfuscation. Students may feel that in order to be accepted as philosophers, they should conform to the writing practices of their published peers. This is a mistake. Remember that it is never better to write a cluttered or confusing sentence than a clear one and that burying your ideas in jargon defeats the effort that you went through to form them.

EXERCISE: Spot the Jargon

Here are some words that are part of philosophical jargon. You will run into a good number of them. Some of them appear deceptively simple; some are difficult to penetrate, since they appear in ordinary language with firm associations; and some are even more impenetrable after years of studying and teaching. See if you can write a sentence or two about some of them, saying what you think they mean: freedom, free will, idealism, pragmatism, rationality, human rights, natural rights, utilitarian, the right to life, a woman's right to choose, epistemology, being, becoming, dread.

Clichés

In the heat of composition, as you are looking for words to help you form your ideas, it is sometimes easy to plug in a cliché—a phrase that has attained universal recognition by overuse. (Clichés differ from jargon in that clichés are part of the general public's everyday language, while jargon is specific to the language of experts in a particular field.) Unless you have some very special reason for using a cliché, don't. They can sap energy out of your prose.

Weasel Words

Weasel words get their name from the practice weasels have of removing eggs from a nest, sucking out the good stuff inside, and replacing the empty shell in the nest. Some examples are "it appears that," "it seems to me to follow that," and "this supports the conclusion that." These and many similar phrases essentially say that something might be the case and that the writer believes it is the case. Weasel words are devices for hiding the fact that you have little or no evidence for a conclusion but advocate a view nonetheless. By using them, you also free yourself from having to offer evidence, since you make only a modest claim and yet leave the impression that you have said something substantial. Besides being intellectually dishonest, weasel words are redundant; a string of them makes for awkward reading. You should not have to tell your audience what seems to be the appropriate conclusion. Just state it. It is your paper. They will know it is your conclusion.

Sexist Language

Language can be a very powerful method of either reinforcing or destroying cultural stereotypes. By treating the sexes in subtly different ways in your language, you may unknowingly be committing an act of discrimination. A common example is the use of the pronoun he to refer to a person whose gender has not been identified. But there are many other writing situations in which sexist bias may appear:

SEXIST: A lawyer should always treat his client with respect.
   CORRECTED: A lawyer should always treat his or her client with respect.
   CORRECTED: Lawyers should always treat their clients with respect.
SEXIST: Man is a political animal.
   CORRECTED: People are political animals.

There are other methods of avoiding sexism in your writing. Some writers, faced with the pronoun dilemma illustrated above, alternate the use of male and female personal pronouns (a strategy used for examples in this manual).

In its more obvious forms, sexist language denies role models to a large number of your readers and so hampers communication. Make sure your writing is not guilty of this subtle form of discrimination. Remember, language is more than the mere vehicle of your thought. Your words shape perceptions for your reader. How well you say something will profoundly affect your reader's response to it.

1.5   REVISING YOUR WRITING

Revising is one of the most important steps in assuring that your essay is a success. While unpracticed writers often think of revision as little more than making sure all the *i*'s are dotted and *t*'s are crossed, it is much more than that. Revising is reseeing the essay, looking at it from other perspectives, trying always to align your view with the view that will be held by your audience. Research in composition indicates that we are actually revising all the time, in every phase of the process, as we reread phrases, rethink the placement of an item in an outline, or test a new topic sentence for a paragraph. Subjecting your entire hard-fought draft to cold, objective scrutiny is one of the hardest activities to master in the writing process, but it is absolutely necessary. You have to make sure that you have said everything that needs to be said, clearly and in logical order. One confusing passage, and the reader's attention is deflected from where you want it to be. Suddenly the reader has to become a detective, trying to figure out why you wrote what you did and what you meant by it. You don't want to throw such obstacles in the path of meaning.

Give yourself adequate time to revise. As discussed earlier, you need time to become "cold" on your paper in order to analyze it objectively. After you have written your draft, spend some time away from it. Try to come back to it as if someone other than you had written it.

Read the paper carefully. This is tougher than it sounds. One good strategy is to read it aloud or to have a friend read it aloud while you listen. (Note, however, that friends do not usually make the best critics. They are rarely trained in revision techniques and are often unwilling to risk disappointing you by giving your paper a really thorough examination.)

Have a list of specific items to check. It is important to revise in an orderly fashion, in stages, looking first at large concerns, such as the overall structure, then rereading the paper for problems with smaller elements, such as paragraph organization or sentence structure.

Check for unity—the clear and logical relation of all parts of the essay to its thesis. Make sure that every paragraph relates well to the whole of the paper and is in the right place.

Check for coherence. Make sure there are no gaps between the different parts of the argument. Look to see that you have adequate transition everywhere it is needed. Transitional elements are markers indicating places where the paper's focus or attitude changes. Transitional elements can be one word long—*however, although, unfortunately, luckily*—or as long as a sentence or a paragraph. Transitional elements rarely introduce new material. Instead, they are direction pointers, either indicating a shift to new subject matter or signaling how the writer wishes certain material to be interpreted by the reader. Because you, the writer, already know where and why your paper changes direction and how you want particular passages to be received, it can be very difficult for you to catch those places in your paper where transition is needed. One place where transitional elements are particularly important, and where they do introduce new material, is in persuasive papers. When you switch from exposition to evaluation and persuasion, you introduce new material and should formulate another paragraph in which you explain how you are about to relate fact to a value decision. Here is an example of this sort of transitional paragraph:

> The major responsibility of the media is to educate viewers. Talk shows are the only place on television where the various ethnic minorities that make up America speak to each other honestly as equals. They also provide a uniquely honest discussion of two crucial areas of contemporary life: sex and drugs. I will argue that Mr. Corbin shirks responsibility by limiting this discussion.

Avoid unnecessary repetition. There are two types of repetition that can annoy a reader: repetition of content and repetition of wording.

Repetition of content occurs when you return to a subject that you have already discussed. Ideally, you want to say what you have to say about a topic once, memorably, and then move on to your next topic. Organizing a paper is a difficult task, however, that usually occurs through a process of enlightenment as to purposes and strategies. It is possible for an early draft to circle back to a subject that you have already dealt with and to begin to treat the same material over again. This sort of repetition can happen even if you have made use of prewriting strategies. What is worse, it can be difficult for you, the writer, to acknowledge the repetition to yourself—to admit to yourself that the material you have worked so hard to shape on page two returns on page five in much the same shape.

As you write and revise, bear this in mind: Any unnecessary repetition of content that you allow into your final draft is potentially annoying to your reader, who is working to make sense of the argument she is reading and does not want to be distracted by a passage repeating material already encountered. You must train yourself, through practice, to read through your draft, looking for material that you have repeated unnecessarily.

Repetition of wording occurs when you overuse certain phrases or words. This sort of repetition can make your prose sound choppy and uninspired.

Avoid a condition known by composition teachers as the I-syndrome. The most characteristic manifestation of the I-syndrome in philosophy papers is the use of the expressions "I think," "I feel," and "I believe." Their use is, of course, redundant. But they also signal to the critical reader that you have just offered a claim that, given the use of these expressions in ordinary language, is probably unsupported. So the occurrence of these expressions in your drafts can be a handy guide for where revision is appropriate.

Not all repetition is bad. You may wish to repeat a phrase for rhetorical effect or special emphasis: *I came. I saw. I conquered.* Just make sure that any repetition in your paper is intentional, placed there to produce a specific effect.

1.5.1   Editing

Editing is sometimes confused with the more involved process of revising. But editing happens later, after you have wrestled through your first draft—and maybe your second and third—and arrived at the final draft. Even though your draft now contains all the information you want to impart and has arranged the information to your satisfaction, there are still many factors to check, such as sentence structure, spelling, and punctuation.

It is at this point that an unpracticed writer might let down his guard. After all, most of the work on the paper is finished; the big jobs of discovering material and organizing and drafting it have been completed. But watch out! Editing is as important as any other job in the writing process. Any error you allow in the final draft will count against you in the mind of the reader. It may not seem fair, but a minor error—a misspelling or the confusing placement of a comma—will make a much greater impression on your reader than perhaps it should. Remember: Everything about your paper is your responsibility. That includes getting even the supposedly little jobs right. Careless editing undermines the effectiveness of your paper. It would be a shame if all the hard work you put into prewriting, drafting, and revising were to be damaged because you carelessly allowed a comma splice.

Most of the tips given above for revising hold for editing as well. It is best to edit in stages, looking for only one or two kinds of errors each time you reread the paper. Focus especially on errors that you remember committing in the past. If, for instance, you know you have a tendency to misplace commas, go through your paper looking at each comma carefully. If you have a weakness for writing unintentional sentence fragments, read each sentence aloud to make sure that it is, indeed, a complete sentence. Have you accidentally shifted verb tenses anywhere, moving from past to present tense for no reason? Do all the subjects in your sentences agree in number with their verbs? Now is the time to find out.

1.5.2   Catching Mistakes

One tactic for catching mistakes in sentence structure is to read the sentences aloud, starting with the last one in the paper and then moving to the next-to-last, then the previous sentence, thus going backward through the paper (reading each sentence in the normal, left-to-right manner, of course) until you reach the first sentence of the introduction. This backward progression strips each sentence of its rhetorical context and helps you to focus on its internal structure.

1.5.3   Miscues

Watch out for miscues—problems with a sentence that the writer simply does not see. Your search for errors is hampered by the fact that, as the writer, you hope not to find any errors with your writing. This desire not to find mistakes can lead you to miss sighting them when they occur. Since you know your material so well, it is easy to supply missing material unconsciously as you read—a word, a piece of punctuation—as if it were present.

EXERCISE: Miscues

How difficult is it to see that something is missing in the following sentence?

Unfortunately, philosophers often have too little regard the niceties of communication.

We can even guess that the missing word is probably *for*, which should be inserted after *regard*. It is quite possible, however, that the writer of the sentence, as he reads it, will supply the missing word automatically, as if he has seen it on the page. This is a miscue, and miscues can be hard for writers to spot because they are so close to their material.

Editing is the stage where you finally answer those minor questions that you put off earlier when you were wrestling with wording and organization. Any ambiguities regarding the use of abbreviations, italics, numerals, capital letters, titles (when do you capitalize the title *president*, for example?), hyphens, dashes, apostrophes, and quotation marks have to be cleared up now. You must check to see that you have used the required formats for footnotes, endnotes, margins, and page numbers.

Guessing is not allowed. Sometimes unpracticed writers who realize that they don't quite understand a particular rule of grammar, punctuation, or format do nothing to fill that knowledge gap. Instead, they rely on guesswork and their own logic—which is not always up to the task of dealing with so contrary a language as English—to get them through problems that they could solve if only they referred to a writing manual. Remember this: It does not matter to the reader why or how an error shows up in your writing. It only matters that, in this instance, you as the writer have dropped your guard. You must not allow a careless error to undo the good work that you have done.

1.5.4   Proofreading

Before you hand in your final version of the paper, it is vital that you check it over one more time to make sure there are no errors of any sort. This job is called proofreading or proofing. In essence, you are looking for many of the same things you checked for during editing, but now you are doing it on the last draft, which has been typed and is about to be submitted to your audience. Proofreading is as important as editing; you may have missed an error that you still have time to find, or an error may have been introduced when the draft was recopied or typed for the last time. Like every other stage of the writing process, proofreading is your responsibility.

At this stage, it is essential that you check for typing mistakes: letters transposed or left out of words, missing words, phrases, or punctuation. If you have had the paper professionally typed, you still must check it carefully. Do not rely solely on the typist's proofreading. If you are creating your paper on a computer or a word processor, you may have unintentionally inserted a command that alters a passage of your document drastically—either slicing out or doubling a word or a line or a sentence at the touch of a key. Make sure such accidental mistakes have not occurred. Even if you use the computer's spell check, it is still important to proofread your paper, since the program, which will catch only those words that are spelled incorrectly, may not find words that are correctly spelled but are wrong in context (such as typing "three" when "there" is meant). I received a paper in philosophy of religion that consistently referred to hysterical religion where the author meant, I hope, historical religion.

Above all else, remember that your paper represents you. It is a product of your best thought, your most energetic and imaginative response to a writing challenge. If you have maintained your enthusiasm for the project and worked through the different stages of the writing process honestly and carefully, you should produce a paper you can be proud of, one that will serve its readers well.

EXERCISE: What Did I Mean?

Here is a way to test the notion that writing is a powerful learning tool: Rewrite the notes you have taken from a recent class lecture. Choose a difficult class—if possible, one in which you are feeling somewhat unsure of the material, and one for which you have taken copious notes. As you rewrite, provide the transitional elements (the connecting phrases, like *in order to, because of, and, but, however*) that you were unable to supply in class because of the press of time. Furnish your own examples or illustrations of the ideas expressed in the lecture.

This experiment forces you to supply necessary coherence out of your own thought processes. See if the loss of time it takes you to rewrite the notes is not more than compensated for by a gain in your understanding of the lecture material.

EXERCISE: Narrowing Topics

The following general topics were assigned to undergraduate students in a course on political philosophy. Their task was to write an essay of 2,500 words on one of the topics. Following each general topic is an example of a way in which students narrowed it to make manageable paper topics.

General Topic	**Paper Topic**
Plato	Plato's philosophy of the role of women in politics
Freedom	A comparison of Rousseau's concept of freedom with John Locke's

Revolution   Arguments for the legitimacy of revolution used by Thomas
                      Paine
Thomas Hobbes   Hobbes's definition of the state in Leviathan

   Without taking time to research them, see what kinds of viable narrowed topics you can make from the following general topics: capital punishment, police use of deadly force, stem cell research, information warfare, Napster, affirmative action, human rights, the right to secede, living wills, the moral responsibilities of talk show hosts.

2

Writing Competently

Students often write patently ungrammatical sentences because that is the way the philosophy they have been reading sounds to them. . . . If you find yourself writing a sentence or paragraph that is grammatically out of control, you are probably trying to express a thought that you do not have under control.

—A. P. Martinich, *Philosophical Writing,* 1989

2.1 GENERAL RULES OF GRAMMAR AND STYLE

2.1.1 Competent Writing

Good writing places your thoughts in your readers' minds in exactly the way you want them to be there. Good writing tells your readers just what you want them to know without telling them anything you do not wish to say. That may sound odd, but the fact is, writers have to be careful not to let unwanted messages slip into their writing. Look, for example, at the passage below. Hidden within the prose is a message that jeopardizes the paper's success. Can you detect the message? What's wrong here?

> Recent articles written on the subject of information warfare have had little to say about the particular problems dealt with in this paper. Since few of these articles focus on the defensive role of information warfare.

Chances are, when you reached the end of the second "sentence," you sensed something missing, a gap in logic or coherence, and your eye ran back through both sentences to find the place where things went wrong. The second sentence is actually not a sentence at all. It does have certain features of a sentence—a subject, for example (*few*), and a verb (*focus*)—but its first word (*Since*) subordinates the entire clause that follows, taking away its ability to stand on its own as a complete idea. The second "sentence," which is properly called a subordinate clause, merely fills in some information about the first sentence.

The sort of error represented by the second sentence is commonly called a sentence fragment, and it conveys to the reader a message that no writer wants to send: that the writer either is careless or, worse, has not mastered the language. Language errors such as fragments, misplaced commas, or shifts in verb tense send up little red flags in readers' minds. The result is that readers lose some of their concentration on the issue being discussed. They become distracted and begin to wonder about the language competency of the writer. The writing loses effectiveness.

Credibility for the majority of your audience still depends upon language competence. Anyone who doubts this should remember the beating that Dan Quayle took in the press when he was Vice President of the United States for misspelling the word "potato" at a Trenton, New Jersey, spelling bee on 15 June 1992.

Although they may seem minor, the fact is that the sort of language errors we are discussing—often called surface errors—can be extremely damaging in certain kinds of writing. Surface errors come in a variety of types, including misspellings, punctuation problems, grammar errors, and the inconsistent use of abbreviations, capitalization, or numerals. These errors are an affront to your reader's notion of correctness, and therein lies one of the biggest problems with surface errors. Different audiences tolerate different levels of correctness. You already know that you can get away with surface errors in, say, a letter to a friend, who will not judge you harshly for them, while those same errors in a job application letter might eliminate you from consideration for the job. Correctness depends to an extent upon context.

Another problem with correctness is that the rules governing correctness shift over time. What would have been an error to your grandparent's generation—the splitting of an infinitive, for example, or the ending of a sentence with a preposition—is taken in stride today by most readers. So how do you write correctly when the rules shift from person to person and over time? Here are some tips.

2.1.1.1 *Consider Your Audience*

One of the great risks of writing is that even the simplest of choices you make regarding wording or punctuation can sometimes prejudice your audience against you in ways that may seem unfair. For example, look again at the old grammar "rule" forbidding the splitting of infinitives. After decades of counseling students to never split an infinitive (something this sentence has just done), composition experts now concede that a split infinitive is not a grammar crime. But suppose you have written a position paper trying to convince your city council of the need to hire security personnel for the library, and half of the council members—the people you wish to convince—remember their eighth-grade grammar teacher's outdated warning about splitting infinitives. How will they respond when you tell them, in your introduction, that librarians are ordered "to always accompany" visitors to the rare book room because of the threat of vandalism? How much of their attention have you suddenly lost because of their automatic recollection of a non-rule? It is possible, in other words, to write correctly and still offend your readers' notions of language competence.

Make sure that you tailor the surface features of your writing to the level of competency that your readers require. When in doubt, take a conservative approach. The same goes for the level of formality you should assume. Your audience might be just as distracted by contractions as by a split infinitive.

2.1.1.2 *Aim for Consistency*

When dealing with a language question for which there are different answers—such as whether or not to place a comma after the second item in a series of three ("In his discourse the young philosopher addressed freedom of religion, the inequities of the slave system, and the question of who holds earthly authority in a frontier community.")—always use the same strategy. If, for example, you avoid splitting one infinitive, avoid splitting all infinitives.

2.1.1.3 *Have Confidence in What You Know*

It is easy for unpracticed writers to allow their occasional mistakes to depress them about their writing ability. The fact is, most of what we know about writing is right. We are all capable, for example, of phrasing utterances that are grammatically sound, even if we cannot list the grammar rules by which we achieve coherence. Most writers who worry about their chronic errors have fewer than they think. Becoming distressed about errors makes writing more difficult.

As various composition theorists have pointed out, the word *grammar* has several definitions. One meaning is "the formal patterns in which words must be arranged in order to convey meaning." We learn these patterns very early in life and use them spontaneously, without thinking. Our understanding of grammatical patterns is extremely sophisticated, despite that few of us can actually cite the rules by which the patterns work.

2.1.1.4 *Eliminate Chronic Errors*

If just thinking about our errors has a negative effect on our writing, then how do we learn to write more correctly? Perhaps the best answer is simply to write as often as possible. Give yourself practice in putting your thoughts into written shape, and get lots of practice in revising and proofing your work. And as you write and revise, be honest with yourself, and patient. Chronic errors are like bad habits; getting rid of them takes time.

You probably know of one or two problem areas in your writing that you could have eliminated but have not done so. Instead, you have "fudged" your writing at the critical points, relying upon half-remembered formulas from past English classes or trying to come up with logical solutions to your writing problems. You may have simply decided that comma rules are unlearnable or that you will never understand the difference between the verbs *lay* and *lie*. And so you guess, and get the rule wrong a good part of the time. What a shame, when just a little extra work would give you mastery over those few gaps in your understanding and boost your confidence as well.

2.2   SENTENCE STRUCTURE

2.2.1   Fused Sentences

A fused sentence is one in which two or more independent clauses (passages that can stand as complete sentences) have been run together without the aid of any suitable connecting word, phrase, or punctuation. There are several ways to correct a fused sentence:

INCORRECT: The philosophers were exhausted they had debated for two hours.

CORRECTED: The philosophers were exhausted. They had debated for two hours. [The linked independent clauses have been separated into two sentences.]

CORRECTED: The philosophers were exhausted; they had debated for two hours. [A semicolon marks the break between the two clauses.]

CORRECTED: The philosophers were exhausted, having debated for two hours. [The second independent clause has been rephrased as a dependent clause.]

INCORRECT: Our policy analysis impressed the committee it also convinced them to reconsider their action.

CORRECTED: Our policy analysis impressed the committee and also convinced them to reconsider their action. [The second clause has been rephrased as part of the first clause.]

CORRECTED: Our policy analysis impressed the committee, and it also convinced them to reconsider their action. [The two clauses have been separated by a comma and a coordinating word.]

2.2.2 Sentence Fragments

A fragment is an incomplete part of a sentence that is punctuated and capitalized as if it were an entire sentence. It is an especially disruptive error, because it obscures the connections that the words of a sentence must make in order to complete the reader's understanding. Students sometimes write fragments because they are concerned that a particular sentence is growing too long and needs to be shortened. Remember that cutting the length of a sentence merely by adding a period somewhere along its length often creates a fragment. When checking your writing for fragments, it is essential that you read each sentence carefully. Determine whether it has a complete subject and a verb. Is there a subordinating word before the subject and verb, which makes the construction a subordinate clause rather than a complete sentence? Some fragments lack a verb:

INCORRECT: The chairperson of our department, having received a letter from the newspaper editor. [Note: The word *having*, which resembles a verb, is here being used as a present participle introducing a participial phrase. Watch out for words that look like verbs but are being used in another way.]

CORRECTED: The chairperson of our department received a letter from the newspaper editor.

Some fragments lack a subject. They are simply continuations of a sentence:

INCORRECT: Our study shows that there is broad support for improvement in the health care system. And in the unemployment system.

CORRECTED: Our study shows that there is broad support for improvement in the health care system and in the unemployment system.

Some fragments are subordinate clauses:

INCORRECT: After the latest edition of the newspaper came out. [This clause has the two major components of a complete sentence: a subject (*edition*) and a verb (*came*). Indeed, if the first word (*After*) were deleted, the clause would be a complete sentence. But that first word is a subordinating word, which acts to prevent the following clause from standing on its own as a complete sentence. Watch out for this kind of construction. It is called a subordinate clause, and it is not a sentence.]

CORRECTED: After the latest edition of the newspaper came out, the chancellor's press secretary was overwhelmed with phone calls. [A common method of correcting a subordinate clause that has been punctuated as a complete sentence is to connect it to the complete sentence to which its meaning is most closely connected.]

INCORRECT: Several congressmen asked for copies of the feminist philosopher's position paper. Because it called for the banning of pornography. [The clause beginning after the first period is a subordinate clause written as if it were a complete sentence.]

CORRECTED: Several congressmen asked for copies of the feminist philosopher's position paper because it called for the banning of pornography.

2.2.3 Dangling Modifiers

A modifier is a word or group of words used to describe—to "modify" our understanding of—another word in the sentence. A dangling modifier appears either at the beginning or ending of a sentence and seems to be describing some word other than the one the writer obviously intended. The modifier therefore "dangles," disconnected from its intended meaning. It is often hard for the writer to spot a dangling modifier, but readers can—and will—find them, and the result can be disastrous for the sentence, as the following examples demonstrate:

INCORRECT: Worried at the cost of the program, sections of the bill were trimmed in committee.

CORRECTED: Worried at the cost of the program, the committee trimmed sections of the bill.

CORRECTED: The committee trimmed sections of the bill because they were worried at the cost of the program.

INCORRECT: To lobby for prison reform, a lot of effort went into the television ads.

CORRECTED: The lobby group put a lot of effort into the television ads advocating prison reform. Often, though not always, the cause of a dangling modifier is the fact that the actor in the sentence is either distanced from the modifier or obliterated by the passive voice verb. It is a good idea to avoid passive voice unless you have a specific reason for using it.

One way to check for dangling modifiers is to examine all modifiers at the beginnings or endings of your sentences. Look especially for *to be* phrases (to lobby) or for words ending in -*ing* or -*ed* at the start of the modifier. Then check to see if the modified word is close enough to the phrase to be properly connected.

2.2.4 Parallelism

Series of two or more words, phrases, or clauses within a sentence should be structured in the same grammatical way. Parallel structures can add power and balance to your writing by creating a strong rhetorical rhythm. Here is a famous example of parallelism from the U.S. Constitution. (The capitalization, preserved from the original document, follows eighteenth-century custom. Parallel structures have been italicized.)

> Preamble to the Constitution
> We the People of the United States, in Order *to form a more perfect Union, Establish Justice, insure Domestic Tranquility, provide for the common defence, promote the general Welfare, and secure the Blessings of Liberty to ourselves and our Posterity,* do *ordain* and *establish* this Constitution for the United States of America.

There are actually two series in this sentence, the first composed of six phrases that each complete the infinitive phrase beginning with the word *to (to form, [to] Establish, [to] insure, [to] provide, [to] promote, [to] secure)*, the second consisting of two verbs (*ordain* and *establish*). These parallel series appeal to our love of balance, of pattern, and give an authoritative tone to the sentence. The writer, we feel, has thought long and carefully about the matter at hand and has taken firm control of it.

Because we find a special satisfaction in balanced structures, we are more likely to remember ideas phrased in parallelisms than in less highly ordered language. For this reason, as well as for the sense of authority and control that they suggest, parallel structures are common in philosophical utterances:

> Whatsoever therefore is consequent to a time of Warre, where every man is Enemy to every man; the same is consequent to the time, wherein men live without other security, than what their own strength, and their own invention shall furnish them withall. In such condition, there is no place for Industry; because the fruit thereof is uncertain: and consequently no Culture of the Earth; no Navigation, nor use of the commodities that may be imported by Sea; no commodious Building; no Instruments of moving, and removing such things as require much force; no Knowledge of the face of the Earth; no account of Time; no Arts; no Letters; no Society; and which is worst of all, continuall feare, and danger of violent death; And the life of man, solitary, poore, nasty, brutish, and short. (Thomas Hobbes, *Leviathan.* Ed. C. B. MacPherson. New York: Penguin, 1968. 186)

If the parallelism of a passage is not carefully maintained, the writing can seem sloppy and out of balance. Scan your writing to make sure that all series and lists have parallel structure. The following examples show how to correct faulty parallelism:

> INCORRECT: The mayor promises not only to reform the police department, but also the giving of raises to all city employees. [Note: Connective structures such as *not only . . . but also* and *both . . . and* introduce elements that should be parallel.]
>
> CORRECTED: The mayor promises not only to reform the police department, but also to give raises to all city employees.

INCORRECT: The cost of doing nothing is greater than the cost to renovate the apartment block.

CORRECTED: The cost of doing nothing is greater than the cost of renovating the apartment block.

INCORRECT: Here are the items on the committee's agenda: (1) to discuss the new property tax, (2) to revise the wording of the city charter, (3) a vote on the city manager's request for an assistant.

CORRECTED: Here are the items on the committee's agenda: (1) to discuss the new property tax, (2) to revise the wording of the city charter, (3) to vote on the city manager's request for an assistant.

2.3   PRONOUN ERRORS

2.3.1   *Its* versus *It's*

Do not make the mistake of trying to form the possessive of *it* in the same way that you form the possessive of most nouns. The pronoun *it* shows possession by simply adding an *s*:

The prosecuting attorney argued the case on its merits.

The word *it's* is a contraction, meaning *it is*:

It's the most expensive program ever launched by the council.

What makes the *its/it's* rule so confusing is that most nouns form the singular possessive by adding an apostrophe and an *s*.

When proofreading, any time you come to the word *it's*, substitute the phrase *it is* while you read. If the phrase makes sense, you have used the correct form.

2.3.2   Vague Pronoun References

Pronouns are words that stand in place of nouns or other pronouns that have already been mentioned in your writing. The most common pronouns include *he, she, it, they, them, those, which, who.* You must make sure that each pronoun reference is clear—in other words, that there is no confusion about the reference. The word that the pronoun replaces is called its antecedent. To check the accuracy of your pronoun references, ask yourself, To what does the pronoun refer? Then answer the question carefully, making sure that there is not more than one possible antecedent.

Consider the following example:

Several special interest groups decided to defeat the new regulation governing the forwarding of electronic mail. This became the turning point of the government's reform campaign.

To what does the word *This* refer? The immediate answer seems to be the words *new regulation* at the end of the previous sentence. It is more likely the writer was referring to the attempt of the special interest groups to defeat the bill, but there is no word in the first sentence that refers specifically to this action. The reference is unclear. One way to clarify the reference is to change the beginning of the second sentence:

Several special interest groups decided to defeat the new regulation governing the forwarding of electronic mail. Their attack on the bill became the turning point of the government's reform campaign.

2.3.3 Pronoun Agreement

Remember that a pronoun must agree with its antecedent in both gender and number:

Crito said that he appreciated Socrates' willingness to explain his decision not to flee from Athens.

The following words, however, can become troublesome antecedents. They may look like plural pronouns but are actually singular: *everybody, nobody, everyone, no one, somebody, each, someone, either, anyone.* A pronoun referring to one of these words in a sentence must be singular too:

INCORRECT: Each of the women in the support group brought their children.

CORRECT: Each of the women in the support group brought her children.

INCORRECT: Has everybody received their ballot?

CORRECT: Has everybody received his or her ballot? [The two gender-specific pronouns are used to avoid sexist language.]

CORRECT: Have all the delegates received their ballots? [The singular antecedent has been changed to a plural one.]

2.3.4 Shift in Person

It is important to avoid shifting unnecessarily among first person (*I, we*), second person (*you*), and third person (*she, he, it, they*). Such shifts can cause confusion.

INCORRECT: Most people [third person] who read philosophy find that if you [second person] read only a few pages at a time, you [second person] will comprehend more than if you [second person] read one hundred pages the night before a test.

CORRECT: Most people who read philosophy find that if they read only a few pages at a time, they will comprehend more than if they read one hundred pages the night before a test.

2.4   PUNCTUATION

2.4.1   Apostrophes

An apostrophe is used to show possession; when you wish to say that something belongs to someone or to another thing, you add either an apostrophe and an *s* or an apostrophe alone to the word that represents the owner. When the owner is singular (a single person or thing), the apostrophe precedes an added *s*:

According to Vice President Moore's memo, the faculty is not allowed to speak to the media.

The same rule applies if the word showing possession is a plural that does not end in *s*. When the word expressing ownership is a plural ending in *s*, the apostrophe follows the *s*:

The new regulation was discussed at the chairs' conference.

When a word that is singular ends in *s*, form its possessive in one of two ways:

1. By adding an apostrophe and an *s*: Adams's policy.
2. By adding only an apostrophe: Adams' policy.

Remember to be consistent with the style you choose.

There are two ways to form the possessive for two or more nouns:

1. To show joint possession (both nouns owning the same thing or things), the last noun in the series is possessive:

   The president and first lady's invitations were sent out yesterday.

2. To indicate that each noun owns an item or items individually, each noun must show possession:

   Plato's and Xenophan's accounts of Socrates' trial took different approaches to the same event.

The importance of the apostrophe is obvious when you consider the difference in meaning between the following two sentences:

Be sure to pick up the dean's mail on your way to the airport.

Be sure to pick up the deans' mail on your way to the airport.

In the first of these sentences, you have only one dean to worry about, while in the second, you have at least two!

2.4.2   Capitalization

2.4.2.1   When to Capitalize

Here is a brief summary of some hard-to-remember capitalization rules.

RULE 1.   You may, if you choose, capitalize the first letter of the first word in a full sentence following a colon. (But remember to use whichever style you choose consistently.)

CORRECT: Our instructions are explicit: Do not allow anyone into the reception without an identification badge.

ALSO CORRECT: Our instructions are explicit: do not allow anyone into the reception without an identification badge.

RULE 2.   Capitalize proper nouns (nouns naming specific people, places, or things) and proper adjectives (adjectives made from proper nouns). A common noun following the proper adjective is usually not capitalized, nor is a common adjective preceding the proper adjective (such as *a, an,* or *the*):

Proper nouns	**Proper adjectives**
Methodist	Methodist officials
Iraq	the Iraqi ambassador
Shakespeare	a Shakespearean tragedy

Proper nouns include

- *Names of famous monuments and buildings*: the Washington Monument, the Empire State Building, Graceland
- *Historical events, certain eras, and certain terms concerning calendar dates*: the Civil War, the Roaring Twenties (but: the sixties), Monday, December, Martin Luther King Day
- *Parts of the country*: North, Southwest, Eastern Seaboard, the West Coast, New England. [Note: When words like north, south, east, west, northwest are used

to designate direction rather than geographical region, they are not capitalized: "We drove *east* to Boston and then made a tour of the *East Coast.*"]

- *Words referring to race, religion, or nationality:* Islam, Muslim, Caucasian, White (or white), Oriental, Negro, Black (or black), Slavic, Arab, Jewish, Hebrew, Buddhism, Buddhists, Southern Baptists, the Bible, the Koran, American, Latino
- *Names of languages:* English, Chinese, Latin, Sanskrit
- *Titles of corporations, institutions, businesses, universities, organizations:* Oracle Systems, the National Endowment of the Arts, Ace Hardware Stores, Fordham University, the Thoreau Society. [Note: Some words once considered proper nouns or adjectives have, over time, become common: french fries, pasteurized milk, arabic numerals, italics, panama hat.]

RULE 3.   Titles of individuals are capitalized if they precede a proper name; otherwise, titles are usually not capitalized:

- Professor Jones
- the professor from New York

2.4.2.2 *When Not to Capitalize*

In general, you do not capitalize nouns when your reference is nonspecific. For example, you would not capitalize the phrase *the senator,* but you would capitalize *Senator Smith.* The second reference is as much a title as it is a term of identification, while the first reference is a mere identifier. Likewise, there is a difference in degree of specificity between the phrase *state university* and *Texas A & M State University.*

The meaning of a term may change somewhat depending on capitalization. What, for example, might be the difference between a *Republican* and a *republican*? (When capitalized, the word refers to a member of a specific political party; when not capitalized, the word refers to someone who believes in the representative form of democratic government that limits majority rule with a bill of rights and a constitution.)

Capitalization depends to some extent on the context of your writing. For example, if you are writing a history of philosophy paper for the Kant Society, you may capitalize words and phrases—the Philosopher of Konigsburg—that would not be capitalized in a paper written for an undergraduate class. Likewise, in some contexts it is not unusual to see titles of certain powerful officials capitalized even when not accompanying a proper noun: The Philosopher was the term Thomas Aquinas used when referring to Aristotle.

Another way that context affects capitalization is when someone capitalizes, or does not capitalize, to make a political or cultural statement. The African American feminist bell hooks chooses not to capitalize her name. You should respect her wishes.

2.4.3   Colons

We all know certain uses for the colon. A colon can, for example, separate the parts of a statement of time (4:25 AM), separate chapter and verse in a biblical quotation (*Psalms* 3:16), and close the salutation of a business letter (Dear Mr. Limbaugh:). But there are other uses for the colon that writers sometimes don't quite learn, yet that can add an extra degree of flexibility to sentence structure. The colon can introduce into a sentence certain kinds of material, such as a list, a quotation, or a restatement or description of material mentioned earlier:

- The committee's research proposal promised to do three things: (1) establish the extent of the problem, (2) examine several possible solutions, and (3) estimate the cost of each solution.
- In his speech, the chair challenged us with these words: "How will your research make a difference in the life of our culture?"
- Ahead of us, according to the provost, lay the biggest job of all: convincing our students and their parents of the benefits of general education.

2.4.4   Commas

The comma is perhaps the most troublesome of all marks of punctuation, no doubt because so many variables govern its use, such as sentence length, rhetorical emphasis, or changing notions of style. The most common problems are outlined below.

2.4.4.1   *The Comma Splice*

A comma splice is the joining of two complete sentences by only a comma. One foolproof way to check your paper for comma splices is to read carefully the structures on both sides of each comma. If you find a complete sentence on each side, and if the sentence following the comma does not begin with a coordinating conjunction (*and, but, for, nor, or, so, yet*), then you have found a comma splice.

Simply reading the draft through to try to "hear" the comma splices may not work, since the rhetorical features of your prose—its "movement"—may make it hard to detect this kind of sentence completeness error. There are five commonly used ways to correct comma splices:

1. Place a period between the two independent clauses.
2. Place a comma and a coordinating connective (*and, but, for, or, nor, so, yet*) between the sentences.
3. Place a semicolon between the independent clauses.
4. Rewrite the two clauses of the comma splice as one independent clause.

5. Change one of the two independent clauses into a dependent clause by beginning it with a subordinating word (*for example, although, after, as, because, before, if, though, unless, when, which, where*), which prevents the clause from being able to stand on its own as a complete sentence.

2.4.4.2   *Commas in a Compound Sentence*

A compound sentence is comprised of two or more independent clauses—two complete sentences. When these two clauses are joined by a coordinating conjunction, the conjunction should be preceded by a comma to signal the reader that another independent clause follows. (This is method two for fixing a comma splice described above.) When the comma is missing, the reader does not expect to find the second half of a compound sentence and may be distracted from the text.

As the following examples indicate, the missing comma is especially a problem in longer sentences or in sentences in which other coordinating conjunctions appear. Notice how the comma sorts out the two main parts of the compound sentence, eliminating confusion:

INCORRECT:	The president promised to visit the hospital and investigate the problem and then he called the press conference to a close.
CORRECT:	The president promised to visit the hospital and investigate the problem, and then he called the press conference to a close.

INCORRECT:	The water board can neither make policy nor enforce it nor can its members serve on auxiliary water committees.
CORRECT:	The water board can neither make policy nor enforce it, nor can its members serve on auxiliary water committees.

An exception to this rule arises in shorter sentences, where the comma may not be necessary to make the meaning clear. However, it is never wrong to place a comma between the independent clauses and before the conjunction. If you are the least bit unsure of your audience's notions about what makes for "proper" grammar, it is a good idea to take the conservative approach and use the comma.

2.4.4.3   *Commas in a Series*

A series is any two or more items of a similar nature that appear consecutively in a sentence. The items may be individual words, phrases, or clauses. In a series of three or more items, the items are separated by commas. The final comma, the one before the *and*, is sometimes left out, especially in newspaper writing. This practice, however, can make for confusion, especially in longer, complicated sentences like the second example above. Without a final comma, the division between the last two items in a series will not be clear. This is the sort of ambiguous structure that can cause a reader to backtrack and lose concentration. You can avoid such confusion by always using that final comma. Remember, however, to follow your chosen style consistently.

2.4.4.4 Commas with Restrictive and Nonrestrictive Elements

A nonrestrictive element is part of a sentence—a word, phrase, or clause—that adds information about another element in the sentence without restricting or limiting the meaning of that element. While the information it carries may be useful, the nonrestrictive element is not needed in order for the sentence to make sense. To signal the inessential nature of the nonrestrictive element, we set it off from the rest of the sentence with commas.

Failure to use commas to indicate the nonrestrictive nature of an element can cause confusion. See, for example, how the presence or absence of commas affects our understanding of the following sentence:

> The dean was talking with the philosopher, who won the Nobel Prize for Literature last year.
> The dean was talking with the philosopher who won the Nobel Prize for Literature last year.

Can you see that the comma changes the meaning of the sentence? In the first version of the sentence, the comma makes the information that follows it incidental: The dean might not even know the philosopher had won the prize. In the second version of the sentence, the information following the word *philosopher* is important to the sense of the sentence. It's suggestive; it leaves us with the expectation that we will be told more about the prize or that the dean has purposely engaged this philosopher in conversation. Here the lack of a comma has transformed the material following *philosopher* into a restrictive element, meaning an element necessary to our understanding of the sentence.

Be sure that in your paper you make a clear distinction between nonrestrictive and restrictive elements by setting off the nonrestrictive elements with commas; otherwise, you will create frustrated expectations in your readers.

2.4.5 Quotation Marks

It can be difficult to remember when to use quotation marks and where they go in relation to other marks of punctuation. When faced with a gap in their knowledge of the rules, unpracticed writers often try to rely on logic rather than referring to a rule book. But the rules governing quotation marks do not always seem logical. The only way to make sure of your use of quotation marks is to memorize the rules.

2.4.5.1 When to Use Quotation Marks

Use quotation marks to enclose direct quotations that are not longer than four typed lines:

> Near the end of the dialogue *Euthyphro*, Socrates tells Euthyphro, "If you had not certainly known the nature of piety and impiety, I am confident that you would never, on behalf of a servant, have charged your aged father with murder."

Longer quotes are placed in a block of double-spaced indented prose—without quotation marks:

> Most of us are acculturated to accept a dichotomy between high and low art. Richard Shusterman attacks this distinction for many reasons. But his most persuasive argument is the following:
>
>> The strongest and most urgent reason for defending popular art is that it provides us (even us intellectuals) with too much aesthetic satisfaction to accept its wholesale denunciation as debased, dehumanizing, and aesthetically illegitimate. To condemn it as fit only for the barbaric taste and dull wit of the unenlightened, manipulated masses is to divide us not only against the rest of our community but against ourselves. We are made to disdain the things that give us pleasure and to feel ashamed of the pleasure they give.

Use single quotation marks to set off quotations within quotations:

> "I intend," said the philosopher, "to use in my article a line from Hamsun's poem 'Island Off the Coast.' " [Note: When the interior quote occurs at the end of the sentence, both single and double quotation marks are placed outside the period.]

Use quotation marks to set off the following kinds of titles:

- Titles of short poems (those not printed as a separate volume): "The Second Coming," by William Butler Yeats (short poem); *The Dark Sister*, by Winfield Townley Scott (long poem published as a book)
- Titles of short stories
- Titles of articles or essays
- Titles of songs
- Episodes of television or radio shows

Use quotation marks to convey irony:

The "neutral" parties covertly contributed funds to the zoning commission.

Use quotation marks to set off a technical term:

To "equivocate" is to use a term, consciously or unconsciously, with at least two different meanings that are essential to the persuasive power of an argument. [Note: Once the term is defined, it is not placed in quotation marks again.]

2.4.5.2 Quotation Marks in Relation to Other Punctuation

Always place commas and periods inside closing quotation marks:

"My fellow Americans," said the president, "we are on a peace mission in Somalia."

Place colons and semicolons outside closing quotation marks:

> In his speech on Afghanistan, the president warned against "mission creep"; he was referring to being drawn into a civil war between hostile factions of the population.
> There are several victims of the government's campaign to "Turn Back the Clock": the homeless, the elderly, and the mentally impaired.

Place question marks, exclamation points, and dashes inside or outside closing quotation marks depending upon context. If the punctuation is part of the quotation, it goes inside the quotation mark:

> "When will Congress recognize the rights of the unborn?" asked the pro-lifer.
> The demonstrators shouted, "More philosophy courses!" and "No more physical education requirements at the university!"

If the punctuation is not part of the quotation, it goes outside the quotation mark:

> Which philosopher said, "Always act so that the maxim of your action can become a universal law"? [Note: Although the quote was a complete sentence, you do not place a period after it. There can only be one piece of "terminal" punctuation (punctuation that ends a sentence).]

2.4.6 Semicolons

The semicolon is another little used punctuation mark that is worth incorporating into your writing strategy because of its many potential applications. A semicolon can be used to correct a comma splice:

INCORRECT: Socrates faced death with equanimity, his arguments had convinced his disciples.

CORRECTED: Socrates faced death with equanimity; his arguments had convinced his disciples.

INCORRECT: Several guests at the fundraiser had lost their invitations, however, we were able to seat them, anyway.

CORRECTED: Several guests at the fundraiser had lost their invitations; however, we were able to seat them, anyway.

Conjunctive adverbs like *however, therefore,* and *thus* are not coordinating words (*such as, and, but, or, for, so, yet*) and cannot be used with a comma to link independent clauses. If the second independent clause begins with a *however*, it must be preceded by either a period or a semicolon.

As you can see from the second example above, connecting the two independent clauses with a semicolon instead of a period strengthens the relationship between the clauses. Use semicolons to separate items in a series when the series items themselves contain commas. Avoid misusing semicolons. For example, use a comma, not a semicolon, to separate an independent clause from a dependent clause:

INCORRECT: Students from the college volunteered to answer phones during the pledge drive; which was set up to generate money for the new philosophy library.

CORRECTED: Students from the college volunteered to answer phones during the pledge drive, which was set up to generate money for the new philosophy library.

Although they are useful, too many semicolons in your writing can distract your reader's attention. Avoid monotony by using semicolons sparingly.

2.5   SPELLING

All of us have problems spelling certain words that we have not yet committed to memory. But most writers are not as bad at spelling as they believe themselves to be. An individual usually finds only a handful of words troubling. It is important to be as sensitive as possible to your own particular spelling problems—and to keep a dictionary handy. There is no excuse for failing to check spelling. But reread your paper after running spell check, or your paper about historical religion might instead address hysterical religion; or your article on women's suffrage might turn into one about women's suffering.

2.5.1   Commonly Confused Words

advice/advise	aisle/isle	an/and
affect/effect	allusion/illusion	angel/angle

ascent/assent
bare/bear
brake/break
breath/breathe
buy/by
capital/capitol
choose/chose
cite/sight/site
complement/compliment
conscience/conscious
corps/corpse
council/counsel
dairy/diary
descent/dissent
desert/dessert
device/devise
die/dye
dominant/dominate
elicit/illicit
eminent/immanent/
imminent
envelop/envelope
every day/everyday
fair/fare
formally/formerly
forth/fourth

hear/here
heard/herd
hole/whole
human/humane
its/it's
know/no
later/latter
lay/lie
lead/led
lessen/lesson
loose/lose
may be/maybe
miner/minor
moral/morale
of/off
passed/past
patience/patients
peace/piece
personal/personnel
plain/plane
precede/proceed
presence/presents
principal/principle
quiet/quite
rain/reign/rein
raise/raze

reality/realty
respectfully/respectively
reverend/reverent
right/rite/write
road/rode
scene/seen
sense/since
stationary/stationery
straight/strait
taught/taut
than/then
their/there/they're
threw/through
too/to/two
track/tract
waist/waste
waive/wave
weak/week
weather/whether
were/where
which/witch
whose/who's
your/you're

2.5.2 Commonly Misspelled Words

acceptable
accessible
accommodate
accompany
accustomed
acquire
against
annihilate
apparent

arguing
argument
authentic
before
begin
beginning
believe
benefited
bulletin

business
cannot
category
committee
condemn
courteous
definitely
dependent
desperate

develop	knowledge	pursuing
different	license	questionnaire
disappear	likelihood	realize
disappoint	maintenance	receipt
easily	manageable	received
efficient	meanness	recession
environment	mischievous	recommend
equipped	missile	referring
exceed	necessary	religious
exercise	nevertheless	remembrance
existence	no one	reminisce
experience	noticeable	repetition
fascinate	noticing	representative
finally	nuisance	rhythm
foresee	occasion	ridiculous
forty	occasionally	roommate
fulfill	occurred	satellite
gauge	occurrences	scarcity
guaranteed	omission	scenery
guard	omit	science
harass	opinion	secede
hero	opponent	secession
heroes	parallel	secretary
humorous	parole	senseless
hurried	peaceable	separate
hurriedly	performance	sergeant
hypocrite	pertain	shining
ideally	practical	significant
immediately	preparation	sincerely
immense	probably	skiing
incredible	process	stubbornness
innocuous	professor	studying
intercede	prominent	succeed
interrupt	pronunciation	success
irrelevant	psychology	successfully
irresistible	publicly	susceptible
irritate	pursue	suspicious

technical	unanimous	various
temporary	unconscious	vegetable
tendency	undoubtedly	visible
therefore	until	without
tragedy	vacuum	women
truly	valuable	writing
tyranny		

2.6 TECHNICAL AND ORDINARY USAGE OF PHILOSOPHICAL TERMS

Unlike scientists, philosophers tend to adopt words from ordinary language to express technical meanings rather than introduce new terminology.

A glossary of important philosophical terms is provided in the back of the text. Following is a list of the most problematic terms. Pay special attention to the ways in which philosophers use them.

absolute	humanism	paradigm
analytic	idea	pragmatic
argument	idealism	pragmatism
authenticity	instrumentalism	rationalism
determinism	intuition	realism
dilemma	materialism	reduction
double effect	metaphysics	synthetic
egoism	naturalism	terrorism
explanation	objectivism	utilitarian

PART TWO

Conducting Research in Philosophy

3

Organizing the Research Process

I am not solitary whilst I read and write, though nobody is with me.

—Ralph Waldo Emerson, *Nature,* 1836

3.1 GAINING CONTROL OF THE RESEARCH PROCESS

Some disciplines are more inclined than philosophy to assign traditional research papers. The type of research paper your philosophy instructor is likely to assign you might be a short expository paper, a compare-and-contrast paper, a case study of an emerging ethical issue, a historical paper, or the traditional research paper with a full bibliography and footnotes. Plenty of guidance on the preparation of these papers will be provided in subsequent chapters, but there are some guidelines for research that will be helpful to you regardless of the nature of your assignment.

Students new to the writing of research papers sometimes find themselves intimidated by the job ahead of them. After all, the research paper adds what seems to be an extra set of complexities to the writing process. Like any other expository or persuasive paper, a research paper should present an original thesis using a carefully organized and logical argument. But a research paper investigates a topic that is outside the writer's own expertise. This means that writers must locate and evaluate information that is new to them, in effect educating themselves as they explore their topics. A beginning researcher sometimes feels overwhelmed by the basic requirements of the assignment or by the authority of the source material being investigated.

In my first year of graduate school I took a course devoted to philosophy of religion. The central historical figures we studied were Immanuel Kant and Georg Wilhelm Hegel. Toward the end of the semester our instructor announced we would have a visiting lecturer, an expert on Hegel who had recently joined the faculty. Professor Blue (not his real name) gave a fine presentation on Hegel's early philosophy of religion. During the discussion, our instructor complimented Blue and then asked why he had restricted his comments to Hegel's early thought and not commented on his lectures on the philosophy of religion. (There is a three-volume collection of Hegel's later lectures on the philosophy of religion available in an English translation.) Blue responded, "I have never read Hegel's lectures on the philosophy of religion."

There was silence. I thought: "Here is an honest person." Even the experts have not read everything. And if they have not read everything, then they may not have thought everything either. Even a beginning student in a subject as remote and specialized as Hegel's philosophy of religion may have information to contribute or opinions to offer that have been overlooked by experts.

You also should be skeptical of experts, especially when they are commenting on each other's views about a historical figure. Also, some concepts from the history of philosophy are resurrected for new purposes. Currently, there is a great deal of interest in the French philosopher Michael Foucault. Foucault borrowed some of his ideas from British philosopher Jeremy Bentham's nineteenth-century proposals calling for social reform through the extension of a social institution Bentham called the Panopticon. Be suspicious of any opinion expressed by experts on Foucault concerning Bentham's view of the Panopticon, since their views of Bentham will be affected by their focus on Foucault. If you are interested in Bentham's ideas or the Panopticon, go to the original source. And check all quotes, particularly those containing ellipses (. . .) indicating that material has been omitted. Sometimes the material omitted changes the entire meaning of the material quoted. (I twisted Emerson's meaning to my own purposes by selecting just one sentence for this chapter's opening quote.)

As you begin a research project, it may be difficult to establish a sense of control over the different tasks you are undertaking. You may have little notion of which direction to search for a thesis, or even where the most helpful sources of information might be located. If you do not carefully monitor your own work habits, you may find yourself unwittingly abdicating responsibility for the paper's argument by borrowing it wholesale from one or more of your sources.

Who is in control of your paper? The answer must be you—not the instructor who assigned you the paper and not the published writers whose opinions you investigate. If all your paper does is paste together the opinions of others, it has little use. It is up to you to synthesize an original idea from a judicious evaluation of your source material. While there are, of course, many elements of your paper about which you are unsure at the beginning of your research project—you will probably not yet have a definitive thesis sentence, for example, or even much understanding of the shape of your argument—you can establish a measure of control over the process you will go through to complete the paper. And if you work regularly and systematically, keeping yourself open to new ideas as they present themselves, your sense of control will grow.

Understand your assignment. It is possible for a research assignment to go bad simply because the writer did not read the assignment carefully. Considering how much time and effort you are about to put into your project, make sure you have a clear understanding of what it is your instructor wants you to do. Be sure to ask your instructor about any aspect of the assignment that is unclear to you—but only after you have read it carefully. Recopying the assignment in your own handwriting is a good way to start, even though your instructor may have given the assignment to you in writing. Before you dive into the project, make sure that you have considered the questions in the paragraphs that follow.

What is your topic? The assignment may give you a great deal of specific information about your topic, or you may be allowed considerable freedom in establishing one for yourself. In a history of modern philosophy class in which you are studying metaphysical or epistemological issues (issues dealing with the ultimate nature of reality and with our ability to acquire knowledge respectively), your professor might give you a very specific assignment—a paper, for example, examining the views of freedom or truth found in the works you are reading by Kant and Spinoza. Or, the instructor may allow you to choose the issue that your paper will address. You need to understand the terms, set up in the assignment, within which you may design your project. Otherwise, you may do a perfectly respectable paper on a topic in political philosophy, such as Hobbes' and Spinoza's views of the social contract, only to be told its focus is inappropriate.

What is your purpose? Whatever the degree of latitude you are given in the matter of your topic, pay close attention to the way in which your instructor has phrased the assignment. Is your primary job to describe a current ethical dilemma or to take a stand on it? Are you to compare several arguments for their views about a particular ethical question and, if so, to what end? Are you to classify, persuade, survey, analyze? Look for such descriptive terms in the assignment in order to determine the purpose of the project.

Some philosophy instructors do not assign argumentative papers in their beginning classes. Instead, they decide to concentrate on developing analytical abilities. So, for example, you might be given the assignment of explaining Kant's and Mill's views of justice but not asked to develop a thesis about their relative merits.

I have never met a philosophy instructor who objected to hearing an opinion after the analytical work had been done. If you are the sort of person who feels a strong need to evaluate the authors you are studying, then ask your instructor if it would be acceptable to include your own opinion in your paper. But do not confuse the acceptability of doing extra work with absolution from doing the work assigned. *You cannot express a reasonable view of Kant's notion of justice without telling the reader what Kant's concept of justice is.*

Who is your audience? Your own orientation to the paper is profoundly affected by your conception of the audience for whom you are writing. Granted, your number one reader is your instructor, but who else would be interested in your paper? Imagining your audience can help you gain an understanding of many elements of your paper. Are you writing about an issue of interest to the voters of a community? You might use your paper as the occasion to formulate a letter to the editor of your local newspaper. A paper that describes a proposal for revising the process for filing a living will may justifiably contain much more technical jargon for an audience of hospital administrators than for a hospital advisory group that includes members of the local community. Your research may serve several audiences, but you will have to rewrite for each audience to communicate effectively.

What kind of research are you doing? Primary research requires you to work firsthand on original published or unpublished texts. For instance, in a course in the history of philosophy you will probably read Descartes' *Meditations on First Philosophy.* Many editions of this classic work contain six sets of objections from philosophers and theologians who were Descartes' contemporaries. The fifth set of objections was formulated by another significant philosopher of the modern period, Thomas Hobbes. You might decide to do your paper on Hobbes' criticism of Descartes' proof of his own existence. And, as part of understanding Hobbes, you will probably want to read the section of his *Leviathan* devoted to the nature of knowledge. Here you will be doing primary research, since both Descartes' *Meditations* and Hobbes' *Leviathan* are considered primary sources.

Other examples of primary sources are such things as manuscripts and notebooks, the dialogues of Plato, or a newly published but original perspective on an ethical issue in a professional journal.

Another sort of primary research students sometimes pursue is looking behind the published works at an author's unpublished material. This type of research can be difficult, since it often requires travel to special collections. But you may be surprised by the holdings your library has available on microfilm.

Finally, you may do primary research that takes you outside the field of philosophy when you venture into interdisciplinary courses or courses on professional ethics. In most professional ethics courses, you will survey existing codes of professional ethics. You might be required to contact the public relations office of a local firm to ask what considerations went into the formulation of the firm's code of ethics and personnel procedures. Or, you might want to write your paper in criminal justice ethics on the question of whether civilians should sit on police review boards. It would be a good idea to interview the local police chief and some patrol officers. Conducting such surveys and interviews is a kind of primary research.

Secondary research makes use of secondary sources—that is, published accounts of primary materials. Many American university courses center on secondary material embodied in textbooks. On the other hand, some material that is considered secondary makes an original contribution to scholarship and understanding. Genevieve Lloyd's *Man of Reason,* for example, brings feminist scholarship to bear on the so-called "dead white males" that used to make up the canon of Western thought. Secondary sources include such items as books dedicated to explaining the work of a historical figure, entries in the *Encyclopedia of Philosophy,* articles in journals devoted to historical figures such as Descartes, or an interpretative paper explaining the re-actions of patrol officers to the proposed inclusion of civilians on review boards.

The most important thing to remember when reading secondary sources is that their authors have their own philosophical allegiances. If possible, select secondary sources from different schools of philosophy. If you are enrolled in a course on Kant's *Critique of Pure Reason*, try to read commentaries from both analytic philoso-phers such as Strawson and continental philosophers such as Heidegger.

Keep your perspective. Whichever type of research you perform, you must keep your results in perspective. There is no way in which you, as a primary researcher, can be completely objective and exhaustive in your research, and your instructor does not expect you to be. She realizes that the state of your library, the availability of materials, the length of the assignment, and even the difficulty of the material all affect how much research you can accomplish. Just choose your sources wisely, consult your instructor, stay on the topic, and select sources with a variety of philo-sophical perspectives. You need not exhaust the field of alternatives.

Likewise, if you are conducting secondary research, you must remember that the articles and journals you are reading are shaped by the aims of their writers, who are interpreting primary materials for their own ends. The further you get from a primary source, the greater the possibility for distortion. Your job as a re-searcher is to be as accurate as possible, and that means keeping in view the limita-tions of your methods and their ends. A good primary source may not be a good secondary source. Giles Deleuze was a prominent French philosopher who pub-lished a book on Spinoza. The book is a good source for understanding Deleuze, but not for understanding Spinoza.

3.2   EFFECTIVE RESEARCH METHODS

In any research project there will be moments of confusion, but you can pre-vent this confusion from overwhelming you by establishing an effective research procedure. You need to design a schedule for the project that is as systematic as possible, yet flexible enough so that you do not feel trapped by it. A schedule will help keep you from running into dead ends by always showing you what to do next. At the same time, the schedule helps you to retain the presence of mind necessary to spot new ideas and new strategies as you work.

You may feel like delaying your research for many reasons: unfamiliarity with the library, the press of other tasks, a deadline that seems comfortably far away. But do not allow such factors to deter you. Research takes time. Working in a library seems to speed up the clock, so that the hour you expected it to take you to find a certain source becomes two hours. You must allow yourself the time it takes not only to find material but to read it, assimilate it, and set it in context with your own thoughts. If you delay starting, you may eventually find yourself distracted by the deadline, having to keep an eye on the clock while trying to make sense of a writer's complicated argument.

The following schedule lists the steps of a research project in the order in which they are generally accomplished. Remember that each step is dependent upon the others and that it is quite possible to revise earlier decisions in the light of later discoveries. After some background reading, for example, your notion of the paper's purpose may change, a fact that may in turn alter other steps. One of the strengths of a good schedule is its flexibility. Note that this schedule lists tasks for both primary and secondary research; you should use only those steps that are relevant to your project.

RESEARCH SCHEDULE

Task	Date of Completion
Determine topic, purpose, and audience	
Do background reading in reference books	
Narrow your topic; establish a tentative conclusion	
Develop a working bibliography	
Write for needed information, such as codes of ethics	
Read and evaluate written sources, taking notes	
Determine whether to conduct interviews	
Draft a thesis and outline	
Write a first draft	
Obtain feedback (show draft to instructor, if possible)	
Do more research, if necessary	
Revise draft	
Correct bibliographical format of paper	
Prepare final draft	
Run spelling check program	
Proofread	
Proofread again, looking for characteristic errors	
Deadline for final draft	

Whether you are doing primary or secondary research, you need to know what kinds of work have already been done in your field of study. A good way to start is by consulting general reference works, though you do not want to overdo it. Be very careful not to rely too exclusively on material taken from general encyclopedias, such as *Encyclopedia Britannica* or even specialized encyclopedias such as the *Encyclopedia of Philosophy* and the *Encyclopedia of Bioethics*. You may wish to consult one for an overview of a topic with which you are unfamiliar, but students new to research are often tempted to import large sections, if not entire articles, from such volumes, and this practice is not good scholarship. One major reason why your instructor has assigned a research paper is to let you experience the kinds of books and journals in which the discourse of philosophy is conducted. General reference encyclopedias are good places for instant introductions to subjects; some even include bibliographies of reference works at the ends of their articles. But to write a useful paper, you will need much more detailed information about your subject. Once you have learned what you can from a general encyclopedia, move on to other sources.

No philosophy instructor is going to let you solve the problem of knowledge by seeing what *Webster's* dictionary offers as a definition.

Narrow Your Topic and Establish a Working Thesis

Before exploring outside sources, it is a good idea to find out what you already know or think about your topic, a job that can be accomplished well only through writing. You might wish to investigate your own attitude toward your topic and your beliefs concerning it, using one or more of the prewriting strategies described in Chapter 1. You might also be surprised by what you know—or don't know—about the topic. This kind of self-questioning can help you discover a profitable direction for your research.

Specific methods for discovering a thesis are discussed in Chapter 1. It is unlikely that you will come up with a satisfactory thesis at the beginning of your project. You need a way to guide yourself through the early stages of research toward a main idea that is both useful and manageable. Having in mind a working thesis—a preliminary statement of your purpose—can help you select material that is of greatest interest to you as you examine potential sources. The working thesis will probably evolve as your research progresses, and you should be ready to accept such change. You must not fix on a thesis too early in the research process, or you may miss opportunities to refine it.

Develop a Working Bibliography

As you begin your research, you will look for published sources—essays, books, encyclopedia articles by experts in the field—that may help you with your project. This list of potentially useful sources is your working bibliography. There are many ways to discover items for the bibliography. The cataloging system in your library will give you titles, as will specialized published bibliographies in your field. (Some of these bibliographies are listed in Chapter 4.) The general reference works in which you did your background reading may also list such sources, and each specialized book or essay you find will itself have a bibliography of sources that may be useful to you. The American Philosophical Society (APA) home page *http://www.apa.udel.edu/apa/index.html* has links to encyclopedias and bibliographies as well as discussion lines devoted to philosophical issues and historical figures, including everyone from Ayn Rand to Charles Peirce to Zarathustra.

It is from your working bibliography that you will select the items for the bibliography that will appear in the final draft of your paper. Early in your research you do not know which of your sources will be of help to you and which will not, but it is important to keep an accurate description of each entry in your working bibliography so that you will be able to tell clearly which items you have investigated and which you will need to consult again. Establishing the working bibliography also allows you to practice using the bibliographical format you are required to follow in your final draft. As you make your list of potential sources, be sure to include all the information about each one in the proper format, using the proper punctuation.

Evaluate Written Sources, Taking Notes

Few research experiences are more frustrating than trying to recall information found in a source that you can no longer identify. You must establish an efficient method of examining and evaluating the sources in your working bibliography. Suggestions for compiling an accurate record of your written sources are described below.

DETERMINE QUICKLY THE POTENTIAL USEFULNESS OF A SOURCE

For books, you can read through the prefatory material (the introduction, foreword, and preface) looking for the author's thesis; you can also examine chapter headings, dust jackets, and indexes. The footnotes of the author you are studying can be particularly fruitful areas to investigate. Often, we assume that if an author footnotes someone else, there is no profit to be gained from studying the cited source. We are charitable and assume that our author has correctly understood the source and conveyed to us all that is worthwhile in the source. We assume that any further research we do should be on material written about our author. Do not make this assumption.

A journal article should announce its intention in its introduction, which in most cases will be a page or less in length. *The Philosopher's Index* publishes abstracts of articles from leading philosophy journals within a few months of their appearance in print. It also is a good source for references to reviews of recent philosophy books. The journal *Philosophical Investigations* is entirely devoted to book reviews.

Look at the index of a potential source first. If I were working on the topic of repeat-offender programs, I would look in the back of the book for entries on due process and repeat offenders. I would hope to find several references, one of which would be at least a couple of pages long. I would then read the longest reference, which usually determines whether I decide to spend more time investigating a potential source. Whatever you decide about the source, copy its title page, making sure that all important publication information (including title, date, author, volume number, and page numbers) is included. Write on the photocopied page any necessary information that is not printed there. Without such a record, later on in your research you may forget that you have consulted a text, in which case you may find yourself repeating your work.

When you have determined that a potential source is worth closer inspection, explore it carefully. If it is a book, you must determine whether you should invest the time it will take to read it in its entirety. Whatever the source, make sure you understand not only its overall thesis, but also each part of the argument that the writer sets up to illustrate or prove the thesis. You need to get a feel for the writer's argument—how the subtopics form (or do not form) a logical defense of the main point. What do you think of the writer's logic and the examples used? Coming to an accurate appraisal may take more than one reading.

As you read, try to get a feel for the larger argument in which this source takes its place. Its references to the works of other writers will show you where to look for additional material and indicate the general shape of scholarly opinion concerning your subject. If you can see the article you are reading as only one element of an ongoing dialogue instead of an attempt to have the last word on the subject, then you can place the argument of the paper in perspective.

USE PHOTOCOPIES

Periodicals and most reference works cannot be checked out of the library. Before the widespread placement of photocopy machines, students could use these materials only by sitting in the library, reading sources, and jotting down information on note cards. While there are advantages to using the old note-card method (see below), photocopying saves you time in the library and allows you to take the source information in its original shape home with you, where you can decide how to use it at your convenience. Record all necessary bibliographical information on the photocopy. If you forget to do this, you may find yourself making an extra trip to the library just to get an accurate date of publication or a set of page numbers. Remember that photocopying a source is not the same thing as examining it. You will still have to spend time going over the material, assimilating it in order to use it accurately. It is not enough merely to have the information close at hand, or even to have read it once or twice. You must understand it thoroughly. Be sure to give yourself time for this kind of evaluation.

THE NOTE CARD: A THING OF THE PAST?

In many ways note cards are an old-fashioned method of recording source material, and for unpracticed researchers they may seem unwieldy and unnecessary, since the information jotted on them—one fact per card—will eventually have to be transmitted again into the research paper. However, using note cards will force you to think productively as you read. In translating the language of the source material into the language of your notes, you are assimilating the material more completely than you would by merely reading it. Note cards also give you a handy way to arrange and rearrange your facts, looking for the best possible organization for your paper. Not even a computer gives you the flexibility of a pack of cards as you try to order your paper.

Draft a Thesis and Outline

No matter how thoroughly you may hunt for data or how fast you read, you will not be able to find and assimilate every source pertaining to your subject, especially if it is a popular or controversial one, and you should not prolong your research unduly. You must bring the research phase of the project to an end—with the option of resuming it later if the need arises—and begin to shape both the material you have gathered and your thoughts about it into a paper. During the research phase of your project, you have been thinking about your working thesis, revising it in accordance with the material you have discovered, and considering ways to improve it. Eventually, you must formulate a thesis that sets out an interesting and useful task, one that can be satisfactorily managed within the limits of your assignment and that effectively employs much, if not all, of the source material you have gathered.

Instructors increasingly require students to make oral presentations in class. An in-class presentation can be a good form for trying out your thesis and the major ideas of your paper. Think of your oral presentation as a first draft and the classroom feedback as an opportunity to revise your work before finalizing it.

Once you have formulated your thesis, it is a good idea to make an outline of the paper. In helping you to determine a structure for your paper, the outline is also testing the thesis, prompting you to discover the kinds of work your paper will have to do in order to complete the task set out by the thesis. Chapter 1 discusses the structural requirements of the formal and the informal outline. (If you have used note cards, you may want to start the outlining process by first organizing your cards according to the headings you have given them and looking for logical connections among the different groups of cards. Experimenting with structure in this way may lead you to discoveries that will further improve your thesis.)

No thesis or outline is written in stone. There is still time to improve the structure or purpose of your paper even after you have begun to write your first draft, or, for that matter, your final draft. Some writers actually prefer to write a first draft of the paper before outlining, then study the draft's structure in order to determine what revisions need to be made. Stay flexible, always looking for a better connection, a sharper wording of your thesis. All the time you are writing, the testing of your ideas goes on.

Write a First Draft

Despite all the preliminary work you have done on your paper, you may feel a resistance to beginning the writing of your first draft. Integrating all your material, your ideas, into a smoothly flowing argument is a complicated task. It may help to think of your first attempt as only a rough draft, which can be changed as necessary. Another strategy for reducing the resistance to starting is to begin with the part of the draft that you feel most confident about instead of with the introduction. You may write sections of the draft in any order, piecing the parts together later. But however you decide to start writing—start.

Obtain Feedback

It is not enough that you understand your argument; others have to understand it, too. If your instructor is willing to look at your rough draft, you should take advantage of the opportunity and pay careful attention to any suggestions for improvement. Other readers may be of help, although having a friend or a relative read your draft may not be as helpful as having it read by someone who is knowledgeable in your field. In any event, be sure to evaluate carefully any suggestions you receive for improvement. Remember, the final responsibility for the paper rests with you.

3.3   ETHICAL USE OF SOURCE MATERIAL

You want to make as effective use of your source material as possible. This will sometimes mean that you should quote from a source directly, while at other times you will recast source information in your own words. At all times, you should work to integrate the source material skillfully into the flow of your written argument.

When to Quote

You should quote directly from a source when the original language is distinctive enough to enhance your argument or when rewording the passage would lessen its impact. In the interest of fairness, you should also quote a passage to which you will take exception. Rarely, however, should you quote a source at great length (longer than two or three paragraphs). Nor should your paper, or any lengthy section of it, be merely a string of quoted passages. The more language you take from the writings of others, the more the quotations will disrupt the rhetorical flow of your own language. Too much quoting creates a "scissors-paste" paper, a choppy patchwork of varying styles and borrowed purposes in which your sense of your own control over your material is lost.

Quotations in Relation to Your Own Writing

When you do use a quotation, make sure that you insert it skillfully. Chapter 2 offers examples of the ways in which to integrate quotations of various lengths into your paper. Remember that quotes of four lines or fewer should be integrated into your text and set off with quotation marks. Quotations longer than four lines should begin on a new line and be indented five spaces from the left-hand margin.

Also, see how skillfully you can place the name of your source in a footnote rather than within the sentence. Papers and articles that contain too many author tags, such as "Heidegger says, '. . .,' " can become tedious. Students tend to write like this whenever they fall in love with a new writer. Bury the names of your saints in the footnotes.

Acknowledge Quotations Carefully

Failing to signal the presence of a quotation skillfully can lead to confusion or choppiness. If you quote from Deleuze's book on Spinoza, make it transparent whether the quoted words are from Deleuze or Spinoza.

The origin of each quote must be indicated within your text at the point where the quote occurs as well as in the list of works cited, which follows the text.

Quote Accurately

If your transcription of a quotation introduces careless variants of any kind, you are misrepresenting your source. Proofread your quotations very carefully, paying close attention to such surface features as spelling, capitalization, italics, and the use of numerals. Occasionally, in order either to make a quotation fit smoothly into a passage, to clarify a reference, or to delete unnecessary material, you may need to change the original wording slightly. You must, however, signal any such change to your reader.

Some alterations may be noted by brackets:

"Several times during his oration, the philosopher said that his stand [on capital punishment] remains unchanged."

Ellipses indicate that words have been left out of a quote:

"The last time the Athenians chose to endorse one of the tyrant's policies . . . they created a disaster for themselves and their city."

When you integrate quoted material with your own prose, it is unnecessary to begin the quote with ellipses:

Benton raised eyebrows with his claim that "nobody in the mayor's office knows how to tie a shoe, let alone work out a compromise."

Paraphrasing

Your writing has its own rhetorical attributes, its own rhythms and structural coherence. Inserting several quotations into a section of your paper can disrupt the patterns you establish in your prose and diminish the effectiveness of your own language. Paraphrasing, or recasting source material in your own words, is one way to avoid the choppiness that can result from a series of quotations.

Remember that a paraphrase is to be written in your language; it is not a near copy of the source writer's language. Merely changing a few words of the original does justice to no one's prose and frequently produces stilted passages. This sort of borrowing is actually a form of plagiarism. In order to fully integrate the material you wish to use into your writing, use your own language.

Paraphrasing may actually increase your comprehension of source material, because in recasting a passage, you will have to think very carefully about its meaning—more carefully, perhaps, than you might if you merely copied it word for word.

Avoiding Plagiarism

Paraphrases require the same sort of documentation as direct quotes do. The words of a paraphrase may be yours, but the idea is someone else's. Failure to give that person credit, in the form of references within the text and in the bibliography, may make you vulnerable to a charge of plagiarism.

Plagiarism is the use of someone else's words or ideas without giving proper credit. While some plagiarism is deliberate, produced by writers who understand that they are guilty of a kind of academic thievery, much of it is unconscious, committed by writers who are not aware of the varieties of plagiarism or who are careless in recording their borrowings from sources. Sometimes plagiarism happens simply because of the passage of time. You read something when you are twenty, and when you think of it again when you are forty, you think you are having an original thought. Plagiarism includes

- Quoting directly without acknowledging the source.
- Paraphrasing without acknowledging the source.
- Constructing a paraphrase that closely resembles the original in language and syntax.
- Turning in someone else's paper as your own work regardless of whether the real author is a family member, friend, or paid ghost writer.

One way to guard against plagiarism is to keep careful notes of when you have quoted source material directly and when you have paraphrased—making sure that the wording of the paraphrases is yours. Make sure that all direct quotes in your final draft are properly set off from your own prose, either with quotation marks or in indented blocks.

What kind of paraphrased material must be acknowledged? Basic material that you find in several sources need not be acknowledged by a reference. For example, it is unnecessary to cite a source for the information that Aristotle was a Greek philosopher and the tutor of Alexander the Great, because these are commonly known facts. Any information that is not widely known, however, whether factual or open to dispute, should be documented.

4

Information in Your Library and Similar Places

A man should learn to detect and watch that gleam of light which flashes across his mind from within, more than the lustre of the firmament of bards and sages. Yet he dismisses without notice his thought, because it is his. In every work of genius we recognize our own rejected thoughts; they come back to us with a certain alienated majesty. . . . God will not have his work made manifest by cowards.

—Ralph Waldo Emerson, *Self-Reliance*, 1841

You will find much valuable information on the library shelves. Topics in philosophy, however, can also offer unusual opportunities to discover information sources outside the library, such as research institutes and political action groups. This chapter describes a variety of research sources in philosophy and in other fields of study that connect with philosophy in interdisciplinary courses.

4.1 INFORMATION RESOURCES IN YOUR COLLEGE LIBRARY

4.1.1 Directories

Adams, Charles J., et al., eds. *The Encyclopedia of Religion.* 16 vols. New York: Macmillan, 1987.

Bahm, Archie, and Robert Thompson, eds. *The Directory of American Philosophers,* 2000–2001. Bowling Green, Ohio: Philosophy Documentation

Center, 1996. This directory lists philosophy programs at all institutions of higher learning in the United States and Canada. It also lists philosophers associated with these institutions along with their areas of specialization. The directory contains a useful section on financial assistance available to graduate students, a description of major philosophical societies, email addresses, Web sites, and information about the major professional journals in philosophy. It is in its twentieth edition, with a new edition projected every two years. The publisher, the Philosophy Documentation Center, is an excellent source of online resources for research in philosophy. The current URL: *http://www.pdcnet.org/ index.html.*

Becker, Lawrence C., et al., eds. *Encyclopedia of Ethics.* 3 vols. New York: Garland, 2001.

Blackwell Guides to Philosophy. Blackwell has recently issued individual guides edited by contemporary philosophers in the areas of ethical theory (Hugh Lafollette), epistemology (John Greco and Ernest Sosa), philosophy of science (Peter MacHamer and Michael Silberstein), business ethics (Norman Bowie), social philosophy (Robert Simon), and modern philosophy (Steven Emanuel.) Certainly, there will be additional Blackwell guides. Check with the library by searching for Blackwell Guide in the title field, or check the Blackwell Web site, an excellent online philosophy resource center: *http://www. blackwellpublishers.co.uk/philos/.* These should prove to be useful tools for advanced undergraduates and graduate students.

Chadwick, Ruth, ed. *The Concise Encyclopedia of the Ethics of New Technologies.* San Diego: Academic Press, 2001.

Chadwick, Ruth, ed. *The Encyclopedia of Applied Ethics.* 4 vols. San Diego: Academic Press, 1998.

Cormier, Ramona, and Robert Thompson, eds. *International Directory of Philosophers, 2001–2002.* Bowling Green, Ohio: Philosophy Documentation Center, 2001. This directory attempts to cover the international scene in a manner similar to the American directory. It lists philosophy programs and faculty at international institutions of higher learning.

DeConde, Alexander, ed. *Encyclopedia of American Foreign Policy.* 3 vols. New York: Scribners, 1978. The essays in these volumes discuss concepts, themes, events, and doctrines in the history of U.S. foreign relations. Contents are organized alphabetically by subject. Volume 3 includes a subject index.

Dey, Alexander, and Kathleen O'Grady, eds. *Philosophy in Cyberspace.* Bowling Green, Ohio: Philosophy Documentation Center, 1998. A compilation and description of mailing lists and newsgroups dedicated to philosophy and allied fields, this collection has an international scope. It lists more than 1,500 philosophy-related Web sites, over 300 mailing lists, approximately 60 newsgroups, and philosophy department home pages.

Edwards, Paul, ed. *Encyclopedia of Philosophy.* 8 vols. New York: Macmillan, 1967. This encyclopedia contains over 1,500 articles on major figures, theories, movements, concepts, and controversies in the history of philosophy. The bibliographies are a little dated, but these volumes are still the best place to begin becoming familiar with philosophical concepts that have shaped Western thought.

Elliott, Stephen P., ed. *A Reference Guide to the United States Supreme Court.* New York: Facts on File, 1986. This volume publishes essays on various topics related to the Supreme Court, including the origin and development of the Court, major issues confronted by the Court, notable jurists, and the Court's relation to other branches of government. There are also summaries of historic cases. A general index is included.

Encyclopedia of Indian Philosophy. 8 vols. Princeton: Princeton University Press, 1977–1999.

Fargis, Paul, and Sheree Bykofsky, eds. *The New York Public Library Desk Reference.* New York: Stonesong Press, 1989. This reference book includes "elemental and frequently sought material" on a vast range of topics, some of interest to political science studies, such as addresses for national, state, county, and city government consumer protection agencies; spoken and written forms of address for government officials and military personnel; brief accounts of events in world history; and descriptions of international organizations. There is an index.

Ferguson, John. *Encyclopedia of Mysticism and Mystery Religion.* New York: Crossroad, 1982.

Gaut, Berys, and Dominic Lopes, eds. *The Routledge Companion to Aesthetics.* New York: Routledge, 2001.

Hall, Kermit, ed. *The Oxford Guide to United States Supreme Court Decisions.* New York: Oxford, 2001.

Hastings, James, ed. *Encyclopedia of Religion and Ethics.* 13 volumes. New York: Scribners, 2000.

Hetherington, Norris S., ed. *Encyclopedia of Cosmology.* New York: Garland, 1993.

Hoffman, Eric, ed. *Guidebook to Publishing in Philosophy.* Bowling Green, Ohio: Philosophy Documentation Center, 1996. Designed to provide information for both new and established writers, this guidebook contains information on journal publishing, book publishing, electronic publishing, and conference presentations in philosophy.

Humana, Charles, comp. *World Human Rights Guide.* 3d ed. New York: Oxford University Press, 1992. This volume uses charts and graphs to profile human rights in a variety of countries. Information comes from the responses of individuals, watch-groups, organizations, and embassy officials to questionnaires based on United Nations instruments. Included are comparative ratings of human rights progress. There is no index.

Kennedy Institute of Ethics. *Bibliography of Bioethics.* 20 vols. Detroit: Gale Research, 2001. This ongoing bibliography contains abstracts of articles, legal decisions, and case studies of interest to bioethicists. There is a topical index.

Lawson, Edward, and Mary Lou Bertucci. *Encyclopedia of Human Rights.* 2d ed. New York: Taylor & Francis, 1996. Various topics concerning international human rights activities from 1945 to 1990 are discussed, and significant government documents reprinted, such as the text of the Convention Relating to the Status of Refugees (1951). The appendixes include a chronological list of international human rights documents and a list of worldwide human rights institutions. There is a subject index.

McGraw-Hill Encyclopedia of World Biography. 12 vols. New York: McGraw-Hill, 1973. This series publishes biographical summaries on notable individuals from different time periods and fields. Each entry includes a list of references. A revised second edition was published by Gale Research in Detroit, 1999. Gale has also published supplementary volumes bringing the encyclopedia to 21 volumes as of 2001.

Malone, Dumas, ed. *Dictionary of American Biography.* 20 vols. New York: Scribners, 1936. This venerable work offers biographical essays on distinguished Americans no longer living. Eight supplementary volumes bring the series up to 1970. A separate volume contains a name index.

Montney, Charles, ed. *Directories in Print.* Detroit: Gale Research. According to the introduction of the two-volume 1994 edition, volume 1 of this annual set "describes 15,900 directories, rosters, guides, and other print and nonprint address lists published in the United States and worldwide" (vii). Each entry includes address, fax number, the price of the directory, and a description of its contents. Arrangement is by subject. Chapter 19 covers "Law, Military, and Government" directories. Volume 2 contains subject and title/keyword indexes.

National Historical Publications and Records Commission. *Directory of Archives and Manuscript Repositories in the United States.* Washington, DC: National Archives and Records Service, 1978. This volume lists and describes 2,675 manuscript repositories in the United States and U.S. holdings. The entries are arranged alphabetically by state, then by city. The types of holdings are characterized for each entry and indexed. There is also an index of repository names.

Reich, Warren T., ed. *Encyclopedia of Bioethics.* 5 vols. New York: Free Press, 1995.

Sheehy, Eugene P. *Guide to Reference Books*, 10th ed. Chicago: American Library Association, 1986. The reference works listed and described in this guide are grouped in chapters according to focus. Chapter titles include "General Reference Works," "The Humanities," "Social and Behavioral Sciences," and "History and Area Studies." The guide lists reference books that cover newspapers and government publications. There is a subject index.

Wiener, Philip P., ed. *Dictionary of the History of Ideas.* 5 vols. New York: Scribners, 1973. The essays in these volumes discuss ideas that have helped to shape and continue to shape human culture. The essays are arranged alphabetically by topic, within a series of broad subheadings. One subheading covers politics and includes sixty essays on such topics as "Authority," "Democracy," "Legal Concept of Freedom," "Liberalism," and "Social Attitudes Towards Women." Volume 5 consists of a subject and name index.

4.1.2   Dictionaries

There is a brief glossary of terms in the appendix of this book, and many introductory textbooks contain glossaries. But if you are a major or minor in philosophy, or are taking an advanced course, you will profit from purchasing an inexpensive dictionary. I recommend the following:

Audi, Robert. *The Cambridge Dictionary of Philosophy.* 2d ed. Cambridge: Cambridge University Press, 1999.

Blackburn, Simon. *The Oxford Dictionary of Philosophy.* Oxford: Oxford University Press, 1996.

Martin, Robert M. *The Philosopher's Dictionary,* 2d ed. Peterborough, Ontario: Broadview Press, 1994.

Another interesting dictionary with its own peculiarities is

Nisbet, Robert A. *Prejudices.* Oxford: Oxford University Press, 1982.

4.1.3   Periodicals

Archie Bahm, ed., *The Directory of American Philosophers,* the Blackwell Web page for resources in philosophy, and the Philosophy Documentation Center are excellent places to find information about philosophy journals dedicated to specific issues or time periods. Following are journals that are appropriate for introductory students (indicated by an asterisk) and journals dedicated to topics generally addressed in introductory, interdisciplinary, or applied philosophy.

Agriculture and Human Values

American Philosophical Quarterly. This journal irregularly runs review articles of current research in areas of philosophy, such as relativism and foundationalism.

*Auslegung. The Philosophy Graduate Student Association at the University of Kansas is the sponsor of this journal, which publishes the work of new Ph.D.s and graduate students.

*Business and Professional Ethics

*Business Ethics

*Business Ethics Quarterly

*Canadian Journal of Philosophy

*Carleton University Student Journal of Philosophy

Criminal Justice Ethics

Eidos: The Canadian Graduate Student Journal of Philosophy

*Environmental Ethics

*Ethics

Film and Philosophy

*Foreign Affairs. Primarily a political science journal, this publication contains cogent discussions of current foreign policy issues and can be especially helpful to students of just-war theory and international politics.

*Foreign Policy

*Free Inquiry

*Hastings Center Report. This is an excellent source for case studies in ethics and the professions.

History of Philosophy Quarterly

Hypatia: A Journal of Feminist Philosophy

*Informal Logic

*International Journal of Applied Philosophy

Journal of Aesthetics and Art Criticism

Journal of Agricultural and Environmental Ethics

Journal of Business Ethics

*Journal of Social Philosophy

*Journal of the History of Ideas

Journal of the History of Philosophy

*Journal of Value Inquiry. This journal covers ethics, social and political philosophy, and aesthetics.

*Kennedy Institute of Ethics Journal

*Kinesis: Graduate Journal in Philosophy. This journal publishes papers by graduate students.

Monist. Published quarterly, this journal arranges each issue around a specific topic.

Philosophical Books. This is a journal of book reviews.

Philosophical Forum

Philosophic Exchange

Philosophy and Literature

Philosophy and Public Affairs

Philosophy and Rhetoric

Philosophy and Social Criticism

Philosophy and Theology

Philosophy East and West

Philosophy of Science

Philosophy of the Social Sciences

Professional Ethics

Public Affairs Quarterly

Reason Papers. This journal focuses on social and political philosophy.

Review of Metaphysics. The September issue of this journal prints a list of recently accepted Ph.D. dissertations. The list is arranged by school and includes statistics on each university's graduate program. The director and committee for each degree are generally listed also. The journal also runs an annual dissertation competition.

Science, Technology, and Human Values

Social Epistemology

Social Philosophy and Policy

Social Theory and Practice

Transactions of the Charles S. Peirce Society. Peirce is often the focus, but essays on all the classical American philosophers are included. Sometimes the editor also prints essays on contemporary philosophy.

This is just a selection from a much larger number of philosophy journals.

4.1.4   Periodical Indexes

Bibliographic Index

Biography Index

Book Review Index

Humanities Index

An Index to Book Reviews in the Humanities

Lineback, Richard H., ed. *The Philosopher's Index.* Vol. 35. Bowling Green, Ohio: Philosophy Documentation Center, 2001. This is "a subject and author index to philosophy articles, books, anthologies, and contributions to anthologies." Begun in 1967 as an index of journal articles, the index began listing anthologies and books in 1978. There are two retrospective indexes covering articles in U.S. publications and in non-U.S. English-language publications between 1940 and 1978. The book review index is especially helpful in finding material that may help you formulate a critical review of a recent book. The subject index can also point you to a wide variety of articles on a pressing paper topic.

Reader's Guide to Periodical Literature
Social Sciences Index

4.2   RESEARCH INSTITUTES

You will find it difficult, if not impossible, to find a topic on which nothing has been written. In fact, for any paper topic you can find, it is highly likely that substantial original research has already been done. Suppose that you could talk to someone who could tell you how to find information, easily and quickly, that might otherwise take you weeks of time to develop. Suppose further that you could take this information and evaluate its importance in view of information on the same topic that you have received from other sources. Your paper would certainly be superior to one for which this information was not available. Private research institutes may provide you with just such an opportunity. From private think tanks like the Brookings Institution to public agencies such as the National Institutes of Health, organizations are continuously conducting research on many topics of interest to students of philosophy. You may want to contact a few of them, tell them what you are doing, and inquire about resources that they may be able to make available to you. In order to find them, look up appropriate organizations for your topic in Dresser, Peter D., and Karen Hill, eds. *Research Centers Directory.* Detroit: Gale Research. Over 11,700 university-related and other nonprofit research organizations are briefly profiled in this annual two-volume publication. The entries are listed in sections by topics. There is a subject index and a master index as well as a supplemental volume.

You will also find a center devoted to issues in applied ethics, professional ethics, and public policy issues on almost every university campus.

5

Philosophy and Cyberspace

As Thoreau said, "We do not ride on the railroad; it rides upon us"; and this is what we must fight, in our time. The question is, indeed, Which is to be master? Will we survive our technologies?

—Bill Joy, "Why the Future Doesn't Need Us," *Wired*, April 2000

Philosophy resources available in virtual reality include encyclopedias, dictionaries, biographies, bibliographies, research centers, newsletters, journals, and electronic versions of classic original sources, discussion groups, interviews, debates, conferences, and courses. Those of you familiar with search engines know how important it is to develop a strategy to narrow searches to the items most relevant to your topic. There are two strategies that are most helpful in filtering the overwhelming amount of information available to you online. One is obvious: Find the most exhaustive overview of the electronic resources available in philosophy and use it to direct you to your area of interest. The other is less obvious. Instead of going to the most general resource, go to a narrowly defined site and follow the links that begin there.

Perhaps the major impediment to research in virtual reality is the phenomenon of broken links. Recently, I edited an anthology of essays devoted to issues in information and computer ethics. Many of the articles included references to material in virtual reality that were given by URL (Uniform Resource Locator), as I did in the previous chapter for Blackwell's home page. Many of these links were broken; but many of the broken links had simply been moved as authors or research centers updated sites. Faced with the problem of including this material in a real-world book in a way that was helpful to other readers I decided to place my home page url, *www.csuchico.edu/~graybosc,* in the preface of the book and to place all the URLs, sorted by chapter, in a link on my home page. I cannot easily update URLs in a book once it is published, but I can keep my URL constant, I hope, and update links there as readers alert me via email of changes.

One consequence of this strategy is that one of the best sources for online material in information ethics is my home page. But if you are searching for a particular article, a research center, or some other resource via URL and encounter a broken link, try the following strategies. Hopefully, these strategies will enable you to locate the source. They certainly will enable you to find material relevant to the same issue.

1. Enter the title of the article in quotes in a search engine. This strategy limits the search to the words in the quotes in the exact order.
2. Alter the URL by deleting the last field. This will take you a step up in the hierarchy of the site and perhaps to an index.
3. Search for the author or source, such as a research center, of the reference material.
4. Connect topical keywords with +'s in a search engine. Simply listing words is connecting them with *or.* Entering *Bill Clinton* will give you all the Bills including Bill Gates and all the Clintons including Clinton Avenue in Bay Shore, New York. The plus sign turns *or* into *and.* It is not a foolproof solution. There may be a Bill who lives on Clinton Avenue. You can narrow your search with additional plus signs. So, if you are interested in Bill Clinton's views on *terrorism,* add that word.

5.1   NARROW SOURCES OF INFORMATION

Professors are increasingly expected by universities to place course syllabi on a home page. Most universities have search engines that allow browsers to locate faculty home pages. University sites generally end in *edu.* If you hear an expert on terrorism from Georgetown University on CNN say something that peaks your interest, and you know her last name, it will be easy enough to guess that you will be able to locate her home page by going to *www.georgetown.edu* and searching for her last name. There you can expect to find a list of publications, works in progress, videos of lectures, links to other sites on terrorism, and whatever else the site owner has felt like putting on her Web page. On my Web site you will find photos I took at Thoreau's retreat, *Walden Pond,* and at Hitler's bunkers in eastern Poland, *Wolf's Lair.* There is generally also an email link. You will be surprised how many experts will answer an email query.

So, one place to start research online is your instructor's home page. This is a particularly good place to start if the instructor is involved in distance education. Such instructors generally make links to supporting material available to students who do not have easy access to university libraries. I teach American philosophy in virtual reality to students all over northern California. On my home page there are links to Web sites with biographies of American philosophers such as Edwards and Emerson, bibliographies, and even online original sources. So, check the home page of your instructor or check the home pages of other significant individuals connected to your course—the editor of your text, the authors of articles in the anthology, the research institutes with which the authors are affiliated or which are mentioned in the text.

It is not just the links on the individual's home page that will interest you but also the links found on the links. Follow the trail.

One link on my home page is to the Berkman Center for Internet and Society at Harvard University. There you will find online discussions, lectures, articles, links, and even job announcements and internship opportunities. Berkman also has an electronic newsletter available, free to anyone with an email address. Such newsletters can provide valuable case studies, research references, and provocative ideas that will help your writing be responsive to work on the cutting edge of the field. Find such institutes relevant to your course early and subscribe. If you do not know the names of the relevant research centers, just do a Web search with plus signs and keywords. Perhaps you are in a course on business ethics. Do a search for +business +ethics +center and see what you get.

Topically oriented societies and conferences are also a good place to find online resources. Some societies maintain archives of conference papers. The Society for Computing and Philosophy, Web site *http://caae.phil.cmu.edu/CAAE/ CAP/CAP-page.html,* casts its meetings and archives presentations for asynchronous viewing. The Society for the Advancement of American Philosophy, *http://www.american-philosophy.org/,* maintains various links, including one to discussion groups on particular American philosophers. At *http://pragmatism.org/programs/undergrad_99.htm* there is an index to the home pages of philosophers who list American philosophy as a specialty.

References to philosophy discussion groups are found on most general philosophy sites, such as Blackwell's. You can also find discussion groups by simply opening your Usenet, displaying all groups, and narrowing the list with a keyword such as *philosophy* or *ethics.* I found thirty-four distinct philosophy groups, including one devoted to heavy metal philosophy, on my server.

Classic individual works are available online. If you know you want Thoreau's "Life Without Principle," just enter the title in quotes in a search engine. Copyright laws will keep more recent work out of virtual reality. Yet some authors choose to make electronic copies of work available. The article by Bill Joy from which this chapter's epigraph was quoted is available online, as are most articles published in *Wired.*

One final type of narrow research you might try online is for the work of a particular philosopher. Philosophers who work on applied issues in ethics and public policy generally maintain or allow Web sites with publications. Noam Chomsky's works in political philosophy are readily available at *http://www.zmag.org/chomsky/index.cfm.* If you are taking an ethics course, you are bound to run into references to Peter Singer; and certainly you will want to include the latest work of this philosopher in a paper on animal rights or euthanasia. By now, you know how to search for this material using plus signs.

I have selected Peter Singer on purpose. Singer's views are controversial enough that his appointment at Princeton University provoked protests. Protestors maintain sites in VR dedicated to refutations and objections to Singer's views. Most of these sites are clearly labeled as *not* being Singer's personal or approved site. But be warned. Some of the first Singer sites you will find are not sympathetic supporters and expositors of his views. These sites are useful to your critical work on Singer, so do not discount them.

Here is as good a place as any to note that VR sources must be regarded with an extra degree of skepticism. Anyone with the basic technical knowledge needed to fill in blanks on a Web page template can publish in VR. It is a good idea to rely on indicators such as university affiliation as a measure of how much faith to put in a VR source.

Interviews, including archived radio discussion, with Peter Singer can be found in VR. There is an hour-long interview at *http://www.greenboffin.com/2000_11_01_archive.html*. The same holds for many other philosophers working in applied and professional ethics. But only one dead philosopher is available for viewing in virtual reality—utilitarian Jeremy Bentham can be found at *http://www.ucl.ac.uk/Bentham-Project/images/auto_il.gif,* in his coffin, waiting to be taken to a meeting.

5.2   GENERAL SOURCES OF INFORMATION

5.2.1   Four Major Directories

The American Philosophical Association, *http://www.apa.udel.edu/apa/index.html,* features links to various philosophy resources, *http://www.apa.udel.edu/apa/resources/,* including

- Philosophy centers and research institutes: *http://www.apa.udel.edu/apa/asp/cent_inst.asp*
- Guides to particular areas of philosophy: *http://www.apa.udel.edu/apa/asp/guides.asp*
- Bibliographies: *http://www.apa.udel.edu/apa/asp/bibliographies.asp*
- Online journals: *http://www.apa.udel.edu/apa/asp/journals.asp*
- Blackwell Publishers' Philosophy Resources, *http://www.blackwellpublishers.co.uk/philos/,* contains links to electronic texts and journals, UseNet and Listserv discussion groups, philosophical dictionaries, professional societies, and virtual reality sites devoted to special areas and topics in philosophy.
- The Philosophy Documentation Center, *http://www.pdcnet.org/,* offers a subscription to an online search engine, Poesis, and electronic access to several

journals. Most university libraries provide free access to Ingenta (formerly Carl Uncover). This is an electronic search engine for professional journals. Use it to find articles on your chosen topic or to search the table of contents of journals in your research area for relevant material.

- Peter Suber's *Guide to Philosophy on the Internet, http://www.earlham.edu/~peters/philinks.htm,* is especially useful for international students. It also features links to quotes from famous philosophers.

5.2.2   Encyclopedias

- *The Internet Encyclopedia of Philosophy: http://www.utm.edu/research/iep/*
- *The Stanford Encyclopedia of Philosophy: http://plato.stanford.edu/contents.html*

5.2.3   Directories of Texts

- *Humanities Internet Resources: http://vax.wcsu.edu/library/h_philosophy.html*
- *The Internet Encyclopedia of Philosophy: http://www.utm.edu/research/iep/philtext.htm*
- *The Internet Classics Archive: http://classics.mit.edu/Browse/index.html*
- Andersen Library at the University of Wisconsin, Whitewater, hosts an Internet resources page with links to electronic journals: *http://library.uww.edu/subject/philos.htm.*

5.2.4   Advice on Writing a Philosophy Paper

Philosopher Richard Field has placed some useful guidelines on how to write a philosophy paper on his home page. Visit *http://www.nwmissouri.edu/~rfield/guide.html.*

5.2.5   Internet Resources for Writing Well

A particularly good place to start your Internet search for writing resources is a Web site called Researchpaper.com: *http://www.researchpaper.com.* Created by an Internet publishing company, Researchpaper.com provides free electronic access to a book entitled *10,000 Ideas for Term Papers, Projects, Reports, and Speeches.*

When you visit Researchpaper.com, you will find

- Information about Infonautics, the Internet publishing company that developed Researchpaper.com.

- Idea Directory, a list of more than 4,000 research topics in over 100 categories. (You can type in a key word, and the directory will find interesting ways of approaching the subject you have chosen.)
- Researchpaper.com Chat, a chat room, which is a site where you will find the thoughts and suggestions of other people and where you can reply to the ideas of others and contribute your own.
- Research Central, a page providing help in searching for information and suggestions about good Web sites.
- Writing Center, a series of guides to more effective writing, containing ideas for writing techniques and answers to commonly asked questions about grammar and style.
- Membership Page, a place to sign up for news, announcements, and other materials related to research and writing.

Researchpaper.com also helps you find many other resources for researching and writing term papers. One of the sites that Researchpaper.com will introduce you to is the Purdue University Online Writing Lab (OWL), at *http://owl. english.purdue.edu.* Several universities now offer their own OWLs, and you may want to check your own college's home page to see if it provides one.

OWL's guide to writing resources on the Web includes such sites as

- Writer's Resources on the Web
- Carnegie-Mellon Online Reference Works for the worldwide Internet community
- The International Federation of Library Associations' Citation Guide for Electronic Documents
- William Strunk's *Elements of Style,* courtesy of the Bartleby project
- Editorial Esoterica
- Grammar Hotline Directory
- Editorial Eye Internet
- Internet Resources for Technical Communicators
- "Punctuation" and "Capitalization," two chapters of *Grammar, Punctuation, and Capitalization—A Handbook for Technical Writers and Editors,* by Mary McCaskill

5.3   ADVICE FOR DISTANCE LEARNERS

Researchers Brundage, Keane, and Mackneson have found that successful distance learners are able to

- Assume responsibility for motivating themselves.

- Maintain their own self-esteem irrespective of emotional support that may or may not be gained from the instructor, other students, family, or friends.
- Understand accurately their own strengths and limitations and become able to ask for help in areas of weakness.
- Take the time to work hard at effectively relating to the other students.
- Continually clarify for themselves and others precisely what it is that they are learning and become confident in the quality of their own observations.
- Constantly relate the course content to their personal experience.

Visit *http://www.onlinelearning.net,* a service of UCLA Extension. This site features answers to a list of commonly asked questions. Reading this material will help you overcome some of your initial trepidation. With respect to UCLA's online courses, you will find, for example, that UCLA extension online courses

- are open to anyone.
- have specific dates of course initiation and completion.
- require regular printed textbooks.
- can be taken anywhere that an average, recent personal computer can operate.
- are accompanied by technical support to help when problems arise.
- are given "asynchronously," which is to say that students are required to send messages frequently to the instructor and other students, and can do so at any time of the day or night.
- have actual instructors who do all the same things over the Web site that instructors in classroom courses do.
- have enrollments that are normally limited to twenty students, allowing adequate access to the instructor.
- feature special software that is provided by UCLA Extension, including an online orientation to this software.

Are you likely to succeed in distance learning courses? Among the factors that will influence your chances of success are how comfortable and happy you are about

- working alone.
- communicating with people without seeing them.
- accomplishing tasks without reminders from others.
- using computers.
- solving occasional technical problems on computers.
- learning how to use new software.

While in classroom courses other students and the instructor have a physical presence, in distance learning your contact with others is in electronic form. Interestingly, many students report spending more time on distance learning courses than on their classroom courses.

Distance learning, therefore, offers several advantages over regular classroom courses. You don't need to commute or relocate. You can sell your car and buy a new freezer, which will afford you several new varieties of frozen pizza. Your distance learning schedule can vary from day to day and week to week. You can connect on a whim or wait until your newborn child awakens you at 2 AM and you are unable to get back to sleep. In addition, the interaction with other students in online courses is often more satisfying than you might first suspect. As messages start streaming back and forth, each student's personality is revealed. Some students send photos of themselves so that you have a better idea of who they are.

There are some disadvantages to online learning. The one factor that seems to irritate distance learners most is that they cannot get instant feedback. As a distance learner, you can't just raise your hand and receive an immediate answer to your questions, as you can in a classroom. A related drawback—subtle but profound—is that the nonverbal responses that students unwittingly come to count on in a classroom are missing from an online course. Is your online instructor frowning or smiling as she makes a certain comment? In other words, the act of communication is sometimes more complex than we think. Sometimes, online course instructions are not sufficiently focused or specific, and it may take several communications to understand an assignment.

Another potential difficulty with distance learning is that online students are less likely to appreciate options than are students in classrooms. Rather than welcome the chance to make their own choices, they tend to want to do exactly what the instructor wants. Other problems appear in online courses occasionally. Sometimes, course materials provide ambiguous instructions and out-of-date links. Testing can be complicated and may require special passwords. Some students must go to their local community college to take examinations, but other online colleges simply remind students of their academic integrity statements.

Some of the disadvantages of distance learning arise from students' personal habits. If you are social by nature, you may suffer from feelings of isolation. You may find that it takes longer to establish rapport with online students with whom you have little in common. There may be some initial confusion as you learn how to run the system and interact effectively, or you may have difficulty interpreting messages from other students. As with your online teacher, so with your classmates: Lack of visual contact means a loss of inflection. Humor and sarcasm are more difficult to detect in written communications. And finally, you may face what seems at times to be an overwhelming volume of email featuring a lot of repetition.

Your local bookstore (as well as *amazon.com* and *barnesandnoble.com*) will offer several guides to distance learning. Among those currently available are:

Peterson's Guide to Distance Learning Programs, 2001

Barron's Guide to Distance Learning: Degrees, Certificates, Courses, 2001

College Degrees by Mail & Internet, 2001

The Independent Study Catalog

The Best Distance Learning Graduate Schools: Earning Your Degree Without Leaving Home

Your Internet search for a suitable course may take some time, since offerings change continuously. Among regular colleges that feature philosophy courses on-line is my RW home institution—California State University, Chico.

Studying for distance learning courses requires the same sort of discipline as studying for classroom courses, with one notable difference. For some people, class attendance is energizing. It helps stimulate their desire to study. This stimulus is, of course, absent for distance learners, but email communication with other students and the instructor may serve the same purpose for some. No doubt your instructor will make use of bulletin boards for online discussion. And although you may live a few hundred miles away from the classroom, a classmate may live nearby. Each semester, I have several students who live in Weed or Lake Tahoe. These students meet and work cooperatively in real life. Ask your instructor, or ask on the bulletin board, if any other students live near you. In general, the same study habits that lead to success in regular courses also lead to success in Web-based courses.

6

Formats for Philosophy Papers

The facts in logical space are the world.

—Ludwig Wittgenstein, *Tractatus Logico-Philosophicus*, 1921

6.1 GETTING STARTED

Your format makes your paper's first impression. Justly or not, accurately or not, the format of your paper announces your professional competence or lack of competence. A well-executed format implies that your paper is worth reading. More than that, however, a proper format brings information to your readers in a familiar form that has the effect of setting their minds at ease. Your paper's format, therefore, should impress your readers with your academic competence as a philosopher by following accepted professional standards. Like the style and clarity of your writing, your format communicates messages that are often more readily and profoundly received than the content of the document itself.

The format described in this chapter is in conformance with standards generally accepted in the humanities, including instructions for the following elements:

General page format
Title page
Abstract
Table of contents
List of tables and figures
Text
Reference page
Appendix

Except for special instructions from your instructor, follow the directions in this manual exactly.

6.2   GENERAL PAGE FORMAT

Philosophy assignments should be typed or printed on 8 1/2-by-11-inch premium white bond paper, 20 lb. or heavier. Do not use any other color or size except to comply with special instructions from your instructor, and do not use an off-white or a poor-quality (draft) paper. Many of your instructors will have reached the stage in life where they need bifocals. Spring for a new ink cartridge or ribbon for your printer or typewriter.

Always submit an original typed or computer-printed (preferably laser) manuscript. Do not submit a photocopy. Always print a second copy to keep for your own files in case the original is lost. If you are using a computer, make sure to back up your paper and your research files onto a disk. Beware: Some instructors no longer fall for the excuse that your paper is done but you cannot turn it in until your printer is fixed. They will ask you for the disk or tell you to email it so they can print it themselves. Never fax a paper without prior permission. Many fax machines still produce low-quality copies.

Margins, except for theses and dissertations, should be one inch from all sides of the paper. (You will need to consult with the appropriate office at your institution for instructions on theses and dissertations.) Unless otherwise instructed, all paper submissions should be double-spaced in a 12-point word-processing font or typewriter pica type. Select a font that is plain and easy to read, such as Helvetica, Courier, Garamond, or Times Roman. Do not use script, stylized, or elaborate fonts.

Page numbers should appear in the upper right corner of each page, one inch from the right side and one-half inch from the top of the page. Numbers should begin appearing immediately after the title page. No page number should actually appear on the title page or on the first page of the text, but these pages should still be counted in the numbering. Numbers should proceed consecutively, beginning with the title page (even though the first number is not actually printed on that page). If you choose to use lowercase roman numerals (i, ii, iii, iv, v, vi, vii, viii, ix, x, and so on) for the pages that precede the first page of text (such as the title page, table of contents, and table of figures), these numerals should be centered at the bottom of the page.

In the absence of further directions, do not bind your paper or enclose it within a plastic cover sheet. Place one staple in the upper left corner, or use a paper clip at the top of the paper. Note that a paper to be submitted to a journal for publication should not be clipped, stapled, or bound in any form.

Professional philosophy journals do not all require the same preparation style of the manuscripts they publish. The simplest way to determine what a journal requires is to consult an issue. Generally, there is an explanation of submission requirements inside the front or back covers. It can become maddening to change styles as you prepare a manuscript for submission to a second or third journal. (Yes, sometimes articles are turned down for publication. It is a good idea to have an alternative journal already in mind when you dispatch your work for consideration the first time.) My experience has been that if you follow a generally accepted style, your manuscript will be reviewed and you will have to reformat it only after it has been accepted for publication.

6.3   TITLE PAGE

The following information is centered on the title page:

- Title of paper
- Name of writer
- Course name, section number, and instructor
- College or university
- Date

The title should clearly describe the issue addressed in the paper. If the paper discusses the implications of act utilitarianism for animal rights and famine control, for example, the title "Act Utilitarianism, Animal Rights, and Famine Control" is professional, clear, and helpful to the reader. Avoid such titles as "Act Utilitarianism," "Animal Rights," or "Meat and Morals," because they are incomplete, vague, or unprofessional.

```
            The Moral Imperative of Vegetarianism

                              by

                        Amber Bovine

              Ethics and Human Happiness

                       Phil 108-03

                     Dr. Hayes Fodder

                       Spring 1997

                     Harvest College

                     March 21, 2001
```

6.4   ABSTRACT

An abstract is a brief summary of a paper, written to allow potential readers to determine if the paper contains information of sufficient interest for them to read. People conducting research want specific kinds of information, and they often read dozens of abstracts looking for papers that contain information relevant to their research topic. Abstracts have the designation "Abstract" centered near the top of the page. Next, the title appears, also centered, followed by a paragraph that precisely states the paper's topic, research and analysis methods, and results and conclusions. The abstract itself should be written in one paragraph that does not exceed 250 words. Remember that an abstract is not an introduction but a summary, as demonstrated in the sample.

```
                      Abstract

           Bertrand Russell's View of Mysticism

     This  paper  reviews  Bertrand  Russell's  writings
on  religion,  mysticism,  and  science,  and  defines  his
perspective  on  the  contribution  of  mysticism  to  sci-
entific  knowledge.  Russell  drew  a  sharp  distinction
between  what  he  considered  to  be  (1)  the  essence  of
religion  and  (2)  dogma  or  assertions  attached  to  re-
ligion  by  theologians  and  religious  leaders.  Al-
though  some  of  his  writings,  including  Why  I  Am  Not
a  Christian,  appear  hostile  to  all  aspects  of  reli-
gion,  Russell  actually  asserts  that  religion,  freed
from  doctrinal  encumbrances,  not  only  fulfills  cer-
tain  psychological  needs,  but  evokes  many  of  the
most  beneficial  human  impulses.  He  believes  that  re-
ligious  mysticism  generates  an  intellectual  disin-
terestedness  that  may  be  useful  to  science,  but  that
it  is  not  a  source  of  a  special  type  of  knowledge
beyond  investigation  by  science.
```

6.5   TABLE OF CONTENTS

A table of contents includes the titles of the major divisions and subdivisions of a paper. Tables of contents are not normally required in papers written as course assignments, but may be included. They usually appear, however, in books, theses, and dissertations. The table of contents should consist of the chapter or main section titles, the headings used in the text, with one additional level of titles, if necessary, along with their page numbers, as the following sample illustrates. (Note that the words "Table of" are not used on the actual contents page; they are used only when referring to it.)

Contents

Chapter 1 An Introduction to Utilitarian
          Ethics 1
    Definitions of Utilitarian Ethics 1
    The Historical Development of Utilitarian Ethics .5
Chapter 2 Applications of Utilitarian Ethics
          to International Relations 11
    International Conflict and Utilitarian Ethics .11
    Specific Applications of Utilitarian Ethics . .17
Chapter 3 Understanding International Politics
          Through Utilitarian Ethics 20
    The Strengths of Utilitarian Ethics Applied
    to International Politics 20
    The Weaknesses of Utilitarian Ethics Applied
    to International Politics 23
Chapter 4 Future Applications of Utilitarian Ethics
          in International Relations 27
    References 31

6.6 LISTS OF TABLES AND FIGURES

A list of tables or list of figures contains the titles of the tables, figures, diagrams, photographs, and pictures included in the paper in the order in which they appear, along with their page numbers. You may list tables, illustrations, and figures together under the title "Figures" (and title them all "Figures" in the text), or, if you have more than a half-page of entries, you may have separate lists for tables, figures, and illustrations (and title them accordingly in the text). The format for all such tables should follow the sample, which is taken from a paper entitled "Ethics, Aesthetics, and Immigration."

```
              List of Figures and Illustrations

1. Photograph of the Author . . . . . . . . . . .1

2. Drawing of Immanuel Kant . . . . . . . . . .3

3. Painting of a Thing-in-Itself by Wilfred

   Sellars . . . . . . . . . . . . . . . . .9

4. "Panopticon" . . . . . . . . . . . . . .15

5. Venn Diagram of Kant's Categorical

   Imperative . . . . . . . . . . . . . . .16
```

6.7   TEXT

Ask your instructor for the number of pages required for the paper you are writing. The text should follow the directions explained in chapters 1 and 2 of this manual. Margins should be set at one inch on all sides.

6.8   CHAPTER HEADINGS

Your papers should include no more than three levels of headings:

- Primary, which should be centered, with each word except articles, prepositions, and conjunctions capitalized:

  The Development of Social Contract Theory

- Secondary, which begin at the left margin, also with each word except articles, prepositions, and conjunctions capitalized:

  Anglo-American Philosophy and the Social Contract

- Tertiary, which should be written in sentence style (with only the first word and proper nouns capitalized) with a period at the end, underlined:

  Two contract theorists: Hobbes and Locke.

6.9   ILLUSTRATIONS AND FIGURES

Illustrations are not normally inserted in the text of a philosophy paper, journal article, or book unless they are necessary to explain the material in the text. Some textbooks and anthologies have begun to include photographs of authors. And certainly, pictures are appropriate to aesthetics papers and journals.

Do not paste or tape photocopies of photographs or similar materials to the pages of the text or the appendix. Instead, photocopy each one on a separate sheet of paper and center each photo or illustration, along with its typed title, within the normal margins of the paper. The format of the illustration titles should be the same as the format for tables and figures.

6.10   REFERENCE PAGE

The format for references is discussed in Chapter 7 of this book.

6.11   APPENDIXES

Appearing at the back of the paper, after the text, appendixes are reference materials that provide information for the convenience of the reader to supplement the important facts contained in the text. Appendixes may include maps, charts, tables, and selected documents. They are rarely used in philosophy.

Do not place in your appendix materials that are merely interesting or decorative. Add in an appendix only items that will answer questions raised by the text or are necessary to explain the text. Follow the guidelines for formats for illustrations, tables, and figures when adding material in an appendix. At the top center of the page, label your first appendix "Appendix A," your second appendix "Appendix B," and so on. Do not append an entire government report, journal article, or other publication, but only the portions of such documents that are necessary to support your paper. The source of the information should always be evident on the appended pages.

7

Citing Sources

Man is timid and apologetic; he is no longer upright; he dares not say 'I think,' 'I am,' but quotes some saint or sage. He is ashamed before the blade of grass or the blowing rose. These roses under my window make no reference to former roses or to better ones; they are for what they are; they exist with God today. There is no time to them. There simply is the rose; it is perfect in every moment of its existence.

—Ralph Waldo Emerson, *Self-Reliance,* 1841

7.1 PRELIMINARY DECISIONS

One of your most important jobs as a research writer is to document your use of source material carefully and clearly. Failure to do so will cause your readers confusion, damage the effectiveness of your paper, and perhaps make you vulnerable to a charge of plagiarism. Proper documentation is more than just good form; it is a powerful indicator of your own commitment to scholarship and the sense of authority that you bring to your writing. Good documentation demonstrates your expertise as a researcher and increases the reader's trust in you and your work; it gives credibility to what you are writing.

Unfortunately, as anybody who has ever written a research paper knows, getting the documentation right can be a frustrating, confusing job, especially for the novice writer. Positioning each element of a single reference citation accurately can require what seems an inordinate amount of time spent thumbing through the style manual. Even before you begin to work on specific citations, there are important questions of style and format to answer.

Footnotes contain references to ranges of pages; footnotes and bibliographies will occasionally refer to multi-volume works published over a series of years.

The numbers in the notes will be connected by a single hyphen and will not have spaces on either side of the hyphen. This special mark is known as an en-dash. It can be inserted with a word processor by holding down the alt key and typing 0150. If you use Microsoft Word with autoformat on an en-dash will be automatically inserted when you type text, a space, one or two hyphens, and then a space or more text.

A double hyphen, called an em-dash, is inserted by Microsoft Word when text is followed by no spaces and one or two hyphens. Or insert an em-dash without using autoformat by holding the alt key down and keying 0151. This type of dash is used to emphasize parenthetical material, to set off appositives that include commas, to signal a list, to provide space to amplify a point, and to provide a shift in thought. So, an em-dash will occur both in text and notes. Single hyphens, en-dashes, also have uses outside of footnotes and bibliographies. Examples are compound words such as "multi-volume" and with certain prefixes—ex-president Clinton. Consult a style manual such as Diana Hacker, *A Writer's Reference* 4th edition, (Boston: Bedford/St. Martin's, 1999) for a full discussion.

7.1.1   What to Document

Direct quotes must always be credited, as must certain kinds of paraphrased material. Information that is basic—important dates; facts or opinions universally acknowledged—need not be cited. Information that is not widely known, whether fact or opinion, should receive documentation.

What if you are unsure whether a certain fact is widely known? You are, after all, very probably a newcomer to the field in which you are conducting your research. If in doubt, supply the documentation. It is better to overdocument than to fail to do justice to a source.

7.1.2   Which Citation System to Use

While the question of which documentation style to use may be decided for you in some classes by your instructor, others may allow you a choice. There are several styles available, each designed to meet the needs of writers in particular fields. The documentary note system, in which superscript numbers ([1]) are placed at the end of sentences in the text, is perhaps the one most widely used in the discipline of philosophy, and it is therefore described here.

7.1.3   The Importance of Consistency

The most important rule to remember is, be consistent. Sloppy referencing undermines your readers' trust and does a disservice to the writers whose work you are incorporating into your own argument.

7.1.4   Using the Style Manual

Unpracticed student researchers tend to ignore this section of the style manual until the moment the first note has to be worked out, and then they skim through the examples looking for the one example that perfectly corresponds to the immediate case at hand. But most style manuals do not include every possible documentation model, so the writer must piece together a coherent reference out of elements from several models. Reading through all the models before using them gives you a feel for where to find different aspects of models as well as for how the referencing system works in general.

7.2   DOCUMENTARY-NOTE SYSTEM: NUMBERED REFERENCES

7.2.1   General Format Rules

In the documentary-note system you place a superscript (raised) number after the passage that includes source material. The number refers to a full bibliographical citation given either at the foot of the page (a footnote) or in a list at the end of the paper (an endnote). Information in this section comes from section 15 of the *Chicago Manual of Style (CMS)*, 14th edition.

7.2.1.1   Numbering System

Number the notes consecutively throughout the entire paper, starting with[1]. In other words, do not restart with[1] at the beginning of each new chapter or section of the paper, as many published works do.

7.2.1.2   Placement of Superscript Numeral

Whenever possible, the superscript numeral should go at the end of the sentence:

Rorty's representation of Sellars as an eliminative materialist is radically mistaken.[1]

If it is necessary to place the reference within a sentence instead of at the end, position the numeral at the end of the pertinent clause.

In his last editorial Bagley denounces the current city administration[13]—and thousands of others feel the same way.

Notice in the example above that the superscript numeral occurs before the dash. For all other pieces of punctuation—comma, semicolon, period, exclamation mark, question mark—the superscript numeral follows the punctuation. The numeral also follows the terminal quotation mark of a direct quote:

"This clause," claimed Lindley, "is the most crucial one in the address."[20]

7.2.1.3 Multiple Notes

When a passage refers to more than one source, do not place more than one superscript numeral after the passage. Instead, use only one numeral, and combine all the references into a single footnote:

> Separate studies by Lovett, Morrison, Collins, and the Anderson Group all corroborate the state's findings.[7]

7.2.2 Models for Documentary Notes and Bibliographical Citations

In each pair of models below, the first model is of a documentary note, and the second is for the corresponding bibliographical entry. A note may appear either as a footnote, placed at the bottom of the page of text on which the reference occurs, or as an endnote, placed in numerical order in a list following the text of the paper. Many word processors are able to change notes from one style to the other.

7.2.2.1 Differences Between Endnotes and Bibliography

In the paper's final draft, your endnotes will precede the bibliography, which is usually the final element in the paper. Because its entries are arranged alphabetically, the order of entries in the bibliography will differ from the order of the endnotes, which are arranged according to the appearance of the references within the text. Pay attention to the basic differences between the note format and the bibliography format. Notes are numbered; bibliographical entries are not. The first line of a note is indented; in a bibliography all lines are indented except the first. While the author's name is printed in normal order in a note, the order is reversed in the bibliography to facilitate alphabetizing. There are also variations within the individual references.

If the note refers to a book or an article in its entirety, you need not cite specific page numbers in your references. If, however, you wish to cite material on a specific page or set of pages, give the page numbers in the note.

7.2.2.2 Books

One author

Note

1. Amanda Collingwood, *Metaphysics and the Public* (Detroit: Zane Press, 1993), 235–38.

Bibliography

> Collingwood, Amanda. *Metaphysics and the Public.* Detroit: Zane Press, 1993.

Two authors

Note

> 6. Delbert P. Grady and Jane Ryan Torrance, *Philosophers and Their Secrets* (New York: Holograph Press, 1989).

Bibliography

> Grady, Delbert P., and Jane Ryan Torrance. *Philosophers and Their Secrets.* New York: Holograph Press, 1989.

Three authors

Note

> 2. Samuel Howard, William J. Abbott, and Jane Hope, *Powerbase: How to Increase Your Hold on Your Fellow Philosophy Students* (Los Angeles: Gollum and Smythe, 1986).

Bibliography

> Howard, Samuel, William J. Abbot, and Jane Hope. *Powerbase: How to Increase Your Hold on Your Fellow Philosophy Students.* Los Angeles: Gollum and Smythe, 1986.

More than three authors

The Latin phrase *et al.*, meaning "and others," appears in roman type after the name of the first author. Note that *al.* (an abbreviation for *alia*) must be followed by a period.

Note

> 21. Angela Genessario et al., *Religion and the Child* (Baltimore: Colgate, 1991), 16–18, 78–82.

Bibliography

> Genessario, Angela, et al. *Religion and the Child.* Baltimore: Colgate, 1991.

Editor, compiler, or translator as author

Note

> 6. Dylan Trakas, comp., *Teaching Philosophy* (El Paso, TX: Del Norte Press, 1994).

Bibliography

Trakas, Dylan, comp. *Teaching Philosophy*. El Paso, TX: Del Norte Press, 1994.

Editor, compiler, or translator with author

Note

15. Ezra Pound, *Literary Essays*, ed. T. S. Eliot (New York: New Directions, 1953), 48.

47. Philippe Aris, *Centuries of Childhood: A Social History of Family Life*, trans. Robert Baldock (New York: Knopf, 1962).

Bibliography

Pound, Ezra. *Literary Essays*. Ed. T. S. Eliot. New York: New Directions, 1953.
Aris, Philippe. *Centuries of Childhood: A Social History of Family Life*. Trans. Robert Baldock. New York: Knopf, 1962.

Untranslated book

Note

8. Henry Cesbron, *Histoire critique de l' hystorie* (Paris: Asselin et Houzeau, 1909).

Bibliography

Cesbron, Henry. *Histoire critique de l' hystorie*. Paris: Asselin et Houzeau, 1909.

Untranslated book with title translated, in parentheses

Note

53. Henryk Wereszyncki, *Koniec sojuszu trzech cesarzy* (The End of the Three Emperors' League) (Warsaw: PWN, 1977).

Bibliography

Wereszyncki, Henryk. *Koniec sojuszu trzech cesarzy* (The End of the Three Emperors' League). Warsaw: PWN, 1977.

Two or more works by the same author

In the notes, subsequent works by an author are handled exactly as the first work. In the bibliography, the works are listed alphabetically, with the author's name replaced, by a three-em dash (six strokes of the hyphen) in all entries after the first.

Bibliography

> Russell, Henry. *Famous Last Words.* New Orleans: Liberty Publications, 1978.
> ————. *Famous Philosophical Debates.* Denver: Axel & Myers, 1988.

Chapter in a multi-author collection

Note

> 23. Alexa North Gray, "American Philosophers and the USIA," in *Current Media Issues,* ed. Barbara Bonnard (New York: Boulanger, 1994), 189–231.

Bibliography

> Gray, Alexa North. "American Philosophers and the Foreign Press." In *Current Media Issues.* Ed. Barbara Bonnard, 189–231. New York: Boulanger, 1994.

You may, if you wish, place the inclusive page numbers in either the note, following the publication information, or in the bibliographical entry, following the name of the editor. If the author of the article is also the editor of the book, you must place her or his name in both locations. If the entire book is written by the same author, do not specify the chapter in the bibliographical reference.

Author of a foreword or introduction

It is not necessary to cite the author of a foreword or introduction in the bibliography unless you have used material from that author's contribution to the volume.

Note

> 4. Issac Singer, foreword to *Hunger,* by Knut Hamsun (New York: Bimini, 1997).

Bibliography

> Singer, Issac. Foreword to *Hunger,* by Knut Hamsun. New York: Bimini, 1997.

Subsequent editions

If you are using an edition of a book other than the first, you must cite the number of the edition, or use Rev. ed. (for Revised edition) if there is no edition number.

Note

> 43. Sarah Hales, *The Coming Ethics Wars,* 2d ed. (Pittsburgh: Blue Skies, 1990).

Bibliography

    Hales, Sarah. *The Coming Ethics Wars.* 2d ed. Pittsburgh: Blue Skies, 1990.

Multivolume work

Note

    49. Charles Logan August Graybosch, *Philosophers Still Write the Darndest Things,* 3 vols. (New York: Starkfield, 1998–99).

Bibliography

    Graybosch, Charles Logan August. *Philosophers Still Write the Darndest Things.* 3 vols. New York: Starkfield, 1998–99.

If you are using only one of the volumes in a multivolume work, follow the format below.

Note

    9. Madeleine Ronsard, *Philosophers on Sabbatical,* vol. 2 of *A History of Philosophy,* ed. Joseph M. Sayles (Boston: Renfrow, 1992).

Bibliography

    Ronsard, Madeleine. *Philosophers on Sabbatical.* Vol. 2 of *A History of Philosophy.* Ed. Joseph M. Sayles. Boston: Renfrow, 1992.

Reprints of older works

Note

    8. Sterling R. Adams, *Debate Strategies* (1964; reprint, New York: Starkfield, 1988).

Bibliography

    Adams, Sterling R. *Debate Strategies.* 1964. Reprint, New York: Starkfield, 1988.

Modern editions of classics

    It is not necessary to give the date of original publication of a classic work.

Note

    24. Edmond Burke, *Reflections on the Revolution in France,* ed. J. G. A. Pocock (Indianapolis: Hackett, 1987).

Bibliography

Burke, Edmond. *Reflections on the Revolution in France.* Ed. J. G. A. Pocock. Indianapolis: Hackett, 1987.

7.2.2.3 Periodicals

Journals are periodicals, usually published either monthly or quarterly, that specialize in printing serious scholarly articles in a particular field. One significant distinction between the note format and the bibliographical format for a journal article is that in the note you cite only those pages from which you took material from the article, while in the bibliography you report the first and last pages of the article.

Journal with continuous pagination

Most journals are paginated so that each issue of a volume continues the numbering of the previous issue. The reason for such pagination is that most journals are bound in libraries as complete volumes of several issues; continuous pagination makes consulting these large compilations easier.

Note that the name of the journal, which is italicized (or underlined if italics are unavailable), is followed without punctuation by the volume number, which is itself followed by the year, in parentheses, then a colon and the page numbers. Do not use "p." or "pp." to introduce the page numbers.

Note

17. Joseph Conlin, "Teaching the Toadies: Cronyism in Academic Philosophy," *Reason Today* 4 (1987): 253, 260–62.

Bibliography

Conlin, Joseph. "Teaching the Toadies: Cronyism in Academic Philosophy." *Reason Today* 4 (1987): 250–262.

Journal in which each issue is paginated separately

Note

8. Buck Rogers, "Toward Ballistic Missile Defense," *Philosophy Revealed* 28, no. 3 (1991): 27, 29.

Bibliography

Rogers, Buck. "Toward Ballistic Missile Defense," *Philosophy Revealed* 28, no. 3 (1991): 27, 29.

The issue number follows the volume number, introduced by "no." It is also permissible to enclose the issue number in parentheses, without the "no.," moving the year to the end of the entry and placing it in a second parentheses: *American Philosophy Digest* 28 (3): 25–34 (1991).

Whichever format you use, be consistent.

Magazines, which are usually published weekly, bimonthly, or monthly, appeal to the popular audience and generally have a wider circulation than journals. *Newsweek* and *Scientific American* are magazines. Note that for entries that cite titles beginning with *The*, this word is dropped in the citation, as in *New Yorker* example below.

Monthly magazine

Note

> 10. Bonnie Stapleton, "I Ate Lunch with Socrates," *Lifelike Magazine*, April 1981, 22–25.

Bibliography

> Stapleton, Bonnie. "I Ate Lunch with Socrates." *Lifelike Magazine*, April 1981, 22–25.

Weekly or bimonthly magazine

The day of the issue's publication appears before the month. If the article cited begins in the front of the magazine and jumps to the back, then according to *CMS* (15.232), there is no point in recording inclusive page numbers in the bibliographical entry after the year. The specific pages used in your paper, however, must still be cited in the note.

Note

> 37. Connie Bruck, "The World of Philosophy," *New Yorker*, 18 October 1993, 13.

Bibliography

> Bruck, Connie. "The World of Philosophy." *New Yorker*, 18 October 1993, 13.

Newspapers

Note that as for magazine titles, *The* is omitted from the newspaper's title, as it is for all English-language newspapers, according to *CMS* (15.242). If the name of the city in which an American newspaper is published does not appear in the paper's title, it should be appended, in italics, as in the second model below. If the city is not well known, the name of the state is added, in italics, in parentheses, as in the second model below.

Notes

> 5. Editorial, *New York Times,* 10 August 1993.
> 14. Fine, Austin, "Hoag on Trial," *Carrollton (Texas) Tribune,* 24 November 1992.

Bibliography

CMS (16.117) says that bibliographies usually do not include entries for articles from daily newspapers. If you wish to include such material, however, you may give the name of the paper and the relevant dates in the bibliography:

> *Carrollton (Texas) Tribune,* 22–25 November 1992.

CMS (15.234–42) offers additional suggestions for citations of newspaper material.

7.2.2.4 *Public Documents*

LAWS AND STATUTES

If you wish to make a formal reference for a statute, you must structure the reference according to the place where you found the published law. Initially published separately in pamphlets, as slip laws, statutes are eventually collected and incorporated first into a set of volumes called *U.S. Statutes at Large* and later into the *United States Code,* a multivolume set that is revised every six years. You should use the latest publication.

Citing to a slip law

Note

> 16. Public Law 678, 103d Cong., 1st sess. (4 December 1993), 16–17.

or

> 16. Public Law 678, 103d Cong., 1st sess. (4 December 1993), *Library of Congress Book Preservation Act of 1993,* 16–17.

or

> 16. *Library of Congress Book Preservation Act of 1993,* Public Law 678, 103d Cong., 1st sess. (4 December 1993), 16–17.

Bibliography

U.S. Public Law 678. 103d Cong., 1st sess., 4 December 1993.

or

U.S. Public Law 678. 103d Cong., 1st sess., 4 December 1993. *Library of Congress Book Preservation Act of 1993.*

or

Library of Congress Book Preservation Act of 1993. Public Law 678. 103d Cong., 1st sess., 4 December 1993.

Citing to the *Statutes at Large*

Note

10. *Statutes at Large* 82 (1993): 466.
    or
10. *Library of Congress Book Preservation Act of 1993, Statutes at Large* 82 (1993): 466.

Bibliography

Statutes at Large 82 (1993): 466.

or

Library of Congress Book Preservation Act of 1993. Statutes at Large 82 (1993): 466.

Citing to the *United States Code*

Note

42. *Library of Congress Book Preservation Act, U.S. Code,* vol. 38, sec. 1562 (1993).

Bibliography

Library of Congress Book Preservation Act. U.S. Code. Vol. 38, sec. 1562 (1993).

UNITED STATES CONSTITUTION

In the documentary-note format, according to *CMS* (15.367), the Constitution is cited by article or amendment, section, and, if relevant, clause. The Constitution is not listed in the bibliography.

Note

23. U.S. Constitution, art. 3, sec. 3.

LEGAL REFERENCES

Supreme Court

Note

> 73. *State of Nevada v. Goldie Warren.* 324 U.S. 123 (1969).

The U.S. in the entry refers to *United States Supreme Court Reports,* which is where decisions of the Supreme Court have been published since 1875. Preceding the *U.S.* in the note is the volume number; following is the page number and year, in parentheses. Before 1875, Supreme Court decisions were published under the names of official court reporters. The following reference is to William Cranch, *Reports of Cases Argued and Adjudged in the Supreme Court of the United States,* 1801–1815, 9 vols. (Washington, DC, 1804–1817). The number preceding the clerk's name is the volume number; following the clerk's name is the page number and year, in parentheses:

> 8. *Marbury v. Madison,* 1 Cranch 137 (1803).

According to *CMS* (15.369), court decisions are only rarely listed in bibliographies.

Lower courts

Decisions of lower federal courts are published in the *Federal Reporter.* The note should give the volume of the *Federal Reporter* (*F.*), the series, if it is other than the first series (2d, in the model below), the page number, and, in parentheses, an abbreviated reference to the specific court (in this case, the Second Circuit Court) and the year.

Note

> 58. *United States v. Sizemore,* 183 F. 2d 201 (2d Cir. 1950).

7.2.2.5 *Electronic Sources*

The 14th edition of *CMS* treats references for electronic sources only sparingly (see 15.424), referring readers to the International Standards Organization (ISO) for further help. At a Web site entitled The Chicago Manual of Style *FAQ (and not so FAQ),* located at the following web address, *http://www.press.uchicago. edu/Misc/Chicago/cmosfaq.html,* the University of Chicago Press, publisher of *CMS,* refers readers to a number of different Web sites, none of which offers satisfactory details for citing electronic sources within a documentary-note format. The following models, therefore, combine *CMS* documentary-note format with citation elements necessary to allow readers to locate the cited sources.

CD-ROM and similar databases

For CD-ROMs and other unchangeable databases, include the type of source, the vender's name, and the electronic publication date, in parentheses, at the end of the note, followed by a period.

Note

> 12. T. J. Greensmoke. "The Internet and Socrates' Ghost," *ePhilosopher,* 4 November 2000, 32–34, *Philosophy Trac: Articles 1995–2001* (CD-ROM. Carmel. Aug. 2001).

Bibliography

> Greensmoke, T. I. "The Internet and Socrates' Ghost." ePhilosopher. 4 November 2000: 32–34. *Philosophy Trac: Articles 1995–2001.* CD-ROM. Carmel. Aug. 2001.

Online sources

In general, a reference for an online source should include as much as possible of the information that would be present in a printed citation, followed by information sufficient to allow a reader to find the source on the Internet.

Online book

For separate publications such as a book or pamphlet, include in parentheses the place of publication, publisher, and date for the printed version, if known, followed by the publisher and date of the online version, the date accessed, and the Web address, or URL.

Note

> 6. Eric C. Withnall, *Wars Just and Unjust: A Catalog* (New York: Grenfell, 1991). Bartleby Republications, 1999, 2 Mar. 2001 <http:// www.utex.bartleby .justwar.com>.

Bibliography

> Withnall, Eric C. *Wars Just and Unjust: A Catalog.* New York: Grenfell, 1991. Bartleby Republications. 1999. 2 Mar. 2001 <http:// www.utex.bartleby. justwar.com>.

The URL should be enclosed in angle brackets (< >)in order to avoid confusion regarding symbols and punctuation marks surrounding it. Use care when breaking a URL at the end of a line to do so only after a forward slash (/) and without adding a hyphen.

Avoiding the creation of hyperlinks. When you type a URL using certain versions of Microsoft Word (Word 97, Word 98, and Word 2000, for example), the word processing program automatically removes the angle brackets and converts the URL into a working link, or hyperlink. It is possible to turn off hyperlinking in Microsoft Word by going to Tools on the menu bar, choosing AutoCorrect, then the AutoFormat As You Type tab, and finally deselecting the check mark next to the phrase "Internet and network paths with hyperlinks." If you wish, instead, to leave the function on and remove each hyperlink individually, right-click your mouse on each URL, then click Hyperlink on the popup menu and, if you are using Word 97, choose Edit Hyperlink and then Remove Link. If you are using Word 2000, simply choose Remove Hyperlink after you have clicked on Hyperlink. The word processing program Word 98 allows you to remove an individual hyperlink by highlighting the URL, clicking Hyperlink on the Insert menu, and then clicking Remove Link.

Personal or Professional Site

Note

> 5. Karla Scaramouche, *Philosopher's Kidneystone*, 14 July 2001 <http://www.ucok.edu/pstone/first.html>.

Bibliography

> Scaramouche, Karla. *Philosopher's Kidneystone*. 14 July 2001 <http:// www.ucok. edu/pstone/ first.html>.

Information database

Note

> 21. Linda L. Steele, ed., *Philosophy of Early Film Database*, 3d ed. (Sarasota: Gnomonics College, 1998), 8 Apr. 2001 <http:// www.sarasota.gnomon.edu/filmphil.htm>.

Bibliography

> Steele, Linda L., ed. *Philosophy of Early Film Database*. 3d ed. Sarasota: Gnomonics College, 1998. 8 Apr. 2001 <http://www.sarasota.gnomon.edu/ filmphil.htm>.

Periodical articles

Because the task of transmitting material from a print version to an electronic version may introduce errors into the text, you should always try to use the print version of a periodical that appears in both print and electronic versions. If the only version available to you is the electronic one, make sure to include in your citation as much information regarding the print version as possible before giving the publication information of the electronic version, the date you accessed it, and its URL.

Note

9. Rachel Harnness and Bonnie Samuelson. "The Philosopher in the Family: William James and his Brother," *Journal of Philosophy and History* 10, no. 2 (1999), 17 February 2001 <http://www.ucavola.edu/jphilohist/home. htm>.

Bibliography

Harnness, Rachel, and Bonnie Samuelson. "The Philosopher in the Family: William James and his Brother." *Journal of Philosophy and History* 10, no. 2 (1999). 17 February 2001 <http://www.ucavola.edu/jphilohist/home. htm>.

E-mail

Personal communications such as email messages should be cited as personal communications in the text and do not appear in the reference list.

7.2.2.6 Interviews

According to *CMS* (15.263), citations to interviews in the documentary-note system should be handled by references within the text. If, however, you wish to include references to interviews, you may use the following formats.

PUBLISHED OR BROADCAST INTERVIEWS

Untitled interview in a book

Note

30. Mary Jorgenson, interview by Alan McAskill, in *Hospice Pioneers,* ed. Alan McAskill (Richmond: Dynasty Press, 1994), 68.

Bibliography

Jorgenson, Mary. Interview by Alan McAskill. In *Hospice Pioneers,* ed. Alan McAskill, 62–86. Richmond: Dynasty Press, 1994.

Titled interview in a periodical

Note

7. John Simon, "Picking the Patrons Apart: An Interview with John Simon," interview by Selena Fox, *Media Week,* 14 March 1993, 43–44.

Bibliography

Simon, John. "Picking the Patrons Apart: An Interview with John Simon." By Selena Fox. *Media Week,* 14 March 1993, 40–54.

Interview broadcast on television

Note

> 4. Clarence Parker, interview by Kent Gordon, *Oklahoma Philosophers*, WKY Television, 4 June 1994.

Bibliography

> Parker, Clarence. Interview by Kent Gordon. *Oklahoma Philosophers*. WKY Television, 4 June 1994.

UNPUBLISHED INTERVIEWS

Note

> 17. Melissa Kennedy, interview by author, tape recording, Portland, ME, 23 April 1993.

Bibliography

> Kennedy, Melissa. Interview by author. Tape recording. Portland, ME, 23 April 1993.

7.2.2.7 *Unpublished Sources*

Dissertation

Note

> 16. Robert Nisbaum, "Sidney Hook's Populism" (Ph.D. diss., University of Virginia, 1980), 88–91.

Bibliography

> Nisbaum, Robert. "Sidney Hook's Populism." Ph.D. diss., University of Virginia, 1980.

Thesis

Note

> 5. Ellspeth Stanley Sharpe, "Black Women in Philosophy: A Troubled History" (Master's thesis, Oregon State University, 1992), 34, 36, 112–114.

Bibliography

> Sharpe, Ellspeth Stanley. "Black Women in Philosophy: A Troubled History." Master's thesis, Oregon State University, 1992.

Paper presented at a meeting

Note

> 82. Kim Zelazny and Ed Gilmore, "Art for Art's Sake: Funding the NEA in the Twenty-First Century" (presented at the annual Conference of Metropolitan Arts Councils, San Francisco, April 1993), 4–7, 9.

Bibliography

> Zelazny, Kim, and Ed Gilmore. "Art for Art's Sake: Funding the NEA in the Twenty-First Century." Presented at the annual Conference of Metropolitan Arts Councils, San Francisco, April 1993.

Manuscript in the author's possession

The entry should include the institution with which the author is affiliated and a description of the format of the work (typescript, photocopy, or the like).

Note

> 16. Rita V. Borges and Alicia Chamisal, "Mexican-American Border Conflicts, 1915–1970" (University of Texas at El Paso, photocopy), 61–62.

Bibliography

> Borges, Rita V., and Alicia Chamisal. "Mexican-American Border Conflicts, 1915–1970." University of Texas at El Paso. Photocopy.

7.2.2.8 Subsequent or Shortened References in Notes

After you have given a complete citation for a source in a note once, it is possible to shorten the reference to that source in later notes. One convenient method of shortening later references to a source, described in *CMS* (15.249), is to give only the last name of the author, followed by a comma and the page number of the reference.

First Reference

> 21. Angela Genessario et al., *Alimony and the Child: A National Survey* (Baltimore: Colgate, 1991), 16–18, 78–82.

Later Reference

> 35. Genessario, 46.

If there are citations to more than one work by the same author, you will have to include a shortened form of the title in all later references.

First References

     23. John George, *Fringe Groups I Have Known: The Radical Left and Right in American Society* (New York: Lear Press, 1995), 45.

     26. John George, "Onward Christian Soldiers: Evangelism on the Plains," *Radical Wind Magazine,* March 1994, 35, 37.

Later References

     32. George, Fringe Groups, 56.
     48. George, "Christian Soldiers," 34.

Government documents

Methods for shortening references to government documents vary, depending on the type of source. One rule is to make sure there is sufficient information in the shortened reference to point the reader clearly to the full citation in the bibliography.

Court decisions

First Reference

     58. *United States v. Sizemore,* 183 F. 2d 201 (2d Cir. 1950).

Later Reference

     67. *United States v. Sizemore,* 203.

Consult *CMS,* sec. 15, for details on shortening other types of references.

Use of Ibid.

Ibid., an abbreviation of the Latin term *ibidem,* meaning "in the same place," can be used to shorten a note that refers to the source in the immediately preceding note:

First Reference

     14. Samuel Howard, William J. Abbott, and Jane Hope, *Powerbase: How to Increase Your Hold on Your Fellow Philosophy Students* (Los Angeles: Gollum and Smythe, 1986), 35–36.

Following Reference

     15. Ibid., 38.

PART THREE

How to Think and Write Like a Philosopher

8

Principles of Argument

If all mankind minus one were of one opinion, and only one person were of the contrary opinion, mankind would be no more justified in silencing that one person, than he, if he had the power, would be justified in silencing mankind.

—John Stuart Mill, On Liberty, 1859

8.1   THE THROWS OF ARGUMENT

Arguments are discussions in which we strive to attain an objective. There are all sorts of objectives: selling our favorite political candidate, gaining a couple of points on an exam, selecting the movie we want to see, returning an item to a department store, or discovering the truth on an important matter. Verbal and non-verbal exchanges of reasons, threats, emotions, or even bricks, in the interest of reaching an objective, are normally called arguments.

The language in which we talk about argument suggests that we conceive argument metaphorically as a war to be won. Words such as *demolished, overwhelmed, destroyed,* and *thrust,* make frequent appearances in our accounts of arguments. And we know that all is fair in love and war. So the very idea that there are rules governing argument may seem questionable from the start, unless the rules are going to show us how to obtain our objectives more effectively.

Protagoras (490–421 BCE), a Sophist, boasted that he could make equally strong cases for any side of an argument. Sophists were in great demand in ancient Athens, just as lawyers are in great demand today. People then, like today, needed to know how to argue to defend their lives and property. Sophists knew how to argue well and made a good deal of money by teaching others and by bringing the rich to court. Protagoras wrote a book about argument that he titled *The Throws,* but only the title has survived. The Greek word used in the title was the same term applied to the throws in the sport of wrestling.

Unlike the Sophists, who argued for money, the Athenian philosopher Socrates argued for truth. He believed that knowing the truth about matters such as the nature of social justice, piety, and God was essential to living a good and happy life.

Socrates was skilled in two strategies essential to good philosophical argument. First, he was adept at keeping the point of an argument from being lost. The Sophists often engaged in long flowery speeches on topics such as the nature of love or justice. Socrates was quick to bring his partners in argument back to the point at issue, a maddening practice for those more interested in style than substance. Second, during an argument, Socrates was skillful at devising examples that undermined definitions offered by his opponents. Socratic dialectic is a method of argument in which a definition of an important concept, such as "justice" or "truth," is subjected to a series of questions aimed at testing it.

In the Socratic dialogues that Plato wrote, Socrates tests definitions offered by other participants in the discussion. For instance, early in Socrates' dialogue with Euthyphro, Euthyphro defines piety as "that which is pleasing to the gods." Socrates tests this definition by pointing out that the traditional stories of the gods are full of conflicts, which suggests that what pleases one god may well displease another. While one god may be pleased by a person's action, another may be offended by that same action. If this is the case, what happens to Euthyphro's definition of piety? Is it possible for one action to be both pious and impious? Of course not, and so the definition must be given up, since it leads to an inconsistency.

Socrates' objective in his dialogues may have been to foster the good life, but despite his public spirit, he acquired many enemies in his pursuit of truth. Two respectable Athenian citizens, Anytus and Meletus, charged that Socrates was an atheist who also believed in and taught about gods that were different from those sanctioned by Athens. In his defense, Socrates pointed out that the charge brought against him contained an inconsistency: Reminding his listeners that an atheist is one who believes in no gods, Socrates asked how he could be an atheist and, at the same time, a believer in gods different from those of the state. You can see that Socrates had a good argument for his innocence of the charge on impiety.

Anytus and Meletus also charged him, however, with corrupting the youth. Perhaps it was this charge that persuaded the Athenian jury to find him guilty and sentence him to death. The point of our discussion of Socrates is that the goal of philosophical argument is to pursue and end an inquiry on a particular issue without regard to practical consequences. And it is the goal of truth, or at least justified belief, that leads to the rules of argument expected in good philosophical writing. In most cases, hopefully, you will not be asked to die for your conclusions. But practical considerations such as the approval of peers should be disregarded in philosophical writing.

Before you can argue effectively, you must know how to identify and analyze arguments presented to you. This requires you first to determine if a series of statements is an argument. If it is an argument, you must then discern if the argument is deductive or nondeductive, valid or invalid, and persuasive or tenuous. In this chapter you will learn

- The definition of an argument
- The two basic types of argument
- How to evaluate arguments
- How to use valid forms to cast your arguments

8.2   THE DEFINITION OF AN ARGUMENT

An *argument* is a series of statements that include at least one premise, a conclusion, and connectives that link the premise(s) to a conclusion. A premise is a statement, offered as evidence for a conclusion, which is assumed or taken for granted in a context. For example, the statements "It is wrong to smoke around pregnant women" and "If it is wrong to smoke around pregnant women, then the unborn have rights" are premises. Some expressions that indicate premises are *if, since, because, on the basis of, on the basis of the following observations,* and *the following observation supports my claim.*

Philosophers use the expression *connective* to designate the basic linking expressions of logic. The basic connectives are *it's not the case that, and, or,* and *if . . . then.* The first connective, which is represented by the negation sign, does not really connect statements. Instead, it negates a statement or a group of statements connected by the other connectives. *And* joins two or more statements. *Or* also joins two or more statements and is understood in logic in its inclusive sense. A better rendering of this connective would be *at least one.*

If . . . then does double duty in arguments. In a conditional statement it connects two statements. The statement before *then* is the antecedent, the statement after *then* is the consequent. Compound sentences formed by *if . . . then* are called conditionals. Conditionals often are found as premises in arguments either expressly stated or implied. But *if . . . then* also functions as the basic connective in any argument connecting the premises to the conclusion. An argument can always be translated into a long conditional sentence in which the conjunction of the premises forms the antecedent, and the conclusion is the consequent.

A *conclusion* is the statement or claim presented as resulting from the premise(s). For example, if we accept the premises that (1) it is wrong to smoke around pregnant women, and (2) if it is wrong to smoke around pregnant women, then the unborn have rights, we must reasonably conclude that the unborn have rights. The conclusion follows whether we like the practical consequences it would suggest or not.

The following are all linking expressions that indicate conclusions: *it follows that, therefore, if . . . then, hence, my conclusion is, consequently, it is (probably) the case that,* and *so.*

Generally, arguments are expressed in a way that requires you to tease out the premises. Sometimes the arguments can be expressed offensively. Someone who remarks that it is ridiculous for pro life advocates to talk about prenatal care both obscures what might be a good argument and infuriates the people whom it might otherwise influence. In ordinary life it takes a lot of patience and charity to reconstruct what others might mean.

Arguments call for us to take the truth or probable truth of the premises for granted for a moment so that we may determine whether the purported truth of the premises is sufficient to guarantee the truth or probability of the conclusion. In addition to premises and conclusions, arguments may contain extraneous material such as jokes, biographical data, or even personal attacks. Philosophers generally avoid such distracting material, and in argument analysis you should simply disregard it. Some style manuals will tell you not to write in the first person. However, some philosophers find that occasional use of the first person serves to emphasize a point.

Narratives, which are simply chronological stories of actions or events, are not arguments. Yet narratives are effective devices for causing someone to accept a conclusion or causing a person to listen with more tolerance to an argument. Perhaps your instructor will be open to such writing and may even use narratives such as *Sophie's World* in her course. Still, you will eventually be required to say in argumentative language what the narrative, Sophie's or yours, seeks to instill.

8.3   THE TWO BASIC TYPES OF ARGUMENT

Arguments are either deductive or nondeductive. An argument is *deductive* if it claims that the conclusion must be true if the premises are true. The conclusion is therefore guaranteed by the truth of the premises. If the premises are true and the deductive form of the argument is arranged properly, then the conclusion must also be true. The argument given above about the unborn is a valid deductive argument. It is an instance of the valid form *modus ponens*.

The following argument is deductive because its conclusion, given its premises, is presented as being an unarguable matter of fact:

Two million and thirty-seven lottery tickets were sold for Wednesday's drawing.
I bought two tickets. So, my chance of winning Wednesday is 2 in 2,000,037.

An argument is *nondeductive (inductive)* if it claims only a high degree of probability for the conclusion. An inductive argument, then, allows for some doubt of the truth of the conclusion, and it bases its claim of accuracy on the very good chance that its premises are correct. Here is an example:

All cats that I have ever seen will eat mice. Jake is a cat. Therefore, Jake will probably eat mice.

It is important to know the difference between deductive and inductive arguments because we must know what an argument demands of us. Does the argument ask us to accept something as true or only as probably true? The actions we take based upon certainty are different from the actions we take based upon mere probability, and we may hold deductive arguments liable for much stronger bases of proof.

8.4   VALIDITY AND SOUNDNESS

8.4.1   Deductive Validity

There are two slightly different definitions of *validity*, which correspond to the two different types of argument, deductive and nondeductive. An argument is *deductively valid* if it is deductive and if the truth of the premises would make it necessary that the conclusion is true also. In other words, an argument is deductively valid if it is deductive and if it cannot be the case that the premises are true and the conclusion is false. The following argument is deductively valid:

> PREMISE 1:   If God knows everything, then God knows what I will do tomorrow before I make up my mind.
>
> PREMISE 2:   God knows everything.
>
> CONCLUSION: God knows what I will do tomorrow before I make up my mind.

The philosopher William James claimed that the second premise is false. Still, the argument is deductively valid; that is, the deduction from the assumed true premises is valid. The argument is deductive because it claims certainty for the conclusion, and it is valid because its conclusion would have to be true if the premises were true.

When you evaluate an argument for deductive validity, you do not yet check for the truth of the premises. The factual truth of the premises is irrelevant to the validity of an argument. Consequently, a deductively valid argument may have false premises and a true conclusion, or it may have false premises and a false conclusion.

In a deductively valid argument the relation between premises and conclusions is not a causal relationship. Premises do not cause a conclusion to be true; they merely explain why, if they are true, the conclusion is also true.

8.4.2   Nondeductive Validity

Nondeductive arguments make claims in their conclusions that go beyond the evidence of the premises. If I claim "since my chances of winning the lottery are 2 million to 1, then I will probably lose the lottery," then I am making a nondeductive argument because I am claiming only the probability, not the certainty, of my conclusion. An argument is *nondeductively valid* if it is nondeductive and if the truth or high probability of its premises make the conclusion highly probable also. My argument about the probability of my losing the lottery is nondeductively valid because the high odds against winning do indeed produce a high likelihood that I will lose.

Checking for validity is important because it is the first step in examining an argument in order to see if it is worthwhile to check the actual truth of the premises. If an argument is not valid, there is no point in finding out whether or not the premises are true. If an argument is valid, however, the premises become important.

Imagine you are a member of the National Science Foundation and someone presents a grant for funding. The grant's hypothesis is that since mosquitoes carry malaria, then the people of Kentucky are vulnerable to malaria. As you read the grant, you realize that the argument guiding the proposed research is not arranged in a valid way. Not all mosquitoes carry malaria, and the mosquitoes that carry malaria have not been found in Kentucky. You would not have to consider funding it, because the project would probably produce invalid information. It needs to be reformulated if it is to be worth funding.

Consider the following deductive arguments. Are they valid?

- If President Clinton did what Paula Jones charged in her deposition that he did, then he is guilty of sexual harassment in the workplace. Paula Jones did indeed speak the truth. Therefore, Clinton is a harasser.
- Republican Bob Dole said he would not raise taxes. But Dole voted many times to raise taxes while he was a senator, even while Republicans were in control of the presidency. So, Dole was lying.
- When I am in Memphis, I always go to the services at Al Green's church. If I go to Al Green's church, then I will visit Graceland afterward, since it is nearby. So, if I go to Memphis, then I will visit Graceland.

If you found yourself asking whether Al Green (soul and gospel singer) has a church, how Dole (former United States Senator and Republican candidate for President in 1996) voted, whether Paula Jones spoke the truth, or if Graceland (Elvis Presley's mansion) is indeed close to Al Green's church (it is), then you missed the point. It does not matter to the question of validity whether the statements you questioned are in fact true or false. It matters only whether, if they and the other premises in their respective arguments were true, the truth of the premise would make it necessary that the conclusion be true also. The anti-Clinton bias of the first argument and the anti-Dole bias of the second argument may irritate you, but these biases have nothing to do with the validity of the arguments. Try to filter your worries about bias out and attend to the arguments.

Are the following nondeductive arguments nondeductively valid?

- The United States has never elected a third-party candidate as President. So, Nader will probably not be elected in 2004.
- When people are transferred to Calvary Hospital, they usually die within a week or two. Helene's physician has recommended that she be transferred to Calvary. So, the physician has decided she is beyond recovery.

8.4.3   Cogency

We have discussed three questions that need to be raised when evaluating a passage to test its credentials as an argument:

1. Does it have the components (at least one premise and a conclusion) of an argument?
2. Is the argument type deductive or nondeductive?
3. Is the argument valid or invalid in the manner appropriate to the argument type?

A fourth question remains to be asked: Is the argument cogent?

We may say that an argument is *deductively cogent* (or sound) if it is deductive, deductively valid, and the premises are in fact true. An argument is *nondeductively cogent* (often called strong or correct) if it is nondeductive, nondeductively valid, and its premises are true or highly probable.

The following argument is deductively cogent:

The electric company charges for electricity. I used electricity from the electric company last month. So, I will be charged for the use of electricity.

The following argument is nondeductively cogent:

Thousands of tickets are sold for each drawing of the California lottery. I bought only one ticket for the next drawing on Wednesday. So, I will probably lose.

8.5   PATTERNS OF REASONING

Now that we know how to ask four questions that will help us test the philosophically relevant credentials of an argument, we can add to our argument-testing capabilities by understanding sound and unsound patterns of reasoning. When we discussed validity, we relied upon simple examples to elicit your agreement on when the premises would guarantee the truth or high probability of a conclusion. There are mathematical demonstrations of which argument forms are valid or invalid, but we will not provide mathematical proofs here, for the attempt to do so would take us too far beyond the compass of this book. If you are interested in mathematical proofs, take a course in symbolic logic or look at a good logic text-book. We will note the major valid forms and invalid forms also. The invalid forms are important because some intuitively appealing forms of argument are invalid.

8.6   VALID FORMS OF ARGUMENT

The practical benefit of learning the valid and invalid argument forms lies in how the forms facilitate argumentative discussion. Once you isolate the author's major thesis and premises for the thesis, you may discover that the author has structured the argument in a valid form, such as *modus ponens* or a *reductio*, and so you would not criticize the author's form of argument, but turn to investigating the premises. But if the author has relied upon eliminative induction, then it may be the case that a possibility has been overlooked and a false dilemma presented. Or, if the author relies upon an invalid form such as affirming the consequent, you can identify her error and criticize or perhaps find a way to repair the argument. And, of course, if you can cast summaries of your own arguments in valid forms, your writing will be more effective.

In sentential logic ordinary language statements are given letters as their names. Each statement gets only one name, one letter. Take the sentence "If this is Tuesday, this must be Brussels." This is a compound sentence containing two state-ments: "This is Tuesday" and "This is Brussels." Some systems of sentential logic use capital letters and begin with the letter A. Others use small letters and begin with p. Whether "This is Tuesday" is named A or p is a convention. The important thing is that in an argument form it keeps the same name and no other statement is given the same name. So "This is Brussels" is going to be B or q, but certainly not A or p. Could we have called it A before we baptized the other statement A? Sure, provided we baptized the other one something else.

When an argument in ordinary language is translated, replacing its state-ments with sentence letters and the connectives with their appropriate symbols, then we have exhibited its form. The connectives in sentential logic connect sen-tences. The connectives are *and, or, it is not the case that*, and *if . . . then*. They are represented by an upside-down v, a right-side-up v, the ~ or −, and an arrow re-spectively. Punctuation is also provided with parentheses and brackets to insure proper grouping.

1. This is Tuesday and this is Brussels

    A ∧ B

    or

    p ∧ q

2. This is Tuesday or this is Brussels.

$A \lor B$

or

$p \lor q$

3. If this is Tuesday then this is Brussels.

$A \rightarrow B$

or

$p \rightarrow q$

4. This is not Tuesday

~A or

~p or

−A or

−p

5. It is not the case that this is Tuesday and this is Brussels

$-(A \land B)$

or

$-(p \land q)$

and you could replace the − in each example with ~.

Two arguments in ordinary language that have the same representation when translated have the same logical or argument form. This is handy because once you know a form is valid and are practiced in recognizing it, you can immediately recognize valid arguments about matters you never heard of.

8.6.1 Tautologies

A *tautology* is a sentence that must be true in all possible worlds. A *contradiction* is a sentence that must be false in all possible worlds. You can recognize tautologies and contradictions by their forms. "A and not A" is a contradiction. "It is snowing in hell and it is not snowing in hell" is a contradiction. Tautologies are redundant and boring, but they are valid. "A or not A" is a tautology: "It is raining right now in Chico or it is not raining right now in Chico." Notice that a tautology requires no premises. It is true on the basis of form alone. So perhaps tautologies are exceptions to the rules we have looked at governing argument: Tautologies are valid argument forms that require no premises. Philosophers disagree on the question of whether tautologies assert any conclusions at all when sentence names are replaced with ordinary language statements. After all, how much information about the weather is included in the tautology about Chico in this example?

8.6.2   Modus Ponens

A common valid form of argument, *modus ponens* is, as its Latin name implies, a "method of putting." A *modus ponens* argument takes the following symbolic form:

> If p, then q.
> P.
> Therefore q.

A simple example of a *modus ponens* would be as follows:

> If July 15 is Graybosch's birthday, then he is a Cancer just like O. J. Simpson, Bill Clinton, and Phyllis Diller.
> July 15 is Graybosch's birthday.
> Therefore, he is a Cancer just like O. J. and the others.

More complicated *modus ponens* follow patterns such as the following:

> If p and q and r, then s or t.
> P and q and r.
> Therefore, s or t.

8.6.3   Hypothetical Syllogisms

Hypothetical syllogisms are arguments that have the following symbolic form:

> If p, then q.
> If q, then r.
> Therefore, if p, then r.

Here is an example of a valid simple hypothetical syllogism:

> If reading someone's personal electronic mail violates the right to privacy, then reading the person's personal electronic mail is wrong.

If reading someone else's personal electronic mail is wrong, then most employers violate employee rights to privacy.

So, if reading someone's personal mail violates the right to privacy, then most employers violate employee rights to privacy.

Syllogisms come in many forms. One is known as the *disjunctive syllogism*, which has the following symbolic form:

P or q.
Not p.
Therefore, q.

Example:

Either you vote or you have no reason to complain. You did not vote. Therefore, you have no reason to complain.

A knowledge of traditional syllogisms will be helpful to you if you are taking a standardized test for graduate or professional school. Here are several valid syllogisms. Notice that traditional syllogisms are not in sentential form.

All A's are B's.
All B's are C's.
Therefore, all A's are C's.

Example:

All rights are valid claims. All valid claims are prima facie moral. Therefore, all rights are prima facie moral.

Another valid syllogism follows:

All A's are B's.
This is an A.
This is therefore also a B.

Example:

All rights are valid claims. Self-defense is a right. Self-defense is a valid claim.

Here is a third valid syllogism:

> All A's are B's.
> No B's are C's.
> Therefore, no A's are C's.

Example:

> All uses of hate speech are violations of civil rights. No violations of civil rights are instances of free speech. So, no uses of hate speech are instances of free speech.

A fourth valid syllogism is:

> No A's are B's.
> Some C's are A's.
> Therefore, some C's are not B's.

Example:

> No ethnic revolutions are democratic revolutions. Some revolutions in the Balkans are ethnic revolutions. So, some revolutions in the Balkans are not democratic revolutions.

8.6.4   Modus Tollens

Modus tollens, Latin for "method of removing," is an argument that takes the following symbolic form:

> If p, then q.
> Not q.
> Therefore, not p.

Example:

> If it is morally wrong to smoke around pregnant women, then the unborn have rights. The unborn do not have rights. So, it is not morally wrong to smoke around pregnant women.

8.6.5   Dilemmas

A *dilemma* is an argument in which there is a choice between two alternatives, neither of which is particularly desirable. A dilemma takes the following symbolic form:

P or q.
If p, then r.
If q, then s.
Therefore, r or s.

Example:

Peter either forgot that it was his son's birthday or did not care enough to buy a gift. If Peter forgot, then he needs to spend less time on work. If Peter did not care enough, then he needs counseling. Therefore, Peter either needs to work less or get counseling.

This is a handy form of argument for use when you know that someone is guilty of one of several offenses but you cannot say which one. You do not have to determine which offense is the real one to convict the person.

8.6.6   Indirect Proof or Reductio ad Absurdum

An *indirect proof*, also known as *reductio ad absurdum*, exhibits that the negation of what it seeks to prove entails a false proposition. Recognition of that logical consequence requires logically the rejection of the proposition that led us to accept the falsity. If that initial proposition must be false, then its negation must be true. *Reductios* have the following form:

To prove p
Suppose: not p.
If not p, then q.
If q, then r.
Not r.
Therefore, not not p.
Therefore, p.

Example:

To prove: Same sex couples should not have the right to marry.

Suppose same sex couples should become legally entitled to marry. If same sex couples marry, then same sex couples will have the right to adopt children. If same sex couples have the right to adopt children, then this will threaten the unique social role of heterosexual marriage. But the unique role of heterosexual marriage ought not to be threatened. Therefore, same sex couples should not be entitled to marry.

The *reductio* looks like an extended version of *modus tollens*. The difference is that the *reductio* is purposely used to throw doubt on a particular premise.

8.6.7   Contradictions

A *contradiction* is a sentence form that must be false no matter what statements are substituted for the statement names. It has the symbolic form "p and not p." For example, the statement "It is raining right now in Chico and it is not raining right now in Chico" is a contradiction. The negation of a contradiction must be true. So, if you find a contradiction, you should conclude that its negation is true: "It is not the case that it is raining and not raining in Chico right now." In the charge of atheism against Socrates, outlined earlier, we would agree with Socrates that it is not the case that he is both an atheist and a believer in gods.

8.6.8   Analogies

In an *analogy* we draw a comparison between the known qualities of a sample population and the partially known qualities of a target population. If, for example, we have several friends who like heavy metal music, alternative rock, mosh pits, and tattoos, and if we make a new friend who likes three of those things, then it would be reasonable to infer by analogy that the new friend will like the fourth thing.

Our analogy works partially on the basis of similarities. If our friends are similar in three respects, they are probably similar in the fourth. The cogency of this reasoning depends in part on the similar qualities being related to each other. Our first three friends might also like falafel, but I would be less inclined to simply infer that the fourth person shares those likes, because an appreciation of falafel does not seem related to an appreciation of mosh pits.

Analogies often lead to unsound conclusions because they are not properly grounded. It is not just the enumeration of common factors that leads us to accept an analogy and take our new friend for a tattoo. It is also that we have background knowledge that these are common elements in a coherent subarea of American culture. This background knowledge is sometimes referred to as a higher order induction and illustrates how beliefs are nested in a wider context. Some philosophers would defend analogies provided that the reasoner possesses no higher order inductive evidence to suggest the lack of a causal connection between the elements in an analogy. Others would argue that the reasoner must possess relevant higher order inductive evidence that a connection does hold before accepting an analogy. For our purpose, philosophical writing, it is enough to note that analogies should be queried for the relevance of the factors enumerated to each other.

8.6.9   Induction by Elimination

Induction by elimination is a popular nondeductive form of reasoning in philosophy. It requires three steps. The first is to canvass the alternative perspectives on a question. The second is to find reasons why all alternatives but one cannot be true. Finally, having eliminated all the unacceptable alternatives, you take step three, which is to accept the remaining alternative as the most probable one. The crucial step in this form of reasoning is the first step. If you have not included all the alternatives, you will commit an informal fallacy called a *false dilemma*. We will talk a little more about false dilemmas in Chapter 9.

8.6.10   Induction by Enumeration

In *induction by enumeration* we infer that a quality probably belongs to a whole population on the basis of a finite number of instances.
Example:

Farmer Jones's turkey believes that Farmer Jones will come to feed him every morning on the basis of a finite number of previous feedings.

This is a fairly reliable inference for the turkey; it is correct every morning except the last.

A *statistical induction* is similar to induction by enumeration. It involves attributing the statistical frequency of a quality in a sample population to the population as a whole.
Example:

Since 75% of the camels we have seen have two humps, we infer that 75% of all camels have two humps.

Both induction by enumeration and statistical induction uncover connections that may be more than coincidences—connections that may be based on an underlying causal relationship.

8.6.11   Inference to the Best Explanation

Some philosophers accept *inference to the best explanation* as a valid form of nondeductive inference. Suppose there is a series of events whose occurrence can be most reasonably explained if you posit another event or fact as their cause. Example:

> You notice that every time you play cards with me, you lose. But when you play cards with other people, you do reasonably well. Your losing streak with me might be best explained if you posit that I am a cheat. Perhaps I have marked the cards.

Or

> Suppose you know there are no perfect vacuums in nature, and you also know that energy in imperfect vacuums is unstable. How did the universe begin? Perhaps the best explanation is that a perfect vacuum transformed into an imperfect vacuum in which energy is unstable and there was an explosion? Here the posit is an imperfect vacuum.

For centuries God was the natural posit for explaining the existence of the universe because a lack of scientific knowledge blocked the suggestion of positing an imperfect vacuum. An explanation, therefore, is only as good as our knowledge of the conditions and circumstances of the phenomenon that we are trying to explain. Good background knowledge might justify our claim that the explanation that occurs to us is the only possible one, but because our knowledge is so often more limited than we think, we should normally give low probability to conclusions from this form of reasoning.

8.6.12   The Hypothetical-Deductive Method

The *hypothetical-deductive method* is usually attributed to Karl Popper but dates at least from the work of the nineteenth-century American philosopher Chauncey Wright. Popper popularized the method with philosophers of science as his original criterion for differentiating science from nonscience. Popper points out that one can never conclusively verify by empirical means a universal statement, but one can falsify it.

For instance, induction by enumeration cannot establish once and for all that all swans are white. One nonwhite swan can falsify the universal claim about white swans. It may sound odd, but *falsifiability* is actually more helpful to science than verification via inductions. After all, if you can falsify a claim, then you need not pursue it any longer and can move on to another claim.

Popper urges that scientific investigators select the hypothesis with the lowest initial probability, given our background beliefs, for further investigation. It is the hypothesis that has the highest likelihood to turn out to be wrong when empirically tested. If it survives frequent tests, it is considered corroborated.

8.7   APPLICATIONS

Argumentation is the means by which most philosophy gets done. As you read philosophical essays, try to determine which particular modes of argumentation the writers are using. The premises may be more complicated than the ones I have used in my examples above, but the basic forms will be there. Remember, learning the throws of argument now will enhance your ability not only to understand philosophical positions but to find ways to question and perhaps improve upon them in your own writing

Most beginning philosophy courses will require you to analyze arguments. Use the valid forms discussed in this chapter to initially lay out the relationship between the author's major thesis and major premises. Then treat each major premise in turn as a conclusion and ask what form of argument is used to support it. Expect that in some cases you will have to supply premises yourself that are taken by the author for granted.

Laying arguments out in argument form will also be useful in compare and contrast papers. It will help you notice the common premises of authors who argue for different conclusions. It will also indicate to you which areas might be most useful to investigate in criticizing one position. Take the valid argument used in this chapter about the rights of the unborn. Most of us agree that it is wrong to smoke in the presence of pregnant women. If we were to evaluate the argument further, we would probably fix our attention on the conditional: If it is wrong to smoke around pregnant women, then the unborn have rights. Perhaps we will argue that this premise is false. It might be that it is wrong to smoke only around pregnant women who want to give birth to a fetus. Or, it might be wrong only if the woman regards the effects of smoking as significantly damaging to her unborn. The rights might not belong to the unborn except through the rights of the woman.

And, of course, as you formulate your own arguments in argumentative papers, you will want to insure they are cogent by casting them in outline in valid forms. If this is not successful, you will know where you need to do more work.

It might seem that some argumentative forms, such as the dilemma, are only useful in criticism. However, a good argumentative paper will anticipate objections and answer them. If you are writing on the immorality of smoking around pregnant women, then you should probably anticipate the objection that such a judgment suggests the unborn have rights, and that conflicts with the right of a woman to choose. The same sorts of argument forms that would help you criticize a real opponent will serve you in criticizing the opponent you anticipate.

At the beginning of this chapter we discussed Socrates' approach to argument and noted that Socrates was adept at coming up with counterexamples to the general definitions offered by his partners in inquiry. In one sense this is an instance of Popper's notion of falsifiability. A definition is a universal statement, and a counterexample, like a single black swan, falsifies a definition. But Socrates' interest in counterexamples was also part of his desire to be clear about the meaning of the concepts he was addressing. The positive message found in the *Apology* is that it is important to be clear about what *atheist* means before investigating whether someone is in fact an atheist.

8.8   A MAP OF HOW TO ARRANGE A PHILOSOPHY PAPER

Let us agree that some philosophy papers, the most basic ones, will be expository papers. Here, your task will be to be clear about the meaning of the key philosophical terms and to present some philosopher's position in its form, hopefully valid. So, if you are assigned an expository paper on William James' concept of freedom, your paper will involve an analytic step in which you explain what James meant by terms such as *determinism* and *indeterminism*. It will also involve exhibiting the structure of his argument against determinism, which seems to this writer to involve use of the dilemma.

In a compare/contrast paper you might address the views of freedom in James, B. F. Skinner, and Jonathan Edwards. In such a paper you would still have to do the analytic steps that make up an expository paper. This time, however, there will be three such expository papers—one for each philosopher under examination. The critical part of the compare/contrast paper will center on the validity or invalidity of each philosopher's argument, the defensibility of key definitions, and the truth of the premises offered for each thesis. So, expository papers are contained within compare/contrast papers.

Argumentative papers likewise contain expository and compare/contrast papers. It is very difficult to address a philosophical issue without considering the work of others. If you are working on the justification of making duties to family members a moral priority over duties to the state, it will be helpful to place your discussion in the context of reasons provided by philosophers who disagree with each other on the issue. Some names that occur to me naturally on this issue are Plato, Aristotle, Marx, Firestone, and Hobbes. The comments you make in comparing the positions of these philosophers will serve as reasons for the position you support in your argumentative paper. Marx, for instance, presented the sentimental family as a means of preserving economic classes through inheritance. If you find yourself objecting that this is rarely the reason why people choose to have children, this objection will serve both as a criticism of Marx and a reason in the position you develop.

Realizing the continuity in these three types of papers, we can map out the steps of a philosophical paper as follows. The different types of papers stop at different places.

1. Expository Step
   a. explain key terms
   b. exhibit the form of the argument under consideration
2. Compare/Contrast Step
   a. address the validity of the arguments under consideration
   b. address the cogency of the arguments by considering the evidence for the various premises and also by attempting to formulate counterexamples
   c. repair the arguments by recasting them in valid forms or adding premises to insure that you address the best possible version of an argument
3. Argumentative Step
   a. state which alternative view seems more likely correct based on the premises available
   b. use the criticisms in the compare/contrast phase to state how close your own view is to the preferred alternative
   c. develop your own view further using the criticisms brought against other alternatives as your initial premises
   d. recast your own argument in a valid form
   e. anticipate and address objections to your view
   f. conclude by stating what has been accomplished and what remains to be investigated

9

Avoiding Fallacies

To say that we should drop the idea of truth as out there waiting to be discovered is not to say that we have discovered that, out there, there is no truth. It is to say that our purposes would be served best by ceasing to see truth as a deep matter, as a topic of philosophical interest, or, "true" as a term which repays "analysis."

—Richard Rorty, *Contingency, Irony, and Solidarity*, 1989

9.1 FORMAL FALLACIES

Fallacies are errors in reasoning that lead us to accept conclusions that we are not entitled to accept on the basis of the premises. Formal fallacies are reasoning errors that occur because the form or structure of an argument is incorrect. There are an infinite number of formal fallacies, yet a few may be identified that are commonly encountered when analyzing arguments. The ability to recognize them may make your job as a critical writer easier.

9.1.1 Denying the Antecedent

Remember the way we formulated arguments in Chapter 8. Consider an argument in this form:

If p, then q.
Not p.
Therefore, not q.

Example:

If Graybosch wins the lottery, then he can take a vacation. Graybosch cannot win the lottery. Therefore, Graybosch cannot take a vacation.

It would be a lot easier to take a vacation if I won the lottery, but maybe I will take one anyway. The error in the argument form is in assuming that the antecedent (winning the lottery) is necessary to my conclusion (taking a vacation). In actuality, my taking a vacation does not depend upon winning the lottery. Winning the lottery is one sufficient, but not necessary, condition of taking a vacation. *Modus ponens* presents an antecedent which is a sufficient, not a necessary, condition of a consequent.

9.1.2   Affirming the Consequent

Here is another invalid form of reasoning:

If p, then q.
Q.
Therefore, p.

Just because p always leads to q does not mean that q always leads to p. Other sufficient conditions may also result in q.

9.1.3   The Exclusive Fallacy

This fallacy takes the following form:

P or q.
P.
Therefore, not q.

The fallacy lies in confusing the inclusive and exclusive sense of *or*. You are at a party and ask who brought the wine. The host says Fred or Jack brought the wine. If *or* is meant exclusively, then once you know that Fred brought wine, you could conclude that Jack did not. But if *or* is used inclusively, then it means at least Fred and possibly Jack brought wine. Since logic uses the inclusive sense of *or*, you ought not to infer from the fact that Fred brought wine that Jack did not.

Here is an example of the exclusive fallacy:

Either Newt Gingrich is guilty of ethics violations or Bill Clinton is guilty of ethics violations.

Newt Gingrich is guilty of ethics violations.

Therefore, Bill Clinton is not guilty of ethics violations.

The inclusive sense of *or* allows both disjuncts to be true. They both could be guilty; both disjuncts could be true.

Of course, we are familiar with detective stories in which each suspect is eliminated until there is only one left who must be guilty. There are eliminative arguments in which the truth or falsity of a disjunct is relevant to the truth or falsity of others. But they must be carefully phrased to show the relevance of the disjuncts to each other. And you will note that the argument example above did not include a premise that said they both could not be guilty. If it did, it would have been a valid argument. But it would also have had a different argument form.

9.2   INFORMAL FALLACIES

Informal fallacies are errors in reasoning based in the content of an argument and not in the argument's form. It is possible to construct arguments with valid forms but still fail to have reasoned properly in one of three general ways. First, the premises of the argument could be false or lack the proper degree of probability. Second, our reasoning could leave out evidence in our possession or evidence that is not in our possession that we are still responsible for gathering. Ignorance of contrary evidence is not automatically an acceptable excuse. Third, our argument could mistakenly assert that the premises give more support to the conclusion than the truth or probability of the premises would warrant.

9.2.1   Susceptibility to Fallacies

Our human desires make us susceptible to fallacies. A common gambling fallacy is to bet on a number that is due because it has not occurred recently. If the dice or the roulette wheel is fair, each outcome has the same probability on each roll or spin regardless of how long it has been since it last occurred. If I throw six snake eyes (two ones) in a row, on the seventh throw it is just as likely that I will throw snake eyes again as it was on the first throw. Snake eyes are not less likely because they have occurred six times in a row, if the dice are fair.

Psychologists have catalogued a number of impediments to reasoning. I am pretty good at math, but I make an increasing number of errors of subtraction in my checkbook toward the end of the month. *Wishful thinking* infects my math. Two other interesting impediments to reasoning are our tendencies to have a *confirmation bias* and to *expect one cause* for any given event. The confirmation bias allows us to accept horoscopes and psychic hot lines because we remember only the instances when the "predictions" come true and forget the times when they do not. The expectation that every event has just one cause blinds us to other contributing causes and makes us especially prone to give up good causal connections when we run into one exception. For example,

> Smoking does not cause cancer, because my Dad smoked until he was 97.

Perhaps your dad was lucky and had a genetic endowment that helped him resist cancer. There is no guarantee (not yet, anyway) you have that same endowment.

There is also an interesting error made consistently with statistical reasoning. Suppose you read of a study that says that 35 percent of people convicted of heroin possession said they had smoked marijuana before becoming involved with heroin. This correlation might lead you to infer that marijuana use causes heroin use; or you might infer that whatever causes marijuana use also causes heroin use. And people commonly make such inferences. The 35 percent is impressive until you notice that 65 percent did not say that they smoked marijuana before becoming involved with heroin. When you are presented with a statistical correlation between two factors such as marijuana use and heroin use, you really want to know four correlations before drawing a conclusion about the relevance of one to the other:

- What percent of marijuana users also use heroin.
- What percent of marijuana users do not use heroin.
- What percent of the population use heroin only.
- What percent of the population use neither marijuana nor heroin.

Our tendency to accept fallacies is, fortunately, counteracted by our ability to identify them. The following list of informal fallacies has been constructed to assist you in identifying fallacies in arguments.

9.2.2   Invalid Appeal to Authority

An invalid appeal to authority occurs when we rely on defective expertise. Defective expertise is a source of knowledge that presents itself as authoritative but is not. Michael Jordan is an expert basketball player, but he does not necessarily know the best brand of ice cream. Experts may be subject to bias that can cause them consciously or unconsciously to render unfair judgment. A Toyota salesman will probably not provide an unbiased evaluation of a Nissan. And sometimes the experts disagree, leaving us forced to reason for ourselves.

The fact that people have positions of authority does not automatically make their beliefs, or our premises, false or unjustified. When the president or the pope speak, they do not commit a fallacy of invalid appeal to authority just by saying something. Perhaps their office does not give them expertise in all matters, but each has a sphere of expertise—politics and religion—where it is appropriate to speak and be cited as an authority. And, when they venture into other areas, such as the philosophy of love, the arguments they offer ought to be considered. It would be simply unfair to convict them of the fallacy of invalid appeal to authority unless they claim that their position gives them some special expertise. In other words, authorities should have the chance to offer arguments and be given a fair hearing.

9.2.3   Straw Person

A straw person is a misrepresentation of the position of an opponent. A straw person is a position or concept that you have formulated because it is more easily attacked than your opponent's real position. The phrase "What so-and-so really means to say" often introduces a straw person argument.

9.2.4   Inconsistency

You commit the error of inconsistency when you use inconsistent premises to support a conclusion. If you accept as a premise the idea that smoking does not lead to death but admit that diseases caused by smoking lead to death, your two premises conflict. You can also commit this fallacy by being inconsistent in your words and actions. Or, you could argue for inconsistent conclusions. Sometimes people change a belief over time without offering an explanation why. And, finally, organizations such as corporations or political parties sometimes take inconsistent positions with different audiences or have spokespersons who take differing stands. You and a friend might take opposing viewpoints on an important issue and send letters to a politician and compare the replies you receive. In many cases, it will look like the politician agrees with both of you.

9.2.5   False Dilemma

A false dilemma occurs when all the available alternatives are not considered. Consider this example of a false dilemma often used by parents: "Do you want to go to bed now or after your bath?" Faced with what seem to be only two possible courses of action, the five-year-old child will take the bath and go to bed, without realizing that there may be other, less undesirable alternatives. When she reaches the age of eight or nine, different courses of action, such as continuing to watch television, may occur to her.

In politics, even in the most sophisticated commentaries, false dilemmas appear in questions such as "Should the United States use military force or economic sanctions against Iraq?"

9.2.6   Complex Question

In this fallacy you ask a question in a way that begs the answer to another, usually negatively perceived, question. The idea is to make your opponents grant a premise that will be useful in constructing an argument against a conclusion they wish to resist. "When are you going to become responsible?" If you answer that question, you admit that you have not been responsible in the past and grant a premise that may then be used against you.

9.2.7   Begging the Question

When you beg the question, you argue for a conclusion by assuming at least part of it in your premises. "Why do you doubt that God is good? Does not the Koran say so?" The question assumes that God exists and that the Koran provides an authoritative description of the deity's characteristics.

9.2.8   Suppressed Evidence

Because we cannot spend all our lives in doubt, we must eventually draw conclusions on the basis of the evidence available to us. But whenever we suppress evidence, whether we have it available or not, we engage in fallacious reasoning. It is easier to know when you have suppressed relevant evidence in your possession than it is to know when you have done enough investigation to conclude that there is no conflicting evidence that you have not uncovered. Do you need to have read everything William James ever wrote to know that he believed in free will? Or is reading "The Dilemma of Determinism" enough? The correct answer depends upon your social role and responsibilities, on whether you are a beginning student or an advanced scholar. We often suppress evidence for good motives. When we tell children that bad things will happen to them when they lie, we suppress evidence that not all lies lead to negative consequences.

9.2.9   Lack of Proportion

When we overestimate or underestimate actions, interests, or outcomes, we are guilty of applying a lack of proportion in our arguments. Consider the following exhortation, addressed to a typical teenager: "Go ahead and buy the Smashing Pumpkins concert ticket for $300.00. You only live once!"

9.2.10   Appeal to Unknowable Statistics

It is tempting to insert into our arguments appeals to unknowable statistics. For example: "Let's have one more drink. Nobody has ever died from a six-pack!" Another example: "Battlefield deployment of tactical nuclear weapons has prevented 17 major wars in Europe since 1950."

9.2.11   Ad Hominem

Ad hominem is Latin for "against the person." It is a fallacy that involves attacking people's character, looks, tastes, or some other irrelevant aspect of their lives to avoid dealing with their arguments.

9.2.12   Guilt by Association

Guilt by association is a form of *ad hominem* argument in which a person's associates are attacked in an attempt to reflect negatively upon that person or her argument. The target person may be beyond reproach, but her associates may be easy targets. Vice presidential candidate Richard Nixon used this strategy in his famous 1951 "Checkers" speech to attack Adlai Stevenson, a politician beyond reproach, by associating Stevenson with Harry Truman, who was very controversial. Although Truman had endorsed Stevenson's candidacy for President, Truman and Stevenson were not constant companions. Politicians commonly employ the opposite of this phenomenon, innocence by association. When wealthy politicians have themselves photographed with the poor, they take advantage of innocence by association.

9.2.13   Two Wrongs Make a Right

A common fallacy involves defending a wrong action by claiming that someone else has done the same thing or has done something just as bad: "Tommy hit me first!" When we base our argument on the wrong behavior of more than two people, this fallacy is called *common practice*: "It's not so bad to cheat on the test; all my friends do it." When a way of doing wrong has become so accepted that it has attained the status of a proverb, it is called *traditional wisdom*: "The real speed limit is ten miles per hour above the posted speed limit."

9.2.14   Equivocation

Equivocation is the practice of using different meanings of a term that has more than one meaning to derive a conclusion: "Jesus loved prostitutes, and so do I. That's why I pay them well for their services."

9.2.15   Appeal to Ignorance

We appeal to ignorance when we try to get someone to believe that his conclusion is false because he has failed to prove it is true. We may even try to get him to believe that because he has failed to prove his conclusion to be true, then the opposite of his conclusion is true. The failure to prove the existence of extraterrestrial humanoids does not demonstrate that there are none, and the failure to prove that there are no extraterrestrial humanoids does not demonstrate that there are some.

9.2.16   Composition

Composition is a fallacy that occurs when we reason that if the members of a group have a property or characteristic, then the whole group has that characteristic. We might believe, for example, that if all the players on the Oklahoma Sooners football team are individually good players, then the team must be good also. They may not, however, play well together.

9.2.17   Division

Division is the fallacy that occurs when we expect a member of a group to have all the characteristics of a group as a whole: "Native Americans care about the environment." Even if most Native Americans do care about the environment, this does not mean that an individual Native American will.

9.2.18   Hasty Conclusion

When you accept a sweeping conclusion on the basis of a single or small number of incidents, you reach a hasty conclusion. For instance, someone may conclude that all New York City taxi drivers are dishonest if she has been overcharged for a ride from the airport to downtown. A hasty conclusion is the result of making a judgment on the basis of too small a sample of experiences.

Sometimes, hasty conclusions are referred to as *small samples*. A sample can be too small to reveal a representative trend. You would probably be less likely to accept the conclusion of a survey about pornography and sexual assault if you found out that only twenty-five offenders were surveyed. A sample can also be faulted for being unrepresentative. A survey of New York City cab drivers ought not to be taken as a fair indication of the behaviors of all cab drivers, no matter how many cabbies are surveyed.

Humans are inclined to make inductions from single experiences, but rationally we ought not to do so. Calculating a sufficiently large sample size depends on both the size of the population we study and its diversity. I heard a psychologist on the radio say that she had spoken to over fifty women before drawing her conclusion about how best to end a relationship. A sample of fifty is not enough to draw a conclusion about such a large group of persons. Also, people are more complex entities than Ping-Pong balls. One may expect a greater diversity of opinions within the population of women or men, and this should affect sample size. Statisticians would want you to check with at least 1,200 people in a rigorous, scientifically designed study before drawing a conclusion about a country like the United States.

The sample should also be representative of the population. So, if you want to talk about women in general, then you should make sure your sample is not just about a particular ethnic or economic group.

9.2.19   Questionable Cause

The questionable cause fallacy is committed when we take an event as the cause of another on the basis of token evidence, such as a correlation that has not been subjected to further investigation. Political candidates are fond of attributing economic improvements to their economic policies. But they rarely consider that there might have been even greater improvements in the economy if their policies had not been followed: that the economy improved despite their policies and not because of them.

9.2.20   Questionable Analogy

A questionable analogy is the result of drawing a conclusion on the basis of similarities while ignoring or overlooking relevant differences. For example, electric discharges occur both in a computer that is processing information and in the human brain when it is thinking. This might lead us to draw analogies between what goes on in the brain and in the computer as support for the conclusion that computers and humans both process information in the same sense. But there are many dissimilarities between human brains and computers; in fact, there may be too many relevant dissimilarities to compare artificial intelligence to human intelligence.

9.2.21   Appeal to Pity

Sometimes we are tempted to accept a conclusion or a premise because we have sympathetic feelings either for the person who advances it or for the person's current situation. Perhaps we may accept a job applicant's argument that he deserves a teaching position because if he does not receive it, he and his family will suffer.

9.2.22   Appeal to the Stick

Appeals to the stick are actions that mistake threats for arguments. When we appeal to the stick, we urge someone to accept a conclusion or else suffer stated or implied negative consequences. "Why should I attend class?" asks the student. "Because if you do not, I will lower your grade one level for each absence in excess of two," replies the authoritarian philosophy instructor. The instructor has not persuaded the student of the reasonableness of attending class but instead has tried to supply a motivation.

9.2.23   Appeal to Loyalty

Sometimes we accept a conclusion because it comes from a revered public figure, or it is crucial to our national interest, or its contradiction reflects unfavorably on our nation or another cherished institution, such as a church, school, or family. Some Americans have refused, for example, to believe that our armed forces have committed atrocities.

9.2.24   Provincialism

Like the appeal to loyalty, provincialism blinds us to the value of beliefs and practices of other cultures. We are provincial when we reject the ideas of others not for verified reasons but simply because we are familiar with our own practices but not with theirs. We may attend a Christian communion service without questioning its value but reject a harvest dance as having no religious value.

9.2.25   Popularity

We rely upon popularity or appeal to the crowd (argument *ad baculum*) when we argue for a conclusion on the grounds of its widespread acceptance or acceptance by an important group that is not composed of appropriate experts

9.2.26   Double Standard

A double standard occurs when we treat similar cases in a dissimilar manner. If we expect men but not women to experience premarital sex, we subscribe to a double standard.

9.2.27   Invincible Ignorance

Some people actually take pride in refusing to listen to argument. This severe form of evading the issue is usually fed by faith, frustration, and self-righteousness. Extremists on both sides of the abortion issue, for example, sometimes exhibit invincible ignorance by demonstrating pride in not listening to arguments of the other side.

9.3   IDENTIFYING FALLACIES

Exercises to sharpen your argumentative skills are waiting for you everywhere. But newspapers and other media, especially those featuring politicians, are good places to look. Your task, to identify the fallacies within arguments, will be easier if you approach each example by taking the following steps, in this order:

1. Identify the conclusion that you are being asked to accept.
2. Identify the reasons (premises) that are offered for accepting the conclusion.
3. Determine the appropriateness of the premises—that is, the extent to which the premises lead to the conclusion.
4. Determine adequacy of the premises—that is, the extent to which the premises provide sufficient reason to accept the conclusion.

5. If the premises are inappropriate or inadequate, select the fallacy from the list above that most adequately explains the error in the argument.

9.4   CALCULATING PROBABILITIES

Now that we understand how valid arguments are formed and how to identify fallacies, we may consider how to calculate the probability that certain types of arguments (those whose elements are quantifiable) may be valid. We stated in the previous chapter that a nondeductive argument is one that claims that a conclusion follows from the premises with a high probability of truth. But how high must the probability of truth be in order for us to believe that a conclusion is sufficiently probable? The answer is not clear.

We may begin, however, with the proposition that the probability's sufficiency depends upon the context. In other words, the strength of the proof that we demand will depend upon the importance of what the conclusion demands of us and the costs to us of ignoring the conclusion. For instance, if I owned a truck whose manufacturer sent a recall notice because one in ten thousand have exploding ashtrays, I would take the truck in for service. Taking the truck in for service is a relatively minor inconvenience compared to the potential damage of an explosion, even if the chance of an explosion is remote.

There are some rules you can use in determining probabilities. If you want to know the probability of winning a lottery, you should find out how many tickets are sold. Your probability of being a winner when the ticket is just pulled out of a drum is equal to the number of tickets you bought divided by the number sold. But lotteries are designed for suspense. They are meant to be presented as television drama. You have seen on television the little Ping-Pong balls floating around until they are sucked into a tube and displayed at the bottom of the television screen. This means of selection allows there to be lotteries with no winner in a given drawing, since no one may have picked the right combination. There can also be several winners, since more than one person may pick the right set of numbers.

The odds of winning in such a lottery depend upon the number of possible values and the number of values you have to pick. Perhaps your state lottery asks you to pick seven numbers from a field of fifty. No lotteries I know of allow a number to repeat. A winning ball is not thrown back in before the next is picked. So, in a lottery with seven values picked from a field of fifty, the odds of any one ticket being the winner would be one in 50 times one in 49 times one in 48 times one in 47 times one in 46 times one in 45 times one in 44. This is because there are fifty candidates for the first pick and one less candidate on each subsequent draw when the selected ball is not replaced. Likewise, the probability of getting heads on two successive tosses of a fair coin is calculated by multiplying the probability of each separate occurrence. One-half times one-half equals one-fourth, a one-in-four chance.

If you wanted to know the probability of a disjunction (a particular number on either of two dice)—let's say the chance of getting a six or a three on a single throw of a single die—you would add the individual probabilities. One-sixth plus one-sixth gives us two-sixths or one-third, which is one chance in three. So, the probability of getting a three or a six on a throw of a die is three to one.

But when events are not independent, we must include the effect of one outcome on the other in the calculation of probabilities. In our fifty-number lottery, each numbered ball has a one-in-fifty chance of being selected on the first draw. After the first draw, the numbers not selected have a one-in-forty-nine chance of being selected on draw two. The joint probability of the selection of any two particular numbers is one in fifty times one in forty-nine, because on the second draw there are only forty-nine candidates left: $1/50 \times 1/49 = 1/2{,}450$. This means you have a one-in-2,450 chance to draw, say, a five and a twenty-six.

The task of calculating probabilities is complex and requires more than one textbook to explain, but we have presented here a sample of the types of considerations that are used in calculation.

9.5   EMOTIVE LANGUAGE

Words are used to do many more things than just describe a factual occurrence or convey our thoughts. When someone says "I promise," she may not be describing what is going on in her head. Perhaps she has no intention at all of doing what she promised. But she promises anyway by saying, "I promise." We also use words to convey feelings of surprise, approval, or disgust. Sometimes, we select and use words in ways that allow us to increase our chances of persuading others to accept a conclusion without doing the hard and honest work required by rational argumentation. Perhaps you noticed how I just used the word "honest" to nudge you in the direction of accepting my view that such forms of nonargumentative persuasion are not only nonrational but immoral. You will be a better critic if you are able to notice these forms of manipulation and a better philosophical writer if you do not use them yourself.

Certain words have positive overtones for the majority of people. It always helps your case if you are an advocate of freedom and self-determination. The positive or negative overtones attached to other words vary with the audience. Certainly, you will be more inclined to grant the presumption of legitimacy to the political actions of a foreign government official if he or she is a premier and not a dictator. A colleague in Israel once remarked that he knew Nicolae Ceausescu, the head of Romania, was doomed the day the Israeli radio began to refer to him as a dictator after calling him premier for years.

A careful choice of words can allow you the opportunity to significantly manipulate others. One common form of manipulation we are all familiar with is doublespeak. Often, doublespeak, using positive or neutral expressions to hide an unpleasantness or a barbarity, actually appears to be a kindness. Corporations "reengineer" or "downsize" instead of firing or laying off workers.

Academics and other professionals often resort to difficult language to convey what could be conveyed in much more straightforward ways. Sometimes, it is because we are expected to write in an unintelligible manner; sometimes, we are trying to demonstrate that we are highly educated and deserve respect. Some writers seem to get a thrill out of making others feel stupid, and some professions actually create employment opportunities by writing in a special jargon. You need a lawyer to interpret the legalese that some other lawyer used to draw up your lease. The first lawyer creates an employment opportunity for the second.

Language can be used to separate you from your money. Disclaimers on contracts are good examples. The most common application seems to be the small print flashed briefly on television screens during automobile leasing commercials. Sure, you can drive a Mustang for $299 a month—if you have $2,000 down, drive only 12,000 miles a year, and do not mind owning nothing when the three-year lease is up.

Legalese is popular with landlords, bureaucrats, and health maintenance organizations. It is a way of depriving clients of just treatment and washing your hands of guilt at the same time. Opponents at a community debate are silenced by procedures that allow only for two-minute statements. Security deposits disappear to cover cleaning expenses. And HMOs seem to enjoy postponing approval of treatment long enough to tell you that since it is more than sixty days since an injury occurred, you are no longer eligible for the treatment you requested.

Besides these manipulative moves that are connected to the choice of particular expressions, there are other ways of nonargumentative persuasion. One way to discount the legitimate arguments of others and strengthen your own position is to be in a position to interpret their remarks in a way that slants them in your favor.

Sometimes, slanting is accomplished just on the basis of social position. Administrators make it clear that opposition to a redeployment of resources will be regarded as a lack of loyalty. It is also fairly easy to convey, through the tone of presentation, that a view should not be taken seriously. There are modes of expression, material that can be juxtaposed, and even rhetorical questions or pictures in the text to suggest that while a reporter is doing her duty in presenting a view, it ought not to be taken seriously.

Another way in which we can make a weak case seem stronger is to claim only a weak degree of justification for a conclusion. "Terrorists may be involved." If we are right, we look good. If we are wrong, we still look good because we only said it was a possibility. Writers making a case also hope that the weak claim they substantiate will be taken as the stronger one they cannot support and will pass unchallenged.

How you handle objections and questions is also important to how strong a case appears to others. If you can wander away from an issue to one you feel more comfortable with, many people will wander with you. You can also dismiss a question with the attitude that it is inappropriate, immoral, insulting, or farfetched.

Finally, I have a word to offer about humor. Ridicule of an opponent is an *ad hominem* attack. It is fallacious. It is also very effective in slanting an argument. If you become the target of humor, you might try to portray your opponent as superficial for using humor in connection with a serious issue. Humor is, however, a very useful way of presenting an objection to those who have more power than you do. It allows you to be heard and provides the other person with the opportunity to retrench while saving face.

10
Writing Sound Arguments

Believe truth! Shun error!—these, we see, are two materially different laws; and by choosing between them we may end, coloring differently our whole intellectual life.

—William James, *The Will to Believe*, 1896

10.1 WHAT IS A POSITION PAPER?

A philosophical position paper is a written argument. It is an attempt to convince someone to accept a conclusion. It contains

- A conclusion, stated in the beginning of the paper.
- Premises that lead to the conclusion.
- Information that supports the premises.

You may not be aware that you encounter position papers every day. They come in many forms. You see them in television commercials. You hear politicians giving campaign speeches. You listen to sermons in church. All of these events are written arguments: They are forms of position papers. The ability to write an effective argument is an essential skill in many professions. A position paper is a basic written argument that may be used for many different purposes and occupations. The directions in this chapter provide help in writing position papers with a method that is applicable to a wide range of topics.

10.2 THE STEPS TO WRITING A POSITION PAPER

There are nine basic steps to writing a position paper:

1. Select a topic.
2. Conduct research.
3. Select a position (a point you wish to make, your conclusion).
4. Identify one or more premises that lead to the conclusion.
5. Construct an outline of the argument you plan to make.
6. Check the outline for fallacies.
7. Write the argument.
8. Test your argument.
9. Revise your argument.

As you write, remember that the writing process is recursive. This means that the steps outlined above, although taken basically in the order in which they are given, may be repeated during the writing process. For example, once you have constructed some premises, you may decide to change your conclusion. Or, when you have tested your argument, you may feel a need to go back and redefine your premises.

10.2.1   Selecting a Topic

Several considerations govern the selection of topics for position papers for courses in philosophy. First, the topic should be a matter of personal concern to you. It should interest you and, even better, be important to you. Topics related to your religious faith, your career choice or major, or your political views are likely to hold your interest, but remember: A position paper assignment is not written merely to confirm your own prejudices. It provides an opportunity for you to consider new information and perhaps even change your opinion, or at least make it a better-informed one.

With that in mind it will still be useful for you to write a brief paragraph outlining your own view at the start of the writing process. This will help you organize the material you consult in the research phase and alert you when your sources have begun to differ with each other and with you. Having your own view in mind as you read will help avoid the common situation of knowing that two philosophers disagree on an issue while feeling that you agree with both of them.

A second parameter for selecting position paper topics is that papers should address current problems and issues, not historical ones. When you write a paper on an issue that is yet to be resolved, you are participating in the relevant discussions of your own times. A current issue is more likely to be of interest than one that has already been decided. There is even a possibility that the paper, properly submitted to a newspaper or magazine editor, may influence the opinions of others. The issue may be current, but the sources used may be historical. Philosophy position papers often involve applying the views of Socrates, Hume, or Kant to contemporary issues. And it is not uncommon for new positions—virtue ethics—to be revivals of historical positions such as Aristotle's ethics.

A third requirement is that philosophy position paper topics should have an appropriate scope. A common mistake of students is to choose topics that are too complex or that require special technical knowledge or skills beyond those normally available. A good general rule for your position paper is to confine the topic to a matter that you can address without special expertise and with only a moderate amount of research. The availability of relevant data is very important to your choice of topic. Here are some examples of topics. Which of them are obviously sufficiently narrow to be suitable for position papers in philosophy courses? Which are obviously too vague or complex? Which might be appropriate if sufficient data are available?

1. "Deterrence Does Not Justify Capital Punishment"
2. "Humans: Innately Good or Evil?"
3. "The Concept of Freedom in Western Thought"
4. "All Parents Should Be Licensed by the State"
5. "The World Views of Plato and Aristotle"
6. "The Morality of In Vitro Fertilization: A Consequentialist Perspective"
7. "Police Use of Deadly Force Against Fleeing Felons Deters Crime"

Topics 1 and 4 are very likely to be suitable; topics 2, 3, and 5 are either too vague or too complex; and topics 6 and 7 are possibly suitable if sufficient data are available.

10.2.2   Conducting Research

No matter how basic your topic is, you will no doubt have to do at least some research on it. Part Two of this manual explains how to conduct research for topics in philosophy. Many arguments are strengthened by the use of factual data and statistics, so in addition to the books and articles that you will find in your college library and the materials you will find on the Internet, be sure to ask the librarian about the statistical data available in government documents and reports from research institutes.

Also, be aware that it is highly unlikely that you are the first person who has ever investigated the topic you have chosen, whatever it may be. Periodicals will contain arguments that have already been written on your topic. This does not mean that your job has been done for you. It does mean that you can select the best elements of other writers' arguments, restate and reorganize them in your own words, add new thoughts that they have overlooked, and produce an argument of your own.

10.2.3   Selecting a Position

Once you have collected some relevant information, you need to identify a conclusion, which is sometimes called a thesis or a position. A position is a declarative statement that sums up the argument you are making. Often, the position gives you the title of your paper, as you can see from the list of positions in the exercise given above. Consider your first attempt to formulate a position to be a hypothesis, a temporary conclusion that allows you to identify premises to support it. As you conduct further research, you may well change your position to reflect the implications of your premises.

10.2.4   Identifying Premises

Let's suppose the conclusion you wish to argue is "Premarital sex is immoral." In order to define the premises for your argument, you need to state why premarital sex is immoral. A good way to begin is to try to define the predicate of your sentence. What is morality? When is something either moral or immoral? Suppose you decide that something is immoral when it results in harm. If this is the case, then you need to demonstrate that premarital sex causes harm. If you can establish that premarital sex has harmful consequences, such as unwanted pregnancy, sexually transmitted diseases, infant mortality, and abortions, then you may construct a list of premises leading to a conclusion. The result may look something like the following:

Main Argument

PREMISE 1:   Activities that cause harm are immoral.

PREMISE 2:   Premarital sex results in unwanted pregnancies.

PREMISE 3:   Premarital sex results in sexually transmitted diseases.

PREMISE 4:   Premarital sex results in infant mortality.

PREMISE 5:   Premarital sex results in abortions.

PREMISE 6:   Unwanted pregnancies, sexually transmitted diseases, infant mortality, and abortions are harmful to the people who experience them.

PREMISE 7:   Premarital sex is a harmful activity.

CONCLUSION: Premarital sex is immoral.

Notice that most, if not all, the premises you list will require supporting evidence. For example, your premise "premarital sex results in unwanted pregnancies" will be strengthened if you provide supporting details like the following ones:

1. Thirty-four percent of pregnancies of unmarried people are terminated in abortions.
2. Thirty-one percent of pregnancies of unmarried people result in adoptions.

Notice further that some of the premises you list may also require arguments to sustain them. For example, Premise 1, which claims that harmful activities are immoral, may not be automatically accepted by your reader and may require a subordinate argument (one that is not the main argument of the paper but that supports a single premise within the main argument) such as the following:

Subordinate Argument

PREMISE 1:   Morality is the knowledge of the difference between right and wrong.

PREMISE 2:   The knowledge of the difference between right and wrong allows us to make choices between moral and immoral actions.

PREMISE 3:   Moral actions are actions taken as a result of choices to decrease or eliminate direct or indirect harm to other living beings.

PREMISE 4:   Immoral actions are actions taken as a result of choices to create or increase direct or indirect harm to other living beings.

CONCLUSION: Activities that cause harm are immoral.

Notice that the conclusion of the subordinate argument directly above becomes a premise (Premise 1) for the major argument.

10.2.5   Constructing an Outline

Your list of premises is the first step in outlining your argument. As the passage on outlining in Chapter 1 makes clear, an outline is an essential step in the process of building your argument because it allows you to see the strengths and weaknesses of the logical structure of your argument.

Construct an outline using the heading format described in Chapter 1. For your convenience, the pattern of a generic paper outline is repeated here:

I. First main idea
   A. First subordinate idea
      1. Reason, example, or illustration
      2. Reason, example, or illustration
         a. Detail supporting reason 2

        b. Detail supporting reason 2
        c. Detail supporting reason 2
     B. Second subordinate idea
  II. Second main idea

The outline for your position paper will follow the principles embodied in the generic outline above. Notice that premises may be supported by any combination of arguments, subpremises, and supporting details. Examine the sample format below:

   I. Premise 1
     A. Argument 1 for Premise 1
       1. Subpremise 1
          a. Detail supporting Subpremise 1
          b. Detail supporting Subpremise 1
          c. Detail supporting Subpremise 1
       2. Subpremise 2
          a. Detail supporting Subpremise 1
          b. Detail supporting Subpremise 1
     B. Argument 2 for Premise 1
       1. Subpremise 1
          a. Detail supporting Subpremise 1
          b. Detail supporting Subpremise 1
          c. Detail supporting Subpremise 1
       2. Subpremise 2
          a. Detail supporting Subpremise 1
          b. Detail supporting Subpremise 1
  II. Premise 2
     A. Detail supporting Premise 2
     B. Detail supporting Premise 2
 III. Premise 3
 IV. Conclusion

If we apply the outline format to our partially developed argument about premarital sex, we have the following partially developed outline:

   I. Activities that cause harm are immoral. [Premise 1]
     A. Morality is the knowledge of the difference between right and wrong.
     B. The knowledge of the difference between right and wrong allows us to make choices between moral and immoral actions.
     C. Moral actions are actions taken as a result of choices to decrease or eliminate, directly or indirectly, harm to other living beings.
     D. Immoral actions are actions taken as a result of choices to create or increase, directly or indirectly, harm to other living beings.

II. Premarital sex results in unwanted pregnancies. [Premise 2]
   A. Thirty-four percent of pregnancies of unmarried people are terminated in abortions.
   B. Thirty-one percent of pregnancies of unmarried people result in adoptions.
III. Premarital sex results in sexually transmitted diseases. [Premise 3]
IV. Premarital sex results in infant mortality. [Premise 4]
V. Premarital sex results in abortions. [Premise 5]
VI. Unwanted pregnancies, sexually transmitted diseases, infant mortality, and abortions are harmful to the people who experience them. [Premise 6]
VII. Premarital sex is a harmful activity. [Premise 7]
VIII. Premarital sex is immoral. [Conclusion]

Construct an outline as soon as you can in the writing process. You may change it several times, but each time you do, you will have a clearer picture of the argument you are forming.

10.2.6 Checking for Fallacies

Chapter 9 of this book provides a description of common fallacies. The following checklist is taken from that chapter. Use it to make sure that your argument is not a victim of any one of them.

Checklist of Fallacies

☐ Denying the Antecedent
☐ Affirming the Consequent
☐ The Exclusive Fallacy
☐ Invalid Appeal to Authority
☐ Straw Person
☐ Inconsistency
☐ False Dilemma
☐ Complex Question
☐ Begging the Question
☐ Suppressed Evidence
☐ Lack of Proportion
☐ Appeal to Unknowable Statistics
☐ Ad Hominem
☐ Guilt by Association
☐ Two Wrongs Make a Right
☐ Equivocation
☐ Appeal to Ignorance

☐ Composition
☐ Division
☐ Hasty Conclusion
☐ Questionable Cause
☐ Questionable Analogy
☐ Appeal to Pity
☐ Appeal to the Stick
☐ Appeal to Loyalty
☐ Provincialism
☐ Popularity
☐ Double Standard
☐ Invincible Ignorance

10.2.7   Writing the Argument

While it is vital to plan adequately, it is also vital that you not plan your paper to death. Once you have what seems to be a viable outline, it is time to begin writing your first draft. The outline, especially in the early stage of your writing, can provide you with the topics—and even the topic sentences—of your paper's individual paragraphs. But writing the first draft also tests your outline, showing you places where the outline holds and places where it may need to be changed. Don't be afraid to depart from the outline if your growing concept of the paper requires you to do so. If such changes do occur, it might be a good idea to pause occasionally in your writing of the first draft to rework the outline, integrating your new insights into it to see where they will finally lead you.

Remember that one of the great benefits of adequate planning is that the confidence it gives you in your material and its organization can transmit itself to your writing. This confidence can help you to write a narrative with a crisp, clear style that allows the reader to understand exactly what you are saying.

10.2.8   Testing the Argument

Test your argument by having someone read your draft and then discuss it with you. Ask the person to state the argument you have made in his own words. This allows you to determine if you have been understood correctly. Ask your reader if your argument is convincing. Ask him to point out both the strengths and weaknesses of your argument, as you see them. Testing the argument is a good exercise to conduct in class. Remember, though, that the classmate who is helping you is very probably not experienced at critiquing a colleague's paper and may feel a bit awkward at trying to help you improve your draft. If time allows, it would be a good idea to let your reader take the draft home and read it more than once in a quiet setting before talking with you about it.

10.2.9   Revising the Argument

After you have tested your argument, revise it. You may have picked up a few points since the time you wrote your draft that are worth including in your paper. Always read the paper again after running spell check lest your paper on historical religions turn into one on hysterical religions.

10.3   THE FORMAT OF A POSITION PAPER

Position papers contain five basic elements:

1. Title page
2. Outline page, which summarizes the paper (usually optional)
3. Text, or body of the paper
4. Bibliography (references to sources of information)
5. Appendixes

The format of each of these elements should follow the directions provided in Chapter 6 of this manual. The outline page (item 2 above) should be the final outline that you write, when your paper is completed. It should resemble the sample outline provided in this chapter and should not exceed two pages in length. Do not exceed three levels of headings in the outline you submit with your position paper, even though you may have had several more levels in the outline you used to write the paper.

Two general rules govern the amount of information presented in the body of the paper. First, content must be adequate for the reader to draw a reasonable conclusion. All the facts necessary to accepting the conclusion must be present. The second guideline for determining the length of a position paper is to omit extraneous material. Include only the information that is relevant to the conclusion at hand.

All sources of information in a position paper must be properly cited. Follow the directions for reference formats given in Chapter 7.

Appendixes can be helpful to the reader of position papers by providing information that supplements the important facts contained in the text. You should attach the appendixes to the end of the paper, after the bibliography. You should not append entire government reports, journal articles, or other publications, but selected charts, graphs, or other pages may be appended. The source of the information should always be evident on the appended pages.

11

History of Philosophy Papers

Nothing so absurd can be said, that some philosopher has not said it.

—Marcus Tullius Cicero, 106–43 BCE

11.1 A VERY SHORT HISTORY OF THE GREAT PHILOSOPHERS

One of the earliest philosophers, Xenophanes of Colphon, was born sometime around 565 BCE. Xenophanes was concerned with the nature of God:

> But if cattle or lions had hands, so as to paint with their hands and produce works of art as men do, they would paint their gods and give them bodies in form like their own—horses like horses, cattle like cattle. Ethiopians make their gods black and snub-nosed, Thracians red-haired and with blue eyes. God is one, supreme among gods and men, and not like mortals in body or in mind. (Milton C. Nahm. *Early Greek Philosophy*. New York: Appleton-Century-Crofts, 1964. 84–85.)

What makes Xenophanes a philosopher, and not a satirist or a critic, is that his criticism of received beliefs is coupled with an attempt to provide a reasoned substitute for them. Xenophanes attempts to answer a major question of human existence without reliance upon a historical text or tradition. His attempt at an answer, then, becomes a suggestion for all reasoning beings and not just for Ethiopians and Thraceans. The god he proposes is a monotheistic god that is identical with the universe. Xenophanes, in other words, was a pantheist. Like Xenophanes, the important historical philosophers are those who propose important alternative answers to one or more of the major questions of human existence.

Buddha is the name by which most of us refer to Siddhartha Gautama. Born around 565 BCE in India, Buddha preached the Four Noble Truths:

1. Life is suffering.
2. Suffering involves a chain of causes.
3. Suffering can cease.
4. There is a path to the cessation of suffering.

The path to happiness, or at least to the end of bodily reincarnation and the suffering that accompanies it, can be reached through following the Buddhist ethic called the eightfold path. The eightfold path is based on the view that suffering can be eliminated through the disappearance of the self. And moral selflessness is the path toward eliminating the psychological self and avoiding bodily reincarnation. Buddhist philosophy may be the first example of a religion that includes immortality without the mediation of a god. It certainly does base its ethics upon the human concern to avoid suffering and not upon a version of God's commandments.

Lao-Tzu lived, if he lived at all, during the sixth or fifth century BCE. Lao-Tzu may, like Homer, simply be the name given to serve as the placeholder for the authors of a collection of writings derived from a preexisting oral tradition—the Tao. Taoist literature consists of both philosophical and religious writings. You may be familiar with Sun Tzu's *The Tao of War* from your management or political theory courses. The writings ascribed to Lao-Tzu tend to be deterministic in nature, meaning that Lao-Tzu is concerned with the ways in which human beings are inextricably led through their lives by natural forces beyond their control.

Chuang-Tzu lived in the fourth century BCE. His writings are more epistemological than those attributed to Lao-Tzu. Chuang-Tzu was less concerned with determinism and more concerned with the ethical implications of skepticism. Chuang-Tzu seems to recommend skepticism as a road to detachment that occasions happiness. And both his skepticism and the detachment he recommends are radical and nonconformist.

Plato lived between 428 and 347 BCE. He was a student of Socrates, and much of what we attribute to Socrates comes from Plato's depiction of his teacher in his early dialogues. It is difficult to pinpoint what was most important about Plato because he wrote upon so many important topics. Plato constructed a blueprint for a utopian state, attempted to put his theoretical views into practice in Sicily, and eventually, in *The Laws,* wrote another blueprint for the best state possible for human beings. Plato wrote on the nature of art and the implications of artistic freedom for a well-ordered state, and Plato was the first philosopher explicitly to formulate the question of the nature of knowledge. The school he founded, the Academy, guaranteed the continued influence of his thought on Western culture and is still considered by many to be the proper model for a university.

A student of Plato, Aristotle (384–322 BCE) was more empirically minded than his teacher, perhaps because his father was a doctor. Alexander the Great sent Aristotle new animals for study that he encountered in his world conquest. Aristotle's empiricism led him to question Plato's idealist realm of the forms. The forms were the objects in a realm existent beyond sense perception that corresponded to the essential natures of particular items in this world. For instance, the truth that we are all human is guaranteed by our sharing an essential form—humanity. Aristotle believed that the forms existed in particulars and not in an ideal realm. Like Plato, Aristotle wrote on a wide variety of important topics, including the nature of the tragic character and the nature of friendship. His great intelligence, however, did not prevent him from defending slavery and the inequality of the sexes.

Thomas Aquinas lived in Italy from 1225 until 1275. Aquinas, who became a saint of the Catholic Church, tried to demonstrate that the Christian faith was compatible with reason. Revelation provides the details that fill in the religious truth available to all humans through the natural light of reason. He wrote many philosophical commentaries and included Aristotle prominently in his studies. Aquinas provided five proofs of the existence of God. And his ethics, still influential today in secular law as well as Christian ethics, was based on the notion of a natural law revealed to all humans by reason. Aquinas's lasting importance, however, is in two areas: the demonstration of a concern to make religious truth compatible with reason and the emphasis of Greek concepts of the deity within Christian religion.

When we reach the period that philosophers call modern philosophy, it is more difficult to decide whom to include in our short history of the great philosophers. René Descartes (1596–1650), the French philosopher and mathematician, is an obvious choice. In previous chapters we have noted his views on several important issues. Modern philosophy is usually presented as an ongoing dialogue between representatives of empiricism and rationalism. Locke, Berkeley, and Hume are the empiricists; Descartes, Spinoza, and Leibniz are the rationalists. A good case could be made for including any of these five thinkers, in addition to Descartes, in our list of major philosophers. John Locke is especially important to Americans, since, to a large extent, the United States of America is constructed along Lockean lines.

Thomas Hobbes (1588–1679) is the most committed physicalist of the modern philosophers. An Englishman, he wrote an effective set of objections to Descartes' *Meditations* in which Hobbes criticized Descartes' attempt to prove that the mind was made of a mental substance. But Hobbes' primary importance is in his attempt to justify government on the ground that it makes us better off than we would be in a state of nature. He carefully circumscribes the responsibility of government as protecting lives and property. All advocates of more extensive government responsibilities must confront Hobbes' political thought. And anyone who wonders why nations are justified in interfering in the affairs of other nations to advance their own national interest at the expense of the client state's interest should consult Hobbes' work *Leviathan*

David Hume (1711–1776), a Scot, was both a philosopher and a historian. Hume is known for his rigorous view of the sources of knowledge. An empiricist, he argued that all knowledge is based in impressions and their faded images, which may be called ideas. Hume's empiricism led him to deny that we have an impression of what men call causality—that is, that one phenomenon causes another. Hume reinterpreted causality to mean a constant conjunction that has become a customary expectation. Hume also posed the philosophical problem of the justification of induction. Basically, Hume noted that induction cannot be used to justify induction, that induction cannot be deductively demonstrated, and that there are no other forms of justification. Hume also formulated an ethics based on empathy that has had a great deal of influence on contemporary ethics, including feminism.

I have now included eight philosophers on the list of the ten most significant historical philosophers. No list of the top ten philosophers should leave out Kant and Hegel. Immanuel Kant (1724–1804), who lived and worked in the Prussian city of Konigsberg, wrote important works in every area of philosophy and originated the idea of a universal political body that is embodied in today's United Nations. Kant was concerned with delimiting the role of reason in human knowledge and in religion and ethics. His *Critique of Pure Reason* sought to answer skeptics and empiricists by providing an account of knowledge that is not wholly dependent upon the senses. Kant argued, in part, that for experience to exist at all, some prior knowledge must be brought to experience by a rational creature. Sensation may serve as the occasion for activating this innate knowledge, but it is not the source of the knowledge itself. Kant also argued that although we cannot know objects in themselves independently of our representations of them, we still possess a form of knowledge of the external world. Knowledge, then, is not of objects, but of objects as they conform to our faculty of knowledge.

In ethics, Kant argued for a universal morality based in the categorical imperative. He believed that some moral rules could be shown to imply something like a contradiction, and that such rules must never be accepted. Just as the denial of a contradiction must be true, the denial of a self-refuting moral maxim must be accepted. So, if I consider lying to you and saying that I have read every book that Kant wrote, I must first consider whether my moral maxim could be universalized. Could there be lying in a world in which everyone lied? The answer, of course, is no. In such a world people would be unable to lie, since no one would believe anything anyone said. Lying, then, is always morally wrong regardless of any consequences that might convince us it is permissible in some special circumstances. Obviously, Kant had a strong sense of the importance of moral duty in living a good life and respecting other human beings.

Finally, the German philosopher Georg Wilhelm Hegel (1770–1831) deserves mention for provoking the incorporation of history into philosophical thought. Hegel sought to acquire metaphysical knowledge of God, or Spirit, in its historical manifestations in social institutions such as the political state. Hegel portrayed human history as passing through necessary stages of advancing and extending human freedom as the Spirit progressed through history. His writings provoked the historical sensitivity of the early work of Karl Marx and the situational commitment of both Christian and atheist existentialists such as Kierkegaard and Nietzsche.

This discussion of philosophers is the barest sort of introduction to the history of philosophy. It is provided only to help you think of the broad range of topics available to you as you set out to find a topic for your paper and to help you select a historically important philosopher whose work may interest and inspire you.

11.2   HOW TO WRITE A HISTORY OF PHILOSOPHY PAPER

Before writing your history of philosophy paper, be sure to read Part One and Part Two of this manual. (Reading this material will save you much more time than it takes to read it.) When you do, you will find there is not one set pattern or process for writing papers. A set of basic tasks (described in chapters 1 and 2) needs to be completed, but you need to experiment to find out how you can best accomplish them.

Also, use the instructions in the previous chapter on position papers. Often, history of philosophy papers are meant to be compare/contrast papers. The description of the history of philosophy given above suggests some major themes—such as the nature of God, free will versus determinism, and whether induction can be justified—that have been addressed by historically important philosophers. These are topics around which you could organize a history of philosophy paper. And so, your history of philosophy paper will often be a position paper designed to show that perhaps Hobbes was more convincing than Locke was in explaining how mathematical knowledge could be based on experience.

Even if you are explicitly instructed not to develop an evaluative conclusion about the relative worth of Hobbes' and Descartes' explanations of self-identity through time, it will help you to write a compare/contrast paper as if you were going to do an evaluative conclusion. The first thing to remember when writing a history of philosophy paper is that your paper must make a point, and it must defend it. In other words, your paper must have a clearly defined thesis, and then it must provide the arguments and supporting materials necessary to defend your thesis.

Thousands of interpretations of the works of the great philosophers have been published. You do not need to generate a new interpretation in order to write a good paper. You merely need to evaluate the interpretations that are available and present your reasons for claiming that some are better than others.

Although all good history of philosophy papers will define and defend a thesis, they may take any one of three approaches: (1) a study of one aspect of a writer's philosophy, (2) a comparison of two or more philosophers on a selected topic, or (3) a study of a philosophical concept.

If you take the first approach and study a single writer's philosophy, you will want to select a philosopher who has written something you find interesting. Let's suppose that you are interested in discrimination. You may want to investigate Aristotle's view of slavery or John Stuart Mill's attitude toward women.

The second approach is a comparison of two or more philosophers on a selected topic. If you decide to compare, say, Hegel and Kant on the subject of ethics, your paper topic will be too broad, but if you select a particular aspect of ethics, such as the permissible uses of violence, you will be able to get a grasp on the topic.

The third way to write a history of philosophy paper is to select a particular topic, such as freedom, and to describe the variety of attitudes toward that subject that are available. If you take this approach, your paper will be much less specific than if you had used one of the first two approaches, but you will be able to sort through many different ideas about a subject and place them in relationship to each other. A paper that describes different concepts of justice, for example, will provide you with an overview that will help you to select more specific topics, such as recidivism or distributive justice, for further research.

11.3   HINTS ON WRITING HISTORY OF PHILOSOPHY PAPERS

One strategy that facilitates writing is to select an applied topic within an historical writer's work that illustrates the writer's important commitments. David Hume argued that the design argument for the existence of God was inconclusive. He suggests that the most reasonable position to take is agnosticism or, perhaps, to believe the universe was designed by a committee. Hume also wrote that it is unreasonable to believe in miracles. Both topics illustrate Hume's views on knowledge, and both topics are generally interesting to students in philosophy. Once you have selected such a topic, you might look for other philosophers who addressed it as a means of constructing a compare/contrast paper.

Aquinas wrote on the design argument, so he is a good choice along with Hume. So did Kant. A little research will uncover the fact that Charles Babbage, the first computer scientist, also wrote on miracles to refute Hume. If you are a computer science major in a history of philosophy course, you may find this an interesting connection. Other such connections exist in the history of philosophy.

Sometimes, the historical connections are obvious. The philosopher under consideration tells the reader via footnotes or references whose views are being refuted or enhanced, so the writer can just follow the trail. Or, secondary sources will point out connections an author does not mention, such as the influence of Emerson on Nietzsche. But you may also find it helpful to contrast philosophers who have not addressed each other, such as Chuang-Tzu and Descartes, to bring out important differences in philosophical movements.

There are some very direct exchanges in the history of philosophy. Aristotle was Plato's student. Plato wrote in the *Republic* about altering the traditional family structure in the interest of social justice; Aristotle offers explicit and pointed criticisms of Plato's plan. Hobbes wrote one of a series of objections to Descartes' *Meditations on First Philosophy*; Descartes replied to these objections. Look in secondary sources or ask your instructor for such connections between philosophers whose lives overlapped.

Influence papers are also interesting ways to approach the history of philosophy. Bertrand Russell wrote a book on Leibniz. Bertrand Russell and G. E. Moore studied with the idealist philosopher F. H. Bradley. Russell and Moore rejected idealism. The poet T. S. Eliot also studied with Bradley and almost completed a Ph.D. in philosophy. Eliot's work on Bradley is published.

A variation on the influence paper is to trace the influence of a discovery in the history of philosophy. The reintroduction of Greek philosophy to the Western world from the Islamic world during the middle ages might be too broad a topic to address in a paper. But certainly, the influence of Aristotle on Christian philosophy or the skeptical writings of Sextus Empiricus on British empiricism are manageable.

There is also a possibility that you will notice a neglected similarity. Augustine's discussion of the proof of his own existence resembles that of Descartes, but there is little written on this connection. It would make a good compare/contrast paper.

Yet another variation is to address the impact of science upon philosophy. Initially, evolution was seen as evidence for the design argument. It was only when the nature of the mechanism of selection, survival of the fittest, was advanced that evolution became regarded as a competitor with the design argument. Newton's physics influenced Descartes' argument for dualism, the view that there are two distinct substances. And Copernican astronomy provoked Kant's theory of knowledge.

American philosophers often address the idea of America. The "discovery" of the new world had an impact on European thinkers as well. New cultures supported cultural relativism, and European philosophy impacted the institutions of the United States. Perhaps you will find Locke's ideas on government helpful to understanding the Declaration of Independence. Jefferson certainly used them, and the ideas of Aristotle, in his political writings.

Finally, an interesting approach to the history of philosophy is to situate the philosopher, or an issue addressed by a philosopher, in its historical context. Aristotle wrote on the nature of tragedy. You could ask how his notion of tragedy squares with that of Shakespeare. Or, you could address how widely his idea was shared by Greeks. Nietzsche wrote such a book about Socrates' values and Greek tragedy—*Philosophy in the Tragic Age of the Greeks*.

These are the ideas that my students have found useful in formulating position papers and compare/contrast papers in the history of philosophy.

11.4 THE CONTENTS OF A HISTORY OF PHILOSOPHY PAPER

History of philosophy papers vary widely in subject matter and approach, but your paper should include the following three elements:

- Title page
- Body of the paper
- Reference page or bibliography

Abstracts, tables of contents, and appendixes are not normally needed.

12

Writing Applied Ethics Papers

We have built for this world a family mansion, and for the next a family tomb. The best works of art are the expression of man's struggle to free himself from this condition, but the effect of our art is merely to make this low state comfortable and that higher state to be forgotten.

—Henry David Thoreau, *Walden*, 1854

There are two different types of ethics courses: ethical theory and applied ethics courses. If you are in an ethical theory course, then you are probably a philosophy major or minor. Your papers will be more akin to the position papers or history of philosophy papers discussed in the previous two chapters.

Applied ethics courses are usually organized either as surveys of current moral issues or as professional ethics courses targeted for students in other departments. Moral issues courses usually target general education students, while professional ethics courses generally are service courses for other majors such as nursing, criminal justice, or business. But of course there are exceptions to these two categories. Some moral issues are so pressing that philosophy departments develop courses that address those concerns. Environmental ethics, peace and war, and family ethics courses are a few examples. Many students in these courses are taking their first, and perhaps last, course in philosophy. If that description fits you, then please read the earlier chapters of this book. In this chapter you will find a discussion of the special aspects of applied ethics position papers.

12.1   WHAT IS ETHICS?

The word *ought* has several meanings. One sense is that of prudence. If I want to avoid an early loss in chess, I ought to castle. If I do not want to pay for a hotel reservation I have guaranteed, I ought to cancel it before 6 PM. A second sense of ought is that of politeness or etiquette. It does not matter if I suck the juice from corncobs at home. That is not proper behavior at the Colonel's. The "ought" of ethics conveys a special type of obligation. It is usually to someone or something outside myself. It is more than personal prudence, and the matters are, at least in the view of the person who feels the obligation, more serious than those covered by etiquette.

Let's take a simple example. The cashier at your supermarket gives you an extra twenty dollars in change. You ought to give her the money back. One sense of ought here is that of prudence. She might discover later that her cash drawer is twenty dollars short and remember that you were the only person to whom she gave that large a bill in change. You are a regular shopper, and next time you visit the store, she might confront you. This would be embarrassing, so you return the extra twenty. It is the prudent thing to do. Now suppose you have had enough of this supermarket and a new supermarket just opened across the street. You intend to shop there in the future. It is no longer prudent to return the twenty, but from a moral standpoint, most people still feel that you ought to return the money.

If the amount of incorrect change is reduced, the matter becomes less significant. Or, take the cup of pennies that has become commonplace in the United States. If you frequent a store regularly, it will not go out of business if every time you need a penny or two, you take it from the penny cup but never drop in your extra pennies for someone else. It does not seem like an immoral way to be, but it does seem impolite. Part of what makes the extra twenty significant is that in order to make the cash drawer balance, the checker will lose the equivalent of three hours work.

There are some people who will feel it is morally correct to simply pocket the twenty. Let's forget about them and make believe that people think it is morally wrong to keep the twenty. Cases where people's intuitions about moral behavior agree will be called simple cases. It is important to notice that even in simple cases, the reasons behind the agreement can differ. For instance, one person gives back the twenty for religious reasons. She believes in the seventh commandment or in karma. Another used to be a cashier in high school and remembers how it felt when his change drawer came up short. He returns the twenty out of empathy, or the golden rule. The third person is a rich capitalist who takes more pleasure in the look of appreciation on the cashier's face than in anything that one more twenty could buy her. And the fourth is a Marxist who believes "from each according to her ability to each according to her need." There is agreement on the level of intuition and disagreement on the level of theory. (For simplicity's sake, I am assuming that causes and reasons are equivalent here.)

Simple cases provide occasions for making moral theory explicit. Simple cases also can illustrate the variety of values, which could theoretically enter into moral reasoning. Simple cases help us understand why we agree on some issues yet disagree on others—that our agreement was on the case, on the level of intuition, and not on the level of theory.

Ethical theory is useful in approaching difficult cases where our own intuitions are unsettled, tentative, or even inconsistent. These cases are the sorts of examples that generally make up the content of applied and professional ethics courses. So, it is useful to have at least a basic knowledge of ethical theory. There is a section on theory immediately below.

Your writing in such courses will generally involve appeal to values justified by ethical theory as opposed to a discussion of the theories themselves. The theories might also be helpful in understanding your own hierarchy of values. Utilitarians and Kantians both value promoting human happiness and respecting human autonomy. But autonomy is higher in the Kantian hierarchy and lower in the utilitarian. Theories are also helpful in analyzing professional codes of ethics, in determining the hierarchy of values of an organization.

It is also important to note that those who disagree on the level of theory often agree on the level of intuition and practice. In professional ethics courses you will often want to propose a policy or institution for handling a problem that not only reflects your hierarchy of values but also allows for the inclusion of those with similar values and different hierarchies.

Difficult cases introduce conflict at the theoretical level to our moral reasoning. The challenges to our current theoretical stance can be created by new technologies, which unsettle our previously consistent ethics. Perhaps you are opposed to abortion on the grounds that it disrespects human life. What position shall you adopt on in vitro fertilization, which allows people to have children but also leads to the disposal of extra embryos?

Another source of hard cases is the conflict of loyalties caused by a complex society in which we have a variety of duties. Professional duties may place a doctor, nurse, or police officer in a situation in which professional ethics requires them to protect the rights of others to engage in behavior deemed immoral in personal life.

There are good reasons to keep personal and professional ethics distinct. And there are good reasons not to criminalize some activities that are ethically wrong. Good applied ethics papers are sensitive to the difference between considering an action morally wrong and considering it appropriate for legal regulation.

So good ethics applied ethics papers will

1. Address a significant moral issue.
2. Address a difficult issue.
3. Develop a solution sensitive to the need to accommodate other value hierarchies.

4. Place the issue in the context of values based in ethical theory.

5. Discriminate between questions of morality and questions of legal regulation.

12.2 THE DISTINCTION BETWEEN FACT AND VALUE

In the eighteenth century David Hume pointed out that ethicists tend to move tacitly from statements of fact to statements of value without justifying the transitions. Examples of statements of fact are "Pain is to be avoided," "Pleasure is regarded as a good," and "Business depends upon the keeping of contracts." Value statements, according to Hume, look quite a bit like statements of fact, except they include the term *ought* or a synonym. Examples are "You ought to choose actions that maximize pleasure and minimize pain," and "You ought to keep your contracts." Hume doubted that we could derive *ought* statements, also called normative statements, from statements of fact. For Hume, moral statements cannot be based upon facts, only upon our emotive reactions to the effects of facts. ". . .[V]irtue is distinguished by the pleasure, and vice by the pain, that any action, sentiment, or character, gives us by mere view and contemplation." (David Hume, *Treatise of Human Nature*, Book 3, Part 1, Section 2. New York: Dutton, 1974. 183.)

Your writing should be sensitive to the distinction of fact and value when you are arguing for a position in applied ethics. People disagree both about the facts of the cases discussed and about what the important values are. If you find yourself realizing that a disagreement is based upon what happened in a case or the statistics about a social practice, then your disagreement is one of fact. Disagreements of fact are more easily settled because, for one thing, they do not have to be settled. You can treat your disagreement as two different hypothetical cases and discuss each in turn. This way, your discussion focuses on the ethical issues.

When you write a paper or an exam, make sure you give a descriptive exposition of your understanding of a case or social practice before launching an evaluative discussion. This will prevent misunderstanding of your position by the instructor when there may not be the opportunity to clear it up at a later time.

Ethical theory is perhaps the means of answering Hume's objection that *ought* cannot be derived from *is*. Ethical theory argues that some aspects of action are morally relevant, and different theories are best viewed as offering different hierarchies of morally relevant characteristics. Hume ultimately placed ethics on the foundation of sentiment, not reason, and so Hume would regard rational ethical theory as a rationalization of the ways in which we are naturally and socially conditioned to feel about actions.

12.3 APPROACHES TO ETHICS

Starting with the opposition between consequentialism and deontology will facilitate our discussion of ethical theory. Consequential theories propose that actions are right or wrong depending upon their outcome. For a consequentialist, an action is good if we reasonably expect it to have good results. Deontological theories hold that the rightness or wrongness of an action depends upon the intent of the actor, and the word *deontologist* comes from the Greek word meaning "having to do with assuming responsibility." For a deontologist, an action is good if my intentions when I commit the act are good.

Suppose that I promise to have dinner with you on Saturday night, but then I am offered a chance to go to the opera with my new friend. I decide to lie and tell you that I had already been invited to the opera. I simply forgot. You and I will have dinner Sunday night. Is it moral to lie, to break my promise? Other things being equal, the consequentialist says it is not only morally permissible but also morally mandatory; the deontologist says it is morally impermissible.

12.3.1 Consequentialism

Among the important varieties of consequentialists are hedonists, eudaemonists, and egoists.

- Hedonists believe the only intrinsic good is pleasure, and by pleasure they mean the pleasant feelings associated with our senses.
- Eudaemonists (a phrase derived from the Greek word for "living well") believe that pleasure is part of happiness but insist that the intrinsic good is more complicated than just pleasure. For instance, they might include intellectual happiness and the companionship of friends as important elements in achieving a good life.
- Psychological egoists believe that humans always choose what appears to be the greatest good for themselves. In other words, they believe that humans act only in their own interests. Psychological egoists deny that humans can act from altruistic motives, but they do not deny that they can commit altruistic actions.

Jeremy Bentham, one of the founders of utilitarianism, wrote, "Nature has placed mankind under the governance of two sovereign masters, pain and pleasure. It is for them alone to point out what we ought to do, as well as to determine what we shall do." (*An Introduction to the Principles of Morals and Legislation*, chapter 1, *The Utilitarians*. Garden City, New York: Doubleday, 1961. 17.) Bentham was a hedonist. Another utilitarian, John Stuart Mill, observed that a beast's pleasures do not satisfy a human being's conception of happiness. Mill was a hedonist also, but remarked that the pleasure of human beings were not equivalent to those of other living beings.

> Human beings have faculties more elevated than the animal appetites, and when once made conscious of them, do not regard anything as happiness which does not include their gratification. . . . [T]here is no known Epicurean theory of life which does not assign to the pleasures of the intellect, of the feelings and imagination, and of the moral sentiments, a much higher value as pleasures than to those of mere sensation. (*Utilitarianism*, chapter 2. *The Utilitarians*. Garden City, New York: Doubleday, 1961. 408)

The Greek philosopher Aristotle was a eudaemonist. He believed that many things were intrinsically good, including pleasure, happiness, knowledge, and friendship. The good life, for the individual and for a society, depended on a proper mixture of these intrinsic goods. Aristotle was not a consequentialist, so Aristotle will be discussed below as a natural law theorist.

Depending upon their concept of the greatest good, psychological egoists may also be acting as either hedonists or eudaemonists. (This does not mean that hedonists and eudaemonists must be psychological egoists. They could also be altruists.) The psychological egoist sees our motivational structure as the result of a combination of genetic and social conditioning. Thus, since people do not choose their parents, society, sexual orientation, ethnicity, religion, or nationality, it is difficult, in the view of the psychological egoist, to hold people responsible for their actions. What makes psychological egoism so difficult to refute is that any human action can be described to make an altruistic action look like it was done for selfish, and not altruistic, motives.

Ethical egoism maintains that we ought to act only in our own interests and that we have a responsibility to maximize our own concept of what is good. There are at least three types of ethical egoism: personal, individual, and universal. All three types believe that people have the right to decide on good for themselves. In regard to the acts of others, however, they differ.

1. A personal egoist makes no claim and has no opinion about what someone else should do.
2. An individual egoist assumes that it is your responsibility to maximize his expected good.
3. A universal egoist declares that your responsibility is to maximize your own happiness.

Just imagine that these persons were on your basketball team. Whenever any one of them got the ball, he would shoot it. But the expectations each of them has of your behavior when you get the ball are very different. The first player does not care what you do. The second wants you to pass it to him so he can shoot. And the third envisions a basketball game in which everyone has a ball and everyone shoots.

Utilitarianism is based on the principle of utility, or usefulness. Utilitarianism tells me that my moral duty is to select from the available alternatives that action which would lead to the greatest amount of happiness for the greatest number of all those with an interest in a matter. The two major historical figures in the development of utilitarianism were nineteenth-century British philosophers Jeremy Bentham and John Stuart Mill.

The first claim of utilitarianism is that pleasure is intrinsically valuable. Both Bentham and Mill were hedonists in that they believed the pleasure of any one person is worth as much or as little as anyone else's pleasure. Bentham proposed that most of us had developed rules by which we could readily decide between pleasures. Further, if an action is going to affect only ourselves, according to Bentham, we need not be concerned with the attitudes of others towards our action. But if my action affects several others as well as myself, I must prefer the interests of others to my own, unless the costs or benefits of my actions to others are far less than the consequences of my actions to myself. John Stuart Mill argued that there are qualitative differences in pleasures. Mill would maximize the pleasure of the greatest number of those with a stake in the matter, but when there are conflicts between pleasures of qualitatively different orders, he urges us to choose the qualitatively better. "Of two pleasures, if there be one to which all or almost all who have experience of both give a decided preference, irrespective of any feeling of moral obligation to prefer it, that is the more desirable pleasure." (John Stuart Mill. *Utilitarianism*, chapter 2. *The Utilitarians*. Garden City, New York: Doubleday, 1961. 409.)

If you believe, for example, that classical music is superior to country music, Mill would probably agree with you. How do we know what pleasures are qualitatively superior? Is it not the case that bowling is as good as philosophy; that Johnny Paycheck is as good as Mozart? Mill says no. When we want to know the nature of something, we should ask the experts, and experts are people with experience. I should not ask someone who has not experienced the pleasures of Mozart whether I should buy Mozart's "Eine Kleine Nachtmusik" or Dolly Parton's "Jolene." I should ask someone who has experienced and appreciated both. So, according to Mill, not everyone has an equal voice in determining which pleasures should be maximized. Perhaps this explains why you are taking a general education course in philosophy.

It is not especially important to utilitarians whom the others affected by your actions are. They could be strangers, illegal aliens, a fetus, an animal. In order to have moral standing, you need only be an organism susceptible to feeling pain and pleasure. You might guess that utilitarians often turn out to be vegetarians. The pleasure of eating chicken nuggets is not great enough to justify the pain to chickens raised under the conditions prevalent on factory farms. But you might not anticipate that they would consider hunting for food morally superior to buying meat at the supermarket. The animal that is killed in the wild at least had a natural life and an opportunity for pleasure, while those raised on factory farms that end up in the meat case had a miserable existence.

We have noted how Mill and Bentham disagree over the question of whether there are qualitative differences in pleasures. But both agree that in most cases we will readily follow utilitarian rules and that when the interests of others are affected, we should count their interests as equal to ours. Of course, Mill would add the proviso that they too are interested in the higher order pleasure. Bentham actually provided a calculus for our use in estimating pleasures when we are uncertain which to prefer.

The six quantitative features of pleasures are intensity, duration, certainty, propinquity, fecundity, and purity. There is the additional seventh condition that when others will be affected by our actions, we consider the extent of pleasure to them also as equals. The first three measures of pleasure are straightforward enough. We should prefer pleasures that are more intensely pleasurable, longer lasting, and more certain to be attained.

Propinquity commits us to choosing, other factors being equal, the nearest of competing pleasures: the "sooner" pleasure. This would leave the time of the more distant pleasures available for filling with another pleasure later. Fecundity refers to the ability of a pleasure to lead to pleasures of the same or similar kind. If I could learn to take pleasure in Green Day, then I might also get other pleasures from many alternative rock bands. Purity refers to the relative amount of pain the pleasure in question is going to cause me. Strictly speaking, the last two factors are not qualities of the pleasure but of the act. Bentham considers them less important factors than the first four.

It might be said that there is no generally accepted way to measure the value of the aspects of pleasures, but this objection misrepresents Bentham. Each person is in the best position, according to Bentham, to estimate the personal value of a pleasure. And the personal value is also its objective value in a world without experts. The simplest way I know to measure the aspects of pleasures is to ask how much I would be willing to pay for a pleasure of this intensity or that duration. By placing dollar amounts on the elements of the calculus, each person gives a public measure to private, subjective preferences.

There are two kinds of utilitarianism. Act utilitarians calculate benefits for each specific situation. Rule utilitarians attempt to define general policies that if consistently followed would lead to the greatest good for the greatest number, and they follow that policy in each situation. Act utilitarians are guided by rules of thumb or the calculus as needed in each situation. Rule utilitarians, again relying on rules of thumb or the calculus, select the general policy that if consistently followed would lead to the greatest good for the greatest number, and they follow that policy in each situation.

Why would they not make an exception to a rule when a situation calls for it? Rule utilitarians point out that each of us is especially prone to make errors of judgment about when an exception is called for in our own cases. They are quick to add that even if you are a person who is not prone to such errors, your action in making an exception to a rule will give a bad example to those who are.

Do not confuse rules with the law. Rule utilitarians believe in following the law in most cases. But if there were a rule that would lead to more happiness than a law, they would be obligated to follow the alternative rule and work for its general acceptance. In some cases they might even have an obligation to follow that rule instead of the law and bear negative consequences.

Another misunderstanding of rule utilitarianism is to think that it commits itself to coming up with perfect rules. It does not. It is committed to the rules that would lead to the greatest good for the greatest number, and those rules may not be perfect. Rule utilitarians may accept the necessity of enduring some pain, and even what non-utilitarians would call injustice, as the price of greater happiness.

Finally, utilitarianism does not claim to work for the happiness of everyone. It works for the happiness of the greatest number of those who have a legitimate interest in a matter.

12.3.2   Deontology: Kant

The most famous deontologist is Immanuel Kant, who believed that we could derive the correct ethical theory from reason alone. In Kant's view the only unconditional and hence intrinsic good is the good intention. Pleasure or happiness is not intrinsically good. Kant understands "good intention" to mean something like respect for duty and law. Yet the law in question is not the law of the state, but moral law. Moral actions are those done with the good intention, with respect for duty and love of the moral law.

> For it is not sufficient to that which should be morally good that it should conform to the law; it must also be done for the sake of the law. Otherwise the conformity is merely contingent and spurious; because though the unmoral ground may indeed now and then produce lawful actions, more often it brings forth unlawful ones. (Immanuel Kant. *Foundations of the Metaphysics of Morals*, trans. Lewis White Beck. Indianapolis: Bobbs-Merrill, 1959. 6.)

Imagine, for example, that you inherit a large sum of money. Kant would commend you if you decide to donate some of it to your college (and maybe some of it to the philosophy department). But Kant would not be sure that your action fits within the moral dimension. It may be the case that you made the donation for the purpose of maximizing your own happiness. Maybe you need the tax deduction. A moral action, for Kant, is one you are obligated to do regardless of the consequences. Now, if the good will is one that acts regardless of consequences, it is not going to be governed by our personal inclinations. Where, then, will the content of our moral duty come from? Kant's position is that morality is based in what he calls the categorical imperative. The categorical imperative is an absolute command, not dependent upon one's inclinations or personal desires or goals; it is the product of reason alone and is capable of being formulated in three ways:

1. Act so that the maxim of your action could be a universal law.
2. Treat all humans as ends in themselves and never as merely means.
3. All humans are universal lawgivers.

According to the categorical imperative, when I consider an action, I should not calculate its consequences to society or myself. Rather, I should submit the action in question to the universalization test: I should ask myself if the maxim (the rule) on the basis of which I am acting could be followed by all rational creatures. So, if I think of breaking a promise, I should ask myself if I could logically imagine a world in which all people broke promises when it suited them.

Perhaps you are the type of person who does not make promises and does not expect others to keep theirs. You might be tempted to accept a world in which people break promises. Kant is asking us if there could be a world in which there were promises and people routinely broke them. He is not asking if the real world is like that or if the real world could be like that. Kant wants you to answer that there could be no world with promising in it in which all people routinely broke promises. And since there can be no world in which people all get to act as you would on the basis of your maxim, you ought not to act that way either in this world. After all, you are not special.

> . . . [W]hile I can will the lie, I can by no means will that lying should be a universal law. For with such a law there would be no promises at all, since it would be in vain to allege my intention in regard to my future actions to those who would not believe this allegation, or if they over-hastily did so, would pay me back in my own coin. Hence my maxim, as soon as it should be made a universal law, would destroy itself. (Immanuel Kant. *Foundations of the Metaphysics of Morals*, trans. Lewis White Beck. Indianapolis: Bobbs-Merrill, 1959. 19.)

There is a sense in which Kant thought humans, or rational creatures, were special. Unlike animals, rational creatures are capable of being motivated by respect for the moral law. So, humans have intrinsic moral standing. Each rational creature is valuable because it possesses something which is intrinsically good—the good will. Animals have derivative value, since they lack the good will. I ought not to harm your dog because it is your dog and it will cause you suffering. But for a utilitarian, intrinsic moral standing belongs to any creature that can suffer pain or enjoy pleasure. A dog does not need to belong to a rational creature for its suffering to count.

But unlike the characteristics that humans ordinarily value in each other, such as wealth or beauty, the characteristic that is the source of moral standing is possessed equally by all rational creatures, and so no rational creature is morally special.

This basic equality underlies Kant's belief that the universalization test could be used to show that various actions were always wrong. These included murder, suicide, lying, stealing, and breaking promises. What he seems to have had in mind is that there is a purely logical inconsistency in advocating ethical principles or maxims that parallels that found in advocating inconsistent factual statements. If I tell you that it is raining in Chico this morning and you want to check the truth of my statement, you have to look or call the National Weather Service. If I tell you that it is raining and it is not raining in Chico this morning, then you do not have to gather any empirical evidence. You know my statement is false because it is a contradiction. You also know that its negation, "It is not the case that it is raining and it is not raining," must be true.

The inconsistency Kant finds in ethical maxims is that if I advocate the maxim of lying when it suits me, I ought also to advocate not only my lying but the lying of all my equals. If I am entitled to lie, then so are my equals. But paradoxically, this involves advocating a world in which there can be no lying, since in this sort of world trust has been destroyed. Therefore, since I cannot advocate a world in which there is and is not lying, such a world is morally unjustified. I ought to advocate its opposite: a world with no lying. And, of course, the way to do what I can to advocate such a world is to tell the truth regardless of consequences. After all, that is what morality is—fulfilling my duties regardless of the consequences.

This way of understanding the universalization test works best with Kant's views on lying and breaking promises. When he discusses suicide and murder, the meaning of the universalization test seems to change to a consideration of whether there would be moral value in a universe in which humanity had been eliminated. And just exactly what Kant meant by the universalization test still occupies scholars. But we can at least agree here that Kant meant to emphasize the equality of human beings, their intrinsic worth, and their special ability to be moral beings.

The second formulation of the categorical imperative is commonly referred to as the respect for persons principle. Kant calls attention to the special worth of human beings as possessors of the good will. Since humans are the source of moral goodness, they should never be treated as merely a means to an end. This does not mean that when you are about to leave Safeway with your groceries, you have to obtain consent from the cashier to pay for your goods. While it is wrong to treat people as merely means, Kant tells us that you can treat them as means to an extent. But if the cashiers were slaves, or were perhaps paid substandard wages, then Kant would urge you to take your business elsewhere.

So, respect for persons will make us opponents of slavery and prostitution perhaps. But more importantly, the respect for persons principle tells us to respect the human ability to direct one's own life. And if I respect persons, I respect their autonomy and creativity. If I am a doctor, I will try to provide opportunities for patients to make informed health care choices. I will do my best to provide others with as much personal autonomy as I can.

The third formulation of the categorical imperative is the one that is most often misunderstood. It does not say that every human creates his or her own ethics; it does not say that each human legislates an ethics he or she wishes to be binding on all others, as the individual ethical egoist. It says that each human has reason and that on the basis of reason alone a person can discover the categorical imperative. The categorical imperative gives people access to the objective moral law that applies to every rational creature. There is one morality that can be discovered by every rational creature.

It probably has not escaped your notice that Kant's morality is similar to the golden rule. There are two ways of stating the golden rule: positive and negative. Some people say, "Do unto others as you would want them to do unto you." Others advise us, "Don't do unto others what you would not want them to do to you." The first formulation, the positive one, is very difficult to satisfy without becoming a saint. Imagine what your life would be like if you took it to be your duty to always treat people exactly the way you would like them to treat you. You would be so busy doing things for others, you would have no time even to think about your own life. The positive golden rule seems to have been advocated by Christ. Bertrand Russell once shocked quite a few people in his essay "Why I Am Not a Christian" by using it to explain why there are so few real Christians. The negative formulation is probably what most people feel is binding. But notice that a hermit could satisfy this version of the golden rule. All it enjoins you to do is leave other people alone. Or, as Pascal pointed out, there would be no trouble in the world if everybody stayed in his or her own room.

Kant was aware of these two ways of looking at the golden rule, and he spoke about duties of justice and beneficence. We are required to do justice to others by never lying or breaking promises. These duties and others are fixed by the categorical imperative. Performing them makes us only a basically good person. If you like, think of someone who follows the specific dictates of the categorical imperative as a C person.

Kant was aware that we could not follow the positive golden rule all the time, but he did feel that we should sometimes aid others. After all, if we are committed to the special value of humans and respect for persons, then we should act in a way that enhances their autonomy and creativity at least on occasion. So Kant does not argue that I have a duty to engage in specific beneficent acts so many times a week or to give ten percent of my income to charity. Rather, his position is that I should act in a beneficiary manner in proportion to my talents and resources. So, although I have no specific duties to benefit others, to give money or time to the AIDS Walk or the United Fund, if I do not give something to some people or charity sometimes, then I am at best a C person. To earn moral praise, I must do more than what is enjoined by the categorical imperative in line with my abilities and means.

Utilitarians regard Kant as a rule utilitarian. The question they put to him is why we should be moral. And the answer they expect is that being moral leads to the greatest good for the greatest number. In other words, Kantianism is justified on the grounds of the principle of utility. But Kant cannot accept that view and keep the moral maxims he bases on the categorical imperative.

12.3.3   Other Ethical Theories

There are other ethical theories that compete with utilitarianism and deontology. Naturalism is the view that organisms fall into categories based upon distinguishing constitutional elements. The moral life is one that leads to the proper use of the essential characteristics. Aristotle saw humans as rational animals and the good life as one in which the satisfaction of the rational nature was given priority over physical pleasures. The good person had both intellectual and moral virtues that enabled the intellectual and physical parts of the self to flourish. A good deal of luck and a well-organized state were necessary to the good life. And despite the name naturalism, social organization is essential to the good life. Aristotle emphasized that humans were meant for society and that friendship was essential to a virtuous life. Aristotle's views had a great deal of influence on the Christian advocates of natural law theories.

> Now if the function of man is an activity of soul which follows or implies a rational principle, and if we say 'a so-and-so' and 'a good so-and-so' have a function which is the same in kind, e. g. a lyre-player, and a good lyre-player, and so without qualification in all cases, eminence in respect of goodness being added to the name of the function (for the function of a lyre-player is to play the lyre, and that of a good lyre-player is to do so well): if this is the case, [and we state the function of man to be a certain kind of life and this to be an activity or actions of the soul implying a rational principle, and the function of a good man to be the good and noble performance of these and if any action is well performed when it is performed in accordance with the appropriate excellence: if this is the case,] human good turns out to be activity of soul in accordance with virtue, and if there are more than one virtue, in accordance with the best and most complete.
>
> But we must add 'in a complete life.' For one swallow does not make a summer, nor does one day; and so too one day, or a short time, does not make a man blessed and happy. (Aristotle, *Nicomachean Ethics*. Ed. Richard McKeon. New York: Random House, 1949. 1098a 5–20.)[1]
>
> . . . And as in the Olympic Games it is not the most beautiful and the strongest that are crowned but those who compete (for it is some of these that are victorious), so those who act win, and rightly win, the noble and good things in life.
>
> Their life is also in itself pleasant. For pleasure is a state of soul, and to each man that which he is said to be a lover of is pleasant; e. g. not only is a

---

[1]There is a special convention in philosophy for citations to the works of selected ancient philosophers. Plato, Aristotle, and Sextus Empiricus are examples. Perhaps due to the proliferation of translations and editions, page citations are made via a common numbering system reproduced in the margins of all editions.

horse pleasant to the lover of horses, and a spectacle to the lover of sights, but also in the same way just acts are pleasant to the lover of justice and in general virtuous acts to the lover of virtue. Now for most men their pleasures are in conflict with one another because these are not by nature pleasant, but the lovers of what is noble find pleasant the things that are by nature pleasant; and virtuous actions are such, so that these are pleasant for such men as well as in their own nature. Their life, therefore, has no further need of pleasure as a sort of adventitious charm, but has its pleasure in itself. For, besides what we have said, the man who does not rejoice in noble actions is not even good; since no one would call a man just who did not enjoy acting justly, nor any man liberal who did not enjoy liberal actions; and similarly in all other cases. If this is so, virtuous actions must be in themselves pleasant. But they are also *good* and *noble*, and have each of these attributes in the highest degree, since the good man judges well about these attributes; his judgement is such as we have described. Happiness then is the best, noblest, and most pleasant thing in the world, and these attributes are not severed as in the inscription at Delos—

> Most noble is that which is justest, and best is health;
> But pleasantest is it to win what we love.

For all these properties belong to the best activities; and these, or one—the best—of these, we identify with happiness. (1099a)

Another alternative account of the good life is an ethics based on empathy or care. David Hume thought morality was based in empathic feelings for others. Hume has received a good deal of attention recently from feminists who see parallels with their emphasis on care as the basis of ethics. Care ethics emphasizes the importance of engaging in some sort of direct caring. It also recognizes that too much care for others can lead to care burnout. And it approaches moral problems with less concern for rights and duties and more concern for arriving at a solution acceptable to all parties involved. There is also a similarity to Kant's duties of beneficence in the recognition that people should follow inclination in selecting the causes to care for.

There is also currently a resurgence of philosophical interest in virtue ethics. Philosophers involved in courses in professional ethics naturally find themselves asking questions about the character that facilitates being a good police officer, businessperson, or medical professional. Their interest has turned to understanding the role of virtues in the particular professions. Western thought is comfortable with the idea that virtues may be relative to different social roles. But Confucian ethics attempted to base all correct behavior on the model provided by the most crucial social institution, the family.

Here, I can only make you aware of these alternatives and urge you to consult a philosophical dictionary, an introductory textbook, *The Encyclopedia of Ethics*, a Web page devoted to ethics, or the writings of the philosophers mentioned for further clarification.

12.4 PERENNIAL ISSUES FOR POLITICAL ETHICS: JUSTICE AND RIGHTS

The study of ethics includes many divisions that are taught not only by philosophy departments but by other disciplines as well. Ethics courses are taught by professors of economics, business, law, medicine, science, sociology, and many other fields. Political science departments offer courses in political philosophy that normally spend considerable time discussing ethical issues. Justice and rights are two concepts that are found at the heart of political philosophy, for they help to define structures of government, the extent of our freedoms, and the patterns of our lives in society. Because they are so important to our daily lives, we shall take a moment to discuss justice and rights.

Many discussions of justice in political philosophy classes begin with Socrates' definition of justice as recorded in Plato's *Republic*. Socrates begins by refuting the definitions of justice most common in Athens in the fifth century BCE. Cephalus, a politically prominent Athenian, has declared that justice is honesty and repaying debt. Socrates, finding this definition inadequate, replies:

> . . . [B]ut as concerning justice, what is it?—to speak the truth and pay your debts—no more than this? And even to this are there not exceptions? Suppose that a friend when in his right mind has deposited arms with me and he asks for them when he is not in his right mind, ought I to give them back to him? No one will say that I ought or that I should be right in doing so, any more than they would say that I ought always to speak the truth to one who is in his condition.
>
> You are quite right he replied.
>
> But then, I said, speaking the truth and paying your debts is not a correct definition of justice. (Plato. *Republic*. Trans. B. Jowett. New York: Random House, 1937. 331.)

Socrates then tackles another definition of justice, this one posed by Cephalus' friend Polemarchus. Polemarchus maintains, "That it is just to render every man his due," which Polemarchus believes means essentially helping friends and harming enemies. Socrates insists, however, that it can never be just to harm someone, because injury diminishes people's lives and abilities, leaving them less just. It cannot be just to make someone less just.

Thrasymachus, a compatriot of Cephalus who dislikes Socrates, then asserts that justice is the will of the stronger. This is the famous "might makes right" argument. Justice, according to this argument, is neither more nor less than the will of the powerful. For Thrasymachus, philosophers can talk all day about different concepts of justice, but their discussions affect nothing in the real world. People in power decide who gets what, who lives and who dies, who is free and who is in slavery. But Socrates is undaunted. Through skillful questioning—that is, through use of the Socratic method—Socrates compels Thrasymachus to admit that the strong are not perfect and that they sometimes harm themselves by not clearly thinking through the consequences of their actions. If justice is always that which is in the interest of the stronger, and if the strong sometimes do that which is not in their own interests, then it is not always just to obey the commands of the strongest. Might does not necessarily make right.

Having destroyed the most common conceptions of justice of his time, Socrates proposes a new definition. Each human being, he asserts, is composed of three aspects, body (physical appetites), spirit (courage), and mind (intelligence, or rationality). Justice occurs within individuals when the mind, which is rational, rules over both the impulse to courage (the spirited nature) and the physical appetites. When the spirited nature rules the mind, the result is excessive courage, which leads to unnecessary conflict. When physical appetites rule over the mind, excessive indulgence in physical pleasure is the result. But when the mind rules, reason can direct courage and appetite to appropriate expression, and justice is achieved.

The same principles that govern individuals govern society. When people who have superior minds govern those who are brave or who have common abilities, then society achieves justice. Socrates says that the logical conclusion of this reasoning is that a philosopher king, the person in any society who has the greatest reasoning abilities, is best qualified to rule society in the interests of all. Justice results when philosophers rule.

Since the time of Socrates, many other definitions of justice have been proposed, and so have many categories for different types of justice. Retributive justice, for example, involves situations in which harm has been done. One set of categories within the concept of retributive justice is a distinction between substantive justice and procedural justice. Suppose that an assassin murders a United States Senator on the floor of the Senate in full view of senators, television cameras, and the nation. There is no doubt that the assassin is guilty. When the police arrest her, however, they do not advise her of her rights. When her case comes to trial, she is set free because her constitutional rights were violated. Has justice been done? Those who answer yes advocate procedural justice, which asserts that justice is achieved whenever the rules of law, such as constitutional rights, have been followed. Those who answer no support substantive justice, which declares that justice is done only when the guilty are punished and the innocent absolved, regardless of the rules of law. Procedural justice focuses upon the means by which cases are decided, whereas substantive justice focuses upon the ends achieved by criminal proceedings.

Students of retributive justice are also interested in justifying punishment. Rehabilitation, deterrence, and retribution are three common justifications for punishing those guilty of committing a harmful act. Advocates of rehabilitation believe that the primary purpose of punishment is to return the guilty to full membership in society. Some rehabilitationists see criminals as diseased and punishment as a cure. Others see the criminal as someone who freely does evil, but they regard the infliction of punishment as justified only if it benefits the criminal or at least does no further harm. Since the purpose of punishment is to cure the criminal, rehabilitationists support indeterminate sentences and alternative forms of punishment like community service.

Advocates of deterrence are convinced that prisons cannot rehabilitate criminals and that the only thing that forestalls further crime is incarceration. In this view, the purposes of prison are (1) to remove criminals from society for a period of time so that the opportunity to commit another crime is not available, and (2) to demonstrate to potential criminals that the penalty for crime is sure and severe. Retributionists, on the other hand, see themselves as respecting the humanity of the criminal by holding the criminal responsible for his or her actions. Criminals are not diseased individuals or even examples to be used to instruct others, but free individuals who intentionally act immorally and illegally. They should be punished according to the damage they have done.

If retributive justice concerns punishment for harmful acts, then distributive justice concerns how to fairly apportion either the resources of society or the access to those resources. Harvard professor John Rawls's book *A Theory of Justice* is a leading recent work on distributive justice. Rawls defines justice as fairness, which is essentially political and social equality. Rawls proposes, "Each person possesses an inviolability founded on justice that even the welfare of society as a whole cannot override. For this reason justice denies that the loss of freedom for some is made right by a greater good shared by others." (John Rawls. *A Theory of Justice.* Cambridge, MA: Belknap Press of Harvard University, 1971. 3.)

If any group of people should come together today to set up the rules for a new society, all of them would naturally strive to protect their own interests. In the struggle to preserve privileges or advantages that already exist, valid principles of fairness would be lost. Rawls proposes, therefore, that to ensure justice for all, the contracting parties make an "original agreement" based upon the principle that "free and rational persons concerned to further their own interests would accept an initial position of equality as defining the fundamental terms of the association" (Ibid, 11). To write this agreement, the people will need to come together under an assumed "veil of ignorance," in which they do not know in advance the attributes they will have in the society that they construct. In a way, they are to write a plan for society as if they have not yet been born. Since they would not know in advance whether they personally will be rich or poor, mentally impaired or highly intelligent, attractive or unattractive, healthy or physically impaired, they will design principles that will be fair to anyone under any of these circumstances. As Rawls explains, the veil of ignorance is not an actual historical condition. If people write the rules for society under this veil of ignorance, Rawls believes, reason will lead them to adopt, as a minimum, the following two principles:

1. Each person is to have an equal right to the most extensive basic liberty compatible with similar liberty for others.

2. Social and economic inequalities are to be arranged so that they are both (a) reasonably expected to be to everyone's advantage, and (b) attached to positions and offices open to all. (Ibid, 60)

Robert Nozick, another Harvard philosopher, disagrees fundamentally with Rawls on the nature of justice. Whereas Rawls is concerned with fairness and equality, Nozick is concerned with the role of the state. Nozick contends that justice maintains maximum freedom for individuals and that an active state constricts freedom. Only a minimal state, therefore, assures justice. Nozick calls his version of justice the "entitlement view." For Nozick, then, individuals are entitled to freedom from government interference, whereas for Rawls, individuals are entitled to an equal opportunity to share the benefits of society.

For both Nozick and Rawls, however, justice is secured by defining, establishing, and respecting rights. Think of rights as valid claims. These valid claims can be based on the kind of entity you are, or a natural characteristic you have, or your membership in a social group; we will call these claims, respectively, human, natural, and social rights. If you believe that all humans have a right not to be slaves, you might base this claim on either their membership in the human species or their possession of the ability to reason. The first approach says that freedom is a human right, the second that it is a natural right. Notice that if you become convinced that animals or computers can reason, then if you advocate natural rights, you should extend freedom to animals and computers. (Of course, the human rights advocate is not immediately committed to enfranchising thinking animals or computers.) Both natural and human rights are commonly regarded as politically valid, which is why President Jimmy Carter felt justified, both during his presidency and afterward, in talking about violations of rights performed within other nations.

Sometimes people assert unalienable rights, as Thomas Jefferson did in the Declaration of Independence. Unalienable rights are intrinsic. Not only may they not be taken from you, but also you may not give them up even if you want to do so. Jefferson said: "We hold these Truths to be self-evident, that all Men are created equal, that they are endowed by their Creator with certain unalienable Rights." Jefferson wrote this, and yet he held slaves. Were Jefferson's actions consistent with his words? What if he believed that unalienable rights are natural rights, and that slaves lack the ability to reason? Some of Jefferson's statements seem to lead to this conclusion. If it is true that Jefferson did indeed believe slaves lacked the ability to reason, he was following a misguided but popular ancient tradition whose proponents included Aristotle.

Another way of looking at rights is to contrast positive and negative rights. Positive rights assume the obligation of others to perform a service for you. For example, you have a positive right to a social security check when the government has a corresponding duty to provide it to you. Negative rights assume a lack of interference by others. You have a negative right to freedom of speech when the government or other people are constrained from interfering with your opportunity to speak. As we can see from our discussion, John Rawls's concern for social equality led him to advocate a positive concept of justice (freedom to enjoy a share of society's benefits), whereas Robert Nozick's interest in individual freedom led him to propose a negative concept of justice (freedom from state control).

Most rights, however, are neither purely positive nor purely negative. They may be compared to coins, which have two sides. Two individuals, for example, are asked if they have a right to travel. One replies, "Yes, I have a right to travel; there are no barriers on the road, and the police do not care where I go." Another replies, "No, you may claim that I have a right to travel, but you mock me. It costs money to travel, and I have no money. I am old and cannot walk beyond a short distance. If I really had a right to travel, the government would be obligated to buy me an airline ticket." The right to travel is therefore positive for some and negative for others, depending upon which side of the coin they are looking at. To consider one further example, it is easy to see that voting is both a positive and a negative right. You exercise the right to vote when the government provides you a ballot (a positive right) and when the Ku Klux Klan is constrained, by the *Voting Rights Acts of 1957 and 1965*, from interfering with your visit to the polls (a negative right).

Considerations of justice and rights such as the ones discussed above are merely the tip of the political ethics iceberg. In your philosophy classes you will have the opportunity to participate in discussions of medical, legal, environmental, and social ethics, and there are more categories of ethics besides these.

12.5 APPLYING ETHICAL THEORIES AND POLITICAL PHILOSOPHY

The values that seem most important to ethicists include human autonomy, individual and community self-reliance, privacy, expected consequences, human flourishing, rights, virtues, equality, opportunities to exercise caring, and even preservation of traditions.[2] These are interrelated values. Roughly, autonomy is the ability to make informed decisions in accordance with a person's own values while free from coercion. Anything that fosters a person's ability to act autonomously respects the person and the person's characteristic ability to act freely. And so, by fostering autonomy, we show respect for a characteristic human ability and humanity in general. And respect for autonomy fosters human flourishing.

A concern for self-reliance recognizes the inherent satisfaction persons find in self-directed personal accomplishments. On the community level it can reflect awareness that individual satisfaction from personal effort is best supplemented and preserved in smaller communities of intimate interaction. A concern for privacy sometimes focuses on establishing places where a person does not need to fear surveillance, such as in the home. And sometimes privacy is interpreted as

---

[2]See the discussion of how to resolve moral dilemmas in Becky Cox White and Eric H. Gampel, "Resolving Moral Dilemmas: A Case-Based Method," *HEC Forum* 8 (1996). 85–102.

control over access to certain types of information. For instance, most people do not desire to have an email address captured by a corporation regardless of accessing email at home, on the job, or in a public Internet cafe.

The brief discussions of ethical theories and political rights above are meant to show how these values are rooted in theoretical philosophy. Applied ethics papers will generally approach problems, cases, and policies directly in terms of some of the values listed above and may not even mention ethical theory. It is generally a good idea to follow the same approach recommended for other position papers and develop your paper out of a compare/contrast paper. It is difficult to know where to start a paper on property rights and Napster from scratch. Let other authors and the Napster home page help you frame the issue. But knowledge of the theories will help your writing by allowing you to place an issue in what may be a larger value context than the ones offered by the authors you consult. The context you advocate will also be influenced by another crucial value rooted in ethical theory. Who, or what, has moral standing—intrinsic, not derivative, moral value? Some will restrict this standing to persons, while others will find moral worth in animals and even the environment.

So, let us regard applied ethics papers as another example of argumentative position papers. Here are the important additional steps to include in applied ethics position papers.

1. The fact–value distinction alerts us to the importance of conveying the important facts of the situation.

2. It is also important to locate the disagreement in the issue between sources as a question of fact or of value.

3. Then, with an eye to the moral values advanced in ethical theory, analyze the opposing views, paying attention both to which values are advanced explicitly or tacitly and to the relative importance of these values to each writer.

4. Consider whether there is a solution to the moral dilemma that can accommodate competing values and value structures.

5. Which moral values are crucial to your analysis of the moral issue under consideration? And how far can you go toward agreement with the authors surveyed and with a compromise decision?

6. Consider whether the issue raises questions of professional ethics. If so, then consult the relevant code of ethics.[3]

7. Clearly label conclusions of personal ethics and professional ethics.

8. Keep considerations of morality and legal regulation separate where appropriate.

9. Political and practical concerns can provide good reason not to regulate activities that conflict with ethical values. You may morally object to a practice and still not favor legal remedies.

---

[3]Codes of Ethics can often be found on the Web sites of corporations and professional associations.

12.6 PROFESSIONAL CODES OF ETHICS

The Center for the Study of Ethics in the Professions at Illinois Institute of Technology *http://www.iit.edu/departments/csep/PublicWWW/codes/* hosts over 850 professional codes of ethics online. CSEP has also posted discussions of the value of professional codes, suggestions on how to use codes with case studies, and links to online sites with case studies.

Here is the Associated Press Managing Editors Code of Ethics.[4] It is also available on the Internet at *http://www.apme.com/about/code_ethics.shtml.* It is selected as an example for various reasons. One reason is the current prominence of information ethics in American culture and news. Another reason is that this code was adopted by the Associated Press Managing Editors Association as a model to be used by newspapers. You can consult the codes of newspapers and see how the model code has been applied, extended, or altered. You may find other codes more directly relevant to this exercise and your writing if you are taking a course in professional ethics. Consult CSEP and you will find an appropriate code. The nine questions on the APME code at the end of the section are easily adapted to other codes.

APME Code of Ethics, Revised and Adopted 1995

These principles are a model against which news and editorial staff members can measure their performance. They have been formulated in the belief that newspapers and the people who produce them should adhere to the highest standards of ethical and professional conduct. The public's right to know about matters of importance is paramount. The newspaper has a special responsibility as surrogate of its readers to be a vigilant watchdog of their legitimate public interests. No statement of principles can prescribe decisions governing every situation. Common sense and good judgment are required in applying ethical principles to newspaper realities. As new technologies evolve, these principles can help guide editors to insure the credibility of the news and information they provide. Individual newspapers are encouraged to augment these APME guidelines more specifically to their own situations.

RESPONSIBILITY

The good newspaper is fair, accurate, honest, responsible, independent and decent. Truth is its guiding principle. It avoids practices that would conflict with the ability to report and present news in a fair, accurate and unbiased manner. The newspaper should serve as a constructive critic of all segments of society. It should reasonably reflect, in staffing and coverage, its diverse constituencies. It should vigorously expose wrongdoing, duplicity or misuse of power, public or private. Editorially, it should advocate needed reform and in-

---

[4]© Copyright 1995 APME/AP. Used with the kind permission of the APME/AP.

novation in the public interest. News sources should be disclosed unless there is a clear reason not to do so. When it is necessary to protect the confidentiality of a source, the reason should be explained. The newspaper should uphold the right of free speech and freedom of the press and should respect the individual's right to privacy. The newspaper should fight vigorously for public access to news of government through open meetings and records.

ACCURACY

The newspaper should guard against inaccuracies, carelessness, bias or distortion through emphasis, omission or technological manipulation.

It should acknowledge substantive errors and correct them promptly and prominently.

INTEGRITY

The newspaper should strive for impartial treatment of issues and dispassionate handling of controversial subjects. It should provide a forum for the exchange of comment and criticism, especially when such comment is opposed to its editorial positions. Editorials and expressions of personal opinion by reporters and editors should be clearly labeled. Advertising should be differentiated from news.

The newspaper should report the news without regard for its own interests, mindful of the need to disclose potential conflicts. It should not give favored news treatment to advertisers or special-interest groups.

It should report matters regarding itself or its personnel with the same vigor and candor as it would other institutions or individuals. Concern for community, business or personal interests should not cause the newspaper to distort or misrepresent the facts.

The newspaper should deal honestly with readers and newsmakers. It should keep its promises.

The newspaper should not plagiarize words or images.

INDEPENDENCE

The newspaper and its staff should be free of obligations to news sources and newsmakers. Even the appearance of obligation or conflict of interest should be avoided. Newspapers should accept nothing of value from news sources or others outside the profession. Gifts and free or reduced-rate travel, entertainment, products and lodging should not be accepted. Expenses in connection with news reporting should be paid by the newspaper. Special favors and special treatment for members of the press should be avoided.

Journalists are encouraged to be involved in their communities, to the extent that such activities do not create conflicts of interest.

Involvement in politics, demonstrations and social causes that would cause a conflict of interest, or the appearance of such conflict, should be avoided.

Work by staff members for the people or institutions they cover also should be avoided.

Financial investments by staff members or other outside business interests that could create the impression of a conflict of interest should be avoided.

Stories should not be written or edited primarily for the purpose of winning awards and prizes. Self-serving journalism contests and awards that reflect
unfavorably on the newspaper or the profession should be avoided.

Questions

1. What is the highest value in the value hierarchy of the APME?
2. What other values are found in the APME code?
3. What ethical theory lies at the bottom of the APME's presentation of the social responsibilities of newspapers?
4. Do you agree with APME's claim, "No statement of principles can prescribe decisions
   governing every situation"?
5. If you were a reporter or editor at a struggling newspaper and had important information that when made public could damage a major advertiser, would you still have a
   duty to report the news in spite of the anticipated effects on the paper and the community through loss of advertising revenue?
6. Why does APME believe "that newspapers and the people who produce them should
   adhere to the highest standards of ethical and professional conduct"? Do you agree?
7. If you knew that a colleague in a news organization had manufactured the information for a story or had accepted favors from a corporation, would you have a duty to
   report that behavior?
8. Could the code violate a media employee's personal ethics in some way? Is it fair, for
   instance, to require a pro-choice reporter to cover an anti-abortion demonstration?
9. Is it good that the APME code avoids specifics? Or can you think of professions in
   which professional behavior should be more exactly spelled out? It would be a good
   idea to consult some other codes at the CSEP address for comparison.

12.7 ANALYZING A PROFESSIONAL CODE OF ETHICS

There is an increasing reliance in professional ethics upon the moral intuitions of competent professionals as a source of moral principles. These moral intuitions are embodied in paradigm cases—situations taken from the actual
experience of professionals—and professional codes of ethics. Cases are not used
merely as tools for understanding a theory but as a source of complex yet practical
ethical principles. We might even say that advocates of the case method see themselves as combating the tyranny of theory. After all, what business does a philosopher have telling a police commissioner when an act of force was unjustified? No
more business than ordinary citizens would have sitting on police review boards!

What "bottom up" advocates of the case study method are asserting is that
professional codes are the outgrowth of years of cooperative engagement by educated and sensitive members of a profession. According to these advocates, the
closest we are going to get to ethical principles that are also practically workable is
to look at the practice of competent professionals. Their practice is a means of
telling us which competing ethical theory is the superior one. But there is a great

deal of disagreement about professional competence. Mayor Goode, the BATF, and Mark Fuhrman all have their supporters. Those who want to exclude them from having a voice in determining what an ethical decision is are covertly relying on either a theory or a tradition.

Also, the admirable behavior of good police officers or good businesspersons almost immediately leads us to ask whether they are examples of exemplary behavior or a professional standard. In other words, should their actions be merely praised, or should they be required as standard behavior? And that question moves us into a theoretical discussion.

One final warning about cases is needed. Whether the case be the short, hypothetical one of the philosopher or the elaborate one of the lawyer, you should be wary of concluding too much on the basis of a case. For instance, when you read about a decision to admit women to a private military academy that would enhance their careers as officers and in civilian life after the military, do not automatically conclude that it also follows that women should be deployed in infantry combat situations.

Note the limits of what a case decision implies. Also, try to see what happens to your intuitions when you add or remove details from the case. Consult CSEP or an alternative source for an appropriate professional code of ethics. Regard the assignment to analyze a professional code of ethics as another example of argumentative position papers. Here are the important additional steps to include:

1. With an eye to the moral values advanced in ethical theory, analyze the code, paying attention both to which values are advanced explicitly or tacitly and to the relative importance of these values to each writer.

2. Consider whether there is any moral dilemma that will be caused by internal inconsistency in values or by inconsistency with personal codes.

3. Which moral values are crucial to your analysis of the code under consideration? And how far can you go toward agreement with the code without compromising your values?

4. Keep considerations of morality and legal regulation separate where appropriate.

5. Political and practical concerns can provide good reason not to regulate activities that conflict with ethical values. You may morally object to a practice and still not favor legal remedies.

6. Rewrite the code in its entirety, or rewrite selected portions, in light of your own views.

7. Justify your revisions in terms of ethical theory or the values rooted in ethical theory.

13

Writing a Personal Ethics Statement

The heart has reasons of which reason knows nothing.

—Blaise Pascal, *Pensees,* 1662

The exercise on codes of ethics that closed Chapter 12, or the discussion of different ethical theories, may have already provoked you to notice your own hierarchy of values as well as where you would disagree with an ethical theory or a professional code. It will be useful for your writing, especially argumentative writing, to have organized your own values early on in your encounters with philosophers. This advice holds for all areas of philosophy. If you are in a philosophy of mind course that addresses free will or dualism, it is a good idea to work your own view out early on in an encounter with Descartes or Searle.

This chapter provides some materials that will help you write your own personal code of ethics. You may have given it little thought, but you have one. Each day, you make many decisions relating to what to do and what not to do. You may lend your friend money for lunch. You may drive through an automated tollbooth without paying the fare. You may volunteer at a hospital or steal to support a drug habit. Whatever you do, you probably justify it to yourself in one way or another. The justifications that you use for your actions all add up to a code of ethics.

When you write your code of ethics, you have an opportunity to understand more clearly the ethical principles by which you live. You have a chance to examine them, review them, and perhaps even revise them.

Before you begin to write your own ethics statement, read some that other people have written. A few examples are provided, but your library contains hundreds of them, which can be found under many headings, including philosophy, religion, theology, and politics. The following examples are not comprehensive, systematic statements of ethics. Instead, they are excerpts from longer statements that address a wide variety of ethical considerations. As you read, write down notes about things you agree with, things you disagree with, and other thoughts that occur to you. You will find these notes very helpful when you begin to write your own code.

But do not be misled by the word *personal.* A personal code is a code for a human being as opposed to a member of a profession. It is not a code in the sense of the personal ethical egoist—what is moral is what I decide is moral for me in light of my own desires and says nothing about how anyone else should live. The most personal of ethicists—Thoreau, Nietzsche, Confucius—offer their ways of life to all.

13.1   EXAMPLES OF FAMOUS STATEMENTS OF ETHICS

13.1.1   Kindergarten Wisdom

All I really wanted to know about how to live and what to do and how to be I learned in kindergarten. Wisdom was not at the top of the graduate-school mountain, but there in the sand pile at Sunday School. These are some of things I learned:

1. Share everything.
2. Play fair.
3. Don't hit people.
4. Put things back where you found them.
5. Clean up your own mess.
6. Don't take things that aren't yours.
7. Say you're sorry when you hurt somebody.
8. Wash your hands before you eat.
9. Live a balanced life—learn some and think some and draw and paint and sing and dance and play and work every day some.
10. Take a nap every afternoon.
11. Be aware of wonder. Remember the little seed in the Styrofoam cup: the roots go down and the plant goes up and nobody really knows how or why, but we are all like that.
12. Goldfish and hamsters and white mice and even the little seed in the Styrofoam cup—they all die. So do we.
13. And then remember the Dick-and-Jane books and the first word you learned—the biggest word of all—LOOK. (Robert Fulghum. *All I Really Need to Know I Learned in Kindergarten.* New York: Ivy Books, 1988. 4–6.)

13.1.2   Ten Commandments

And God spoke all these words:
I am the Lord your God, who brought you out of Egypt, out of the land of slavery.

You shall have no other gods before me.

You shall not make for yourself an idol in the form of anything in heaven above or on the earth beneath or in the waters below. You shall not bow down to them or worship them; for I, the Lord your God, am a jealous God, punishing the children for the sin of the fathers to the third and fourth generation of those who hate me, but showing love to a thousand generations of those who love me and keep my commandments.

You shall not misuse the name of the Lord your God, for the Lord will not hold anyone guiltless who misuses His name.

Remember the Sabbath day by keeping it holy. Six days you shall labor and do all your work, but the seventh day is a Sabbath to the Lord your God. On it you shall not do any work, neither you, nor your son or daughter, nor your manservant or maidservant, nor your animals, nor the alien within your gates. For in six days the Lord made the heavens and the earth, the sea, and all that is in them, but He rested on the seventh day. Therefore the Lord blessed the Sabbath day and made it holy.

Honor your father and your mother, so that you may live long in the land the Lord your God is giving you.

You shall not murder.

You shall not commit adultery.

You shall not steal.

You shall not give false testimony against your neighbor.

You shall not covet your neighbor's house. You shall not covet your neighbor's wife, or his manservant or maidservant, his ox or donkey, or anything that belongs to your neighbor.

13.1.3   Man is Born in Tao

Fishes are born in water
Man is born in Tao.
If fishes, born in water
Seek the deep shadow
Of pond and pool,
All their needs
Are satisfied.
If man, born in Tao,
Sinks into the deep shadow
Of non-action
To forget aggression and concern,
He lacks nothing
His life is secure. (*The Way of Chuang-Tzu.* Trans. Thomas Merton. New York: New Directions Press, 1969. 65.)

13.1.4   Declaration of Independence

When in the course of human events it becomes necessary for one people to dissolve the political bands which have connected them with another and to assume among the powers of the earth, the separate and equal station to which the Laws of Nature and of Nature's God entitle them, a decent respect to the opinions of mankind requires that they should declare the causes which impel them to the separation.

We hold these truths to be self-evident, that all men are created equal, that they are endowed by their Creator with certain unalienable rights, that among these are life, liberty and the pursuit of happiness. That to secure these rights, governments are instituted among men, deriving their just powers from the consent of the governed. That whenever any form of government becomes destructive to these ends, it is the right of the people to alter or to abolish it, and to institute new government, laying its foundation on such principles and organizing its powers in such form, as to them shall seem most likely to effect their safety and happiness. *(Preamble to the Declaration of Independence.)*

13.1.5   Humanist Manifesto II

In the best sense, religion may inspire dedication to the highest ethical ideals. The cultivation of moral devotion and creative imagination is an expression of genuine "spiritual" experience and aspiration. . . .

We believe, however, that traditional dogmatic or authoritarian religions that place revelation, God, ritual, or creed above human needs and experience do a disservice to the human species. Any account of nature should pass the tests of scientific evidence; in our judgment, the dogmas and myths of traditional religions do not do so. Even at this late date in human history, certain elementary facts based upon the critical use of scientific reason have to be restated. We find insufficient evidence for belief in the existence of a supernatural; it is either meaningless or irrelevant to the question of survival and fulfillment of the human race. As nontheists, we begin with humans not God, nature not deity. Nature may indeed be broader and deeper than we now know; any new discoveries, however, will but enlarge our knowledge of the natural. . . .

We affirm that moral values derive their source from human experience. Ethics is autonomous and situational needing no theological or ideological sanction. Ethics stems from human need and interest. To deny this distorts the whole basis of life. Human life has meaning because we create and develop our futures. Happiness and the creative realization of human needs and desires, individually and in shared enjoyment, are continuous themes of humanism. We strive for the good life, here and now. The goal is to pursue life's enrichment despite debasing forces of vulgarization, commercialization, and dehumanization. (American Humanist Association. *Humanist Manifesto II*, 1973 23 January 2002, http://www.americanhumanist.org/documents/.)

13.1.6   Thus Spake Zarathustra

What *is* great in man *is* that he *is* a bridge and not an end: what can be loved in man is that he *is* an *overture* and a *going under.*

I love those who do not know how to live, except by going under, for they are those who cross over.

I love the great despisers because they are the great reverers and arrows of longing for the other shore.

I love those who do not first seek behind the stars for a reason to go under and be a sacrifice, but who sacrifice themselves for the earth, that the earth may some day become the overman.

I love him who lives to know, and who wants to know so that the overman may live some day. And thus he wants to go under.

I love him who works and invents to build a house for the overman and to prepare earth, animal, and plant for him: for thus he wants to go under.

I love him who loves his virtue, for virtue is the will to go under and an arrow of longing.

I love him who does not hold back one drop of spirit for himself, but wants to be entirely the spirit of his virtue: thus he strides over the bridge as spirit.

I love him who makes his virtue his addiction and his catastrophe: for his virtue's sake he wants to live on and to live no longer.

I love him who does not want to have too many virtues. One virtue is more virtue than two, because it is more of a noose on which his catastrophe may hang.

I love him whose soul squanders itself, who wants no thanks and returns none: for he always gives away and does not want to preserve himself.

I love him who is abashed when the dice fall to make his fortune, and asks, "Am I then a crooked gambler?" For he wants to perish. . . . (Frederick Nietzsche, *Thus Spoke Zarathustra: A Book for All and None.* Trans. Walter Kaufmann. New York: Viking, 1959. 15.)

O you higher men, it was *your* distress that this old soothsayer prophesied to me yesterday morning; to your distress he wanted to seduce and tempt me. "O Zarathustra," he said to me, "I come to seduce you to your final sin."

"To my final sin?" shouted Zarathustra, and he laughed angrily at his own words; "*what* was it that was saved up for me as my final sin?"

And once more Zarathustra became absorbed in himself, and he sat down again on the big stone and reflected. Suddenly he jumped up. "Pity! Pity for the higher man!" he cried out, and his face changed to bronze. "Well then, *that* has had its time! My suffering and my pity for suffering—what does it matter? Am I concerned with *happiness?* I am concerned with my *work.*

"Well then! The lion came, my children are near, Zarathustra has ripened, my hour has come: this is *my* morning, *my* day is breaking: *rise now, rise, thou great noon!*"

Thus spoke Zarathustra, and he left his cave, glowing and strong as a morning sun that comes out of dark mountains. (Ibid, 327.)

13.1.7   The Unabomber Manifesto

1. The Industrial Revolution and its consequences have been a disaster for the human race. They have greatly increased the life-expectancy of those of us who live in "advanced" countries, but they have destabilized society, have made life unfulfilling, have subjected human beings to indignities, have led to widespread psychological suffering (in the Third World to physical suffering as well) and have inflicted severe damage on the natural world. The continued development of technology will worsen the situation. It will certainly subject human beings to greater indignities and inflict greater damage on the natural world, it will probably lead to greater social disruption and psychological suffering, and it may lead to increased physical suffering even in "advanced" countries. . . .

2. . . . Furthermore, if the system survives, the consequences will be inevitable: There is no way of reforming or modifying the system so as to prevent it from depriving people of dignity and autonomy. . . .

4. We therefore advocate a revolution against the industrial system. This revolution may or may not make use of violence: it may be sudden or it may be a relatively gradual process spanning a few decades. . . . This is not to be a POLITICAL revolution. Its object will be to overthrow not governments but the economic and technological basis of the present society. . . . (The Unabomber, *Industrial Society and Its Future*, 19 September 1995. 23 January 2002 http://www.panix.com/~clays/Una/index.html.)

13.2   WRITING YOUR OWN PERSONAL CODE OF ETHICS

How do you write a code of ethics? There is no one set way, but this chapter has some suggestions. The suggestion offered here is what might be called a top-down approach. Other ways of making your moral code explicit suggested earlier are to develop it in response to a moral problem, a case study, or a professional code. First, construct a list of questions pertaining to right and wrong, or the basis on which you might determine right or wrong. Your list may have many entries but should include at least the following questions:

1. Is there an objective basis for ethics? In other words, is there a set of universal moral principles available for everyone to find?
2. If there is an objective basis for ethics, what is that basis?
3. Are any of the supposed objective bases really subjective?
4. If there is no objective basis for ethics, is there another reasonable basis for ethics?
5. What are my most important ethical values?

6. What do my ethical values have to say about the value of human life?

7. What do my ethical values have to say about the value of nonhuman life, of the environment?

8. What do my ethical values have to say about my obligations to others?

9. What do my ethical values have to say about my obligations to myself?

10. What do my ethical values have to say about what I am free to do?

11. What do my ethical values have to say about what I am not free to do?

After you have written your list of questions, take some time to answer each one. This whole exercise can be much more fun if you do it with others, who may have ideas very different from your own.

Next, explore the implications of your answers by applying them to concrete situations. You may begin with the following hypothetical situations, but do not feel confined to them. Read each of the following situations and explain on paper what you would do in each situation and the ethical basis or reasons for your actions. When you finish, reread with the values in mind listed in Chapter 12: human autonomy, individual and community self-reliance, privacy, expected consequences, human flourishing, rights, virtues, equality, opportunities to exercise caring, and preservation of traditions. Have you considered all these major values in developing your personal code?

13.2.1   Situation 1

You are driving Route 66 in your 1962 Corvette. It's a beautiful day. The speed limit is 55, but, hey, everyone drives 65 on this road, and it sure would be nice to go over 55. What will you do?

13.2.2   Situation 2

Your cousin Alfred is a computer whiz. You are virtually helpless when it comes to things that run with electricity. Alfred notices that on your new PC you are running Windows 95, and he just happens to have a CD-ROM that carries Windows XP. He offers to install it on your computer for free, even though doing so is a violation of copyright law. Of course, Microsoft will never know that you are using its product without paying for it. Will you accept the software?

13.2.3   Situation 3

Late at night you hear an intruder breaking into your home. You grab your grandfather's shotgun, hastily load it, and wait as the intruder breaks down the door. You shout a warning but the intruder surges toward you with a knife. Do you fire the gun?

13.2.4   Situation 4

You are a newspaper reporter. A politician you know and respect utters certain racially charged phrases to you while speaking off the record. Not only do you respect this politician's social programs, but also you share the politician's ethnicity. Making the conversation public will damage the politician's effectiveness and harm your ethnic group. Use a professional code of ethics in addition to your personal code in handling this example.

13.3   THE CONTENTS OF A PERSONAL ETHICS STATEMENT

Your personal ethics statement may be very different from those of your classmates, for your concerns will in many ways be different from theirs. Your paper, however, should conform to the format described in Chapter 6 of this manual and should include a title page and the text of the paper. References to sources are necessary if you quote from or derive ideas from authors to whom credit is due. Your paper should be in essay form and should address at least the following three issues:

1. From what or whom do you derive the basis of your ethical principles?
2. What are your most important ethical principles?
3. How do your ethical principles apply to situations you have encountered or may encounter in life (provide some examples)?

You will find printed below two sample student essays dealing with the first three situations. Situation 4 is left for you to complete. Notice that it combines material from this chapter and Chapter 12. Each student approaches ethical problems differently; but both students begin the attempt to define their own ethical systems.

13.4   TWO SAMPLE STUDENT ETHICS STATEMENTS

13.4.1   Jeremy Scott's Essay

Jeremy Scott, who, at the time he wrote it in the fall of 1996 had not yet had a course in the history of philosophy but used this assignment as an opportunity to sort out his own values, wrote the following essay. He achieved the objective of the assignment because, rather than attempting to copy someone's philosophy, he explored his own beliefs and experiences and arrived at some new insights about them.

A Statement of Personal Ethics

Jeremy Scott

University of Kansas

October 1996

I have a problem when it comes to ethics. My actions do
not always line up with my beliefs. My beliefs come from
many places, most notably my experiences in life and people
I have known. The most simple daily decisions I make, such
as deciding what I will eat, seem to influence my beliefs. I
find that I can examine each of the questions asked in the
directions to this writing assignment and arrive at a conclusion that seems to be rational and ethical. However, when
I find myself in situations that call for an ethical decision, I do not always do what my personal ethics seem to demand. I would, for example, break the speed limit because I
always do. Since I am a student with a limited budget, and
Bill Gates is so rich, I would be tempted to install Win-
dows95 on my computer illegally and not feel like I am a
terrible person. The more I think about doing this, however,
the more uncomfortable I feel. I need a reason to pay for
the software. Why shouldn't I take the Windows95 when it is
offered to me: because it is illegal, or because I would be
stealing?

Since I need some way to answer these questions, I will
try to get to the bottom of my ideology, my ethical system.
I guess it all begins with happiness. Sorting through my
values has led me to a relatively simple conclusion. Happiness is the foundation of my ideology, which is my personal

set of ethical values. Without happiness life is not life at all, but is merely existence controlled by emotions and the decisions of other people. First, I must decide what happiness is and then I must determine what ethical decisions I should make to promote happiness.

The times I am happiest are when I am relatively independent, making my own decisions for myself. When I find myself feeling like I have to make most of my decisions in an effort to make someone else happy, that is when I am the least happy. It's not that I don't want to do things to make other people happy. Ironically, I also find happiness when I do something for someone spontaneously, completely of my own free will, like when I help someone pick something up that she just dropped. I feel good about myself because I have helped someone. Maybe I helped brighten someone's day. I feel this way because if I drop something and someone picks it up for me, then I feel a certain amount of gratitude towards that person. I therefore experience happiness when someone appreciates what I have done. The times when I am most unhappy are the times when I experience guilt and grief. What I am saying is that I am not happy when I find myself constantly worried about someone else, like my girlfriend. When I start thinking about her needs all the time, I start to get resentful. Happiness is having the choice to do something for someone when I want to, not because I feel I have to.

If happiness is the basic principle of my ideology, and if happiness is freedom to do things for others and myself when I want to, what then can I say about ethical problems such as exceeding the speed limit or stealing software? Should I abide by the law because a group of individuals decided that it was best for me not to drive more than 65 miles per hour? No, I am too independent for that. Following other people's wishes is what makes me unhappy. Would I be happier going 130 miles per hour and spending the night in jail, or abiding by the rules and going 65 miles per hour? Since I don't have the money to pay the fine, or would have to borrow it, I will not drive 130 miles per hour. Maybe 80. And should I "borrow" Windows from my friend? I don't know what the penalty is for copyright infringement. I know I can't afford it.

Getting caught speeding or stealing does not make me happy, or increase my freedom to do what I want; it brings me grief and makes me do what other people want. I do not necessarily agree with all the laws that I live by, but until I can change them, I will abide by most of them, because the less grief I experience, the happier I am.

Another problem I have not resolved is this: does my happiness come first when it is in conflict with someone else's happiness? Certainly I would be happy if you sold me your father's brand new Porsche for five dollars. Would your father be happy? Do I care? Since my happiness is the most important thing in my life, I do care because I care about other people. Therefore, my own happiness cannot be the single most important value in my life. I realize that I have no set formulas for how to treat others in various situations. My obligations to other people are therefore hazy at best. But part of my happiness is affected by whether my loved ones are happy. I know from experience that a few kind words or actions from a loved one, friend, or stranger, can completely change the way I visualize life. This does not mean I feel obligated to make other people, friends or strangers, happy. I realize their happiness is out of my control.

Furthermore, simple ethical dilemmas like speeding and stealing cannot be compared to decisions that other people have confronted. For example, the decision to drop an atom bomb that would kill thousands of people is certainly not one that anyone should be able to make. How can I choose the happiness of one group of people over the happiness of another group? I do not know. It has taken me a while to figure out what makes me happy, and I certainly cannot assume that I know what makes other people happy.

I understand that I have a lot more thinking to do about my personal ethics. I have come, however, to one preliminary conclusion: ethics needs to begin with allowing people the freedom to find their own happiness as much as possible. Maybe the more I am allowed to find out what truly makes me happy, the more able I will be to solve the problem with which I started this essay: I will be better able to have my actions agree with my personal ethical standards.

13.4.2 Chris Allen's Essay

Chris Allen, who, at the time she wrote it in the fall of 1996, was studying sociology and ethics, wrote the second essay. Chris used this assignment as an opportunity to clarify her ethical values. She also achieved the objective of the assignment because she defined in clear and simple terms her current understanding of the origin and implications of her personal ethical system.

A Statement of Personal Ethics

Chris Allen

Mount Holyoke College

October 1996

Ethics creates the fabric of who we are as human beings, affecting every decision that we make and every objective we pursue. We need a personal code of ethics the most when the need for it is least apparent; it is the most difficult yet important aspect of life to develop. It forms who we are as individuals and as members of society. If we fail to define our personal ethical code, we will live by expediency, justifying our actions with pretexts rather than principle. For this assignment I tried at first to outline my code of ethics by setting up a list of rules to live by, but I found rules are a poor substitute for ethical character. Ethics are broader and deeper than rules, and yet I must find some guiding principles, so this is what I came up with:

Treat others as you would want to be treated.

Be sincere to everyone, including yourself.

Use sound judgment.

Listen objectively before you pass judgment.

These are the values that express, most accurately, how I try to live my life. It is important to value others' lives in the same way that you expect your life to be valued. If you live in a manner that expresses kindness towards others, in most cases you will be treated kindly. Kindness makes you responsible for following laws and abiding by regulations because your conscience tells you it's right, not because you are afraid of being caught. My ethics have not come from a single experience in life or from something that people have told me. They were formed from a number of experiences, from reading the simple teachings of the Bible to walking in the woods, where I learned not to touch the wild flowers so that others could appreciate them as I had. Everyone learns these ethical ideas, but they are important in shaping how I respond to the world. The most important ethical principle is treating other people as I would want to be treated. I cannot clarify this principle by saying, "do not kill" or "it is always wrong to steal" because situations will inevitably arise in which I would have to break my code. If someone breaks into my home and threatens my life, I might have to make the decision to protect myself, but the intruder also made an ethical decision by threatening me. If I threatened someone else's life, I would expect her to protect herself. It is important to remain sincere and objective when making ethical decisions. As long as I am protecting myself because I know it's right and not to get revenge, then I will know that I have not broken my code.

Protecting my life may be difficult in practice, but it does not pose a challenging ethical problem, for violence clearly violates a basic principle: treat others as you would be treated. Ironically, the more subtle the situation, the greater the ethical complexity. When considering if I would exceed the speed limit on the open highway, for example, I face an ethical dilemma greater than the one posed by self-defense.

What are the forces that prevent me from speeding? Are they bigger than the forces that are encouraging me to

speed? A criminal with a gun presents a problem that seems
ethically clear cut. Driving on the highway presents a more
difficult issue because I am not affecting anyone by speeding, and following the rules, therefore, seems less important. The effects of speeding would be detrimental, however,
if a small child ran out in the road in front of my car. The
possibility of a child entering my path seems to present an
extreme scenario, because it does not happen very often, but
the thought of a child being killed because of my reckless-
ness forces me to realize that speeding is wrong. It is true
that driving five miles an hour over the speed limit would
probably not affect my reaction time, but going thirty miles
an hour over the speed limit certainly would.

Other ethical issues are even less clear because they
arise from actions for which there are no real ramifications. In these cases it seems that the only motivating
force is honor. Illegal use of software is an example. If I
copy Windows onto my computer, and have not paid for the
software license, I will not be physically hurting anyone or
putting anyone in danger. I will most likely avoid getting
caught and even if I am caught the punishment will probably
not be severe. But does this justify theft? In this subtle
ethical situation I cannot escape my nagging conscience.
While most people would probably copy the software, and feel
little remorse for it, I don't think any one of them would
say that what they did was right.

Problems like stealing software confront us every day.
Our ethical code, therefore, is something that arises in
some manner in virtually every situation we face, whether we
recognize it or not. We cannot escape ethics, for we must

consider and take into account the ramifications and implications of every action we take. We neglect ethics at our
peril, and when we seem to need a code of ethics the least
is when we need it most.

13.5 WRITING A CRITIQUE OF A BRIEF ETHICS STATEMENT

We noted above that another way, a bottoms-up way, to write a personal ethics statement is by reflecting on a case study. This process is facilitated when you already have on hand a statement of the ethics of the main players in the case, so we will use a case involving the Unabomber.

John Hauser had been accepted into NASA's astronaut training program. An Air Force pilot and student at the University of California at Berkeley, Hauser was working on a research project on May 15, 1985, when he opened a box that exploded, obliterating the fingers of his right hand and ending his long-cherished dream of a career exploring the last frontier. He was, however, fortunate to be alive, for he was one of twenty-two victims of the Unabomber who had been injured and yet survived. Hugh Scrutton, who had owned a computer store; Thomas Mosser, who was in advertising; and Gilbert Murray, an executive in the lumbering business, all died when the Unabomber's packages exploded in their hands. It took the efforts of dozens of federal agents to catch Theodore Kaszynski, in his cabin in Montana in 1996, but before he was apprehended, he was able to get major newspapers to publish his letters and what is now known as his "manifesto," a statement entitled "Industrial Society and its Future."

The Manifesto is a statement of social and political ethics. It is a commentary on what is right and wrong in the world, and what should and should not be done about social problems. It provides you, as student of ethics, with an opportunity to define more clearly your own social and political ethics by writing an applied ethics paper which critiques the manifesto. Kaszynski's manifesto also provides an opportunity for you to address other considerations, such as the circumstances under which it was written and its author. Is the document merely a pretext for murder? It would be difficult to write an analysis and critique of the Unabomber without making your personal ethics explicit. An applied ethics paper is a writing exercise in which you analyze and evaluate someone's ethical statement by applying to it the principles of your own ethical system or another system that you have selected. This process occurs in seven steps:

1. Target statement selection
2. Target statement analysis
3. System definition

4. Criteria definition
5. Verity identification
6. Error identification
7. Conclusion

13.5.1   Target Statement Selection

The first step in the process of writing an applied ethics paper is to select a statement to be analyzed and evaluated. The *Unabomber Manifesto* is a potential target statement, but be sure to ask your instructor if it is acceptable or if you should select another statement. Please be aware that the authors of this text do not in any way endorse the ideas contained in the manifesto. It is selected only because it provides an opportunity to discover fallacies and to generate interesting class discussions. Any essay, proclamation, or editorial that contains significant ethical content may be an appropriate target statement for an ethical analysis paper. The more substantial the statement, the more opportunities it affords for analysis. If you select a major work of philosophy as your target statement, however, be prepared to write a very substantial paper.

You should select a paper that addresses a topic that personally interests you. Excerpts from several statements are included at the end of this chapter. You may select one of them, or simply read them to get an idea of the types of ethics statements that are appropriate subjects for your critique.

13.5.2   Target Statement Analysis

Analyze the target statement by precisely describing what it says and explaining its major implications. The best way to begin this analysis is to outline the target statement. Construct a useful outline that identifies the target statement's premises, the supporting premises, and its conclusion. Once you have completed your outline, it is time to begin writing a first draft. Your primary job is to describe the major elements of the target statement in such a manner that your readers understand clearly what the target statement proposes.

13.5.3   System Definition

Your next job is to describe the hierarchy of ethical values (we shall call this "the system") that you will use to evaluate the target statement. This section need not be more than two or three pages in length, but it should contain a series of statements that summarize the philosophy you will use as a guide in judging the target statement. If you consider yourself to be a utilitarian (or a stoic, or a Platonist), then briefly describe your fundamental ethical beliefs. If you wish, you may adopt, for the purposes of this paper, a set of beliefs you do not actually hold, so that when you apply them to the target statement, you will gain a better understanding of the belief system you have adopted. Examining the target statement from the point of view of an ultra-right-wing conservative, for example, may give you insights not only into the nature of the target statement but also into the nature of political conservatism.

13.5.4   Criteria Definition

Once you have described the belief system within which you will operate for the purposes of this assignment, you must deduce from your ethical system a list of specific criteria to use to evaluate the target statement. Make your criteria as specific as possible.

13.5.5   Verity Identification

By completing the tasks above, you will have chosen a target statement and established criteria by which to judge it. The next challenge is a two-step process through which you will apply your criteria to the target statement. First, identify the elements of the target statement that are "correct"—that is, those elements that meet the qualifications established by your criteria—and then explain why they are correct. Second, proceed to error identification.

13.5.6   Error Identification

Identify the elements of the target statement that are "incorrect"—that is, those that conflict with or fail to conform to your evaluation criteria—and explain why they are incorrect. These two steps, verity identification and error identification, will be the longest sections of your paper.

13.5.7   Conclusion

Finally, write a general summary evaluation of the target statement, based upon the insights you have gained in the steps above. Tell your reader the specific strengths and weaknesses of the target statement and then make some general evaluative comments.

At this point you will have produced an applied ethics paper that critiques a case study in light of the Unabomber's personal ethical statement. It will be a relatively easy task to produce at this point your own personal ethical statement by reflecting upon the system you identified in step 3, the criteria selected in step 4, and the summary comments made in step 7.

14

Sample Student Papers

Here are three papers written by students for general education courses at California State University, Chico. These are not cooked examples. These are papers written by real undergraduate students and recommended by their professors.

14.1 A PAPER FROM PERSONAL VALUES: THE MATRIX

Here is what Professor Marcel Daguerre wrote about the first paper:

A paper was assigned as the capstone project in my introductory philosophy course Personal Values. The main objective of the course is to examine various conceptions of the good life. Ms. Parish crafts a clear explanation of a moral dilemma from the movie, *The Matrix*, and evaluates it in light of issues and philosophers discussed throughout the semester. She takes a clear position on the issue, offers a positive argument to support her stance and defends her position against objections. She treats the assignment as an opportunity to demonstrate the breadth and depth of her understanding.

Author Katherine Parish was 19 when she wrote the paper. She aspires to either practice law or become a college professor. Parish is a speech communications major from Clayton, California.

Red or Blue? Which Pill Would You Take and Why?

By Katherine Parish

In the movie, *The Matrix*, Thomas A. Anderson lives in what I will term the "normative society." What I intend in using the phrase "normative society" is to describe the place where the values, beliefs and customs that are held by society to be the norm, or are considered to be "normal," are followed. On the surface, Anderson lives the life that society wants him to live. On a deeper level, he lives the secret life of Neo, an identity he assumes under his computer alias. This other life, or the secret alternative life, goes against what society would like for him to do with his time and energy.

Then, Morpheus contacts Neo and takes him away from normative society. Morpheus reveals to Neo that the world he lives in is not really what it seems. The world that Neo lives in is what is termed by Morpheus "the matrix." This is the world that has been pulled over people's eyes to make them believe something that is not the truth. Morpheus gives Neo the opportunity to take either a red or a blue pill. The red pill will show Neo the truth about the matrix, while the blue pill will send him back into the matrix with no recollection of anything that he has been told by Morpheus. If Neo takes the red pill, he is promised only the truth. Morpheus does not promise happiness or love to Neo with the red pill. If he takes the blue pill, he will go on with his life oblivious to the fact that there is anything more to life than what he sees going on.

My position is that I would take the red pill because it will show me the truth. I believe that in order for a person to live "the good life," he or she must be living an honest life, or in other words, a life of truth. Without knowledge about the truth of one's life, I do not believe it is possible to live the good life. If one is living in a world other than the world of absolute reality, one is not actually living his or her own life, but a projected image of what life "should be," but cannot actually be.

The only way for me to be truly happy is to be happy, or at least content, with the truth. For example, say I have grown up believing that Santa Claus is real. When I say that he is "real" I do not mean merely that he is real in the spiritual sense, but that he is real in the sense that he is a jolly fat man with a sleigh and reindeer. This is something that makes me happy. However, because this happiness is based on a false premise, I am not truly happy. In order to be truly happy I must be happy with the actual truth. For me to go on with life basing my happiness on the premise that Santa Claus is real would be to live a life of superficial happiness. An essential part of living the good life *is* happiness, although I also believe that it is not possible for a person to be truly happy without knowledge of the truth. Therefore, while it is true that I may be content in the matrix, I will never be really happy if my happiness is based on a lie or a false reality.

In Nozick's *The Experience Machine*, a machine is described that would allow people to program in whatever experiences they so desire while plugged in. However, Nozick concluded that most people, if not all, would not plug in because they actually want to do things with their lives rather than just experience them with the bad parts edited out. If people merely wanted to experience happiness they would plug in and live lives filled with happy events rather than real ones. But since the experience machine would only allow them to live in a false reality (or a reality that is based on a lie), people would not choose to plug in.

One argument against my viewpoint is that the truth may end up causing a person more *angst* than ignorance. What if, for example, I am living the life that I have always wanted to live? I have the perfect husband, the perfect children, the perfect job and the perfect friends. I am sickeningly happy. However, without my knowledge, my husband is having an affair with my best friend. If I take the blue pill, I can live my life oblivious to the fact that my life really isn't perfect. I will continue living in complete bliss and will eventually die a "happy" woman. If I take the red pill, I will find out that my husband is having an affair, my marriage will most likely end and therefore a large part of what I base my immediate happiness on is gone. Am I really better off taking the red pill even though taking the blue pill will predictably produce more desirable consequences for me? Is knowing the truth really worthwhile if it could result in the destruction of my present happiness?

In order to live the good life is knowledge of the truth really necessary? According to Voltaire, yes, it is both worthwhile and necessary. Voltaire wrote "The Story of the Brahmin" and explains that a wise, old Brahmin who is miserable because he knows the truth is living a better life than is his ignorant neighbor who is blissfully happy. The Brahmin would not choose to trade places with the neighbor in order to be happy. It is better for a person to be tormented and miserable with the truth than it is to be happy and ignorant. There is something more important for us to achieve than happiness. This higher and more enriching goal is truth.

Some people may say that the point of life is to live, and that examining life for truth is a waste of time. We should just live our lives according to what is in our own best interests. However, in response to this egoist claim, I say that in order to know the best way to live life, we must evaluate what kind of life is the good life. If we do not examine what it is to live the good life, our options become too broad for people to actually follow this maxim. That is, if we do not somehow evaluate what it is to live the good life, some may say that the good life, to them, is to sit around and scratch themselves all day. Therefore, it is necessary to come to some agreement on what it is to live the good life.

According to Plato in *The Apology*, in order to live the good life, one must examine life. Wisdom for Socrates meant that a person knew what it was he or she did not know. I agree with this completely because I believe that it is not possible for one to really live life without trying to come to an understanding of what life really is, or in other words, to realize the truths of life. In the movie *The Matrix*, Morpheus shows Neo what it is that he does not know.

Neo then must choose if he wants to learn more. This is his opportunity to become awakened and to really be able to examine life.

In Nietzsche's Introduction to *Thus Spoke Zarathustra*, the three metamorphoses of a spirit are illustrated through the camel, the lion, and the child. The camel represents the spirit that bears the heavy load of knowledge and travels away from the crowd. The spirit in the stage of the camel then becomes educated and transforms into the spirit of the lion, who has the willingness to destroy what has come before. The lion must break the rules and understand that there are new boundaries. The spirit then converts into a child. The stage in which the spirit is a child is representative of creating a new way. Nietzsche believes that in order to "overcome man" and live the good life, one must undergo this process. This theory also supports my statement that one must search for the truth in order to live the good life. It is important to realize that the truths that we know are not necessarily truths. We have to examine more than what we have been taught by society in order to truly see reality. We must be willing to explore the fact that there are other truths out there besides the ones that have been handed to us in order to live the good life.

The movie, *The Matrix*, does present a valid and reasonable argument to support the idea that we should examine life and realize that there are other truths out there. If we choose not to do this, we could be missing out on a higher quality of life.

14.2 A PAPER FROM BIOMEDICAL ETHICS: STEM CELL RESEARCH

Beth Lanam's paper uses a five-step method for systematic analysis, justification, and resolution of moral dilemmas formulated by Becky White and Eric Gampel. Professor White was her instructor in Biomedical Ethics. A full explanation of this method can be found in the article referenced in footnote two, page 202. Each letter of CARVE represents the nature of the concern: *C* stands for consequences, the expected results of an action. Three moral principles are involved: (1) the principle of nonmaleficence (PNM) indicates the importance of refraining from causing harm; (2) the principle of positive beneficence (PPB) reflects the importance of expected benefits; and (3) the principle of utility (PU) weighs the harms and benefits experienced by different people to promote the best outcome for the whole group. *A* stands for autonomy and is used when an individual's action is preserved, promoted, protected, or obstructs that of another's self-determination. *R* represents a person's rights and is used when a person's rights are respected or disrespected. *V* represents virtues and constitutes that of integrity, honesty, compassion, courage, tolerance, and any other important virtues. And *E* stands for equality/fairness/justice (EFJ).

You can find the reference to White and Gampel's method in the notes to Chapter 12. It is designed to facilitate resolution of moral conflict. If you are working on a cooperative paper or are unsure of where you stand on an issue due to conflicting values, the method is sure to help your writing.

Biomedical ethics is an upper division general education course in a thematic cluster at CSU, Chico. Most students are pursuing careers in health care.

```
                    Stem Cell Research?

                       Beth Lanam
```

Moral Dilemma:

Is it morally permissible for stem cell research to be federally funded?

Reasons For and Against:

If allowed, society benefits by enabling cures to be found for today's life threatening diseases. (PU)

By allowing stem cell research to be funded by the federal government it uses a taxpayer's money whether he/she is for or against the research. (R, J, F)

Step 1: Creative Problem Solving

Allowing the federal government to fund stem cell research would anger a lot of taxpayers. The federal government does not use its own money to assist in the research; instead it would be using every person's money who pays taxes to our government regardless of whether he or she believed stem cell research is moral. My solution would be to have a box on the tax return indicating to the government your position on stem cell research. The government should have the right to only dip into those tax-paying dollars in which have been indicated that they are for stem cell research. This solution would be an additional complication for our government, but would diminish the violation of the people's right to withhold support from policies they find objectionable, while still benefiting our society by continuing to fund health care research to cure disease.

Step 2: Pros and Cons

Listed below are the prevailing intuitive reasons, the pros and cons of stem cell research. The parenthetical notations indicate the common moral concerns and or principles of CARVE that each reason falls under.

Step 3: Evaluating Pros and Cons

The two strongest and/or most important reasons will be taken and further evaluated for their strengths and weaknesses. The number scales for strength are 1–3 and for probability 0–1. After assigning numbers to each important

OPTIONS	PRO	CON
Stem cell research	1. Society benefits by finding cures and may lead to further medical breakthorough. (PU) 3. Compassion—aid to decrease suffering. (V—compassion, PPB, R)	2. Kills embryos. (R, PNM) 4. Transitivity of respect if federally funded. (R, F, J) 5. Religious objection. (J) 6. Eugenics (mad scientist). (PNM, PU) 7. Misallocation of scarce resources. (PU) 8. Playing god. (A) 9. Expensive. (EFJ) 10. Wrong motives for embryo donation. (E, F, J)

reason, I then multiply the numbers and in the end can clearly make a distinction of which reason was the strongest.

Pro #1 Society benefits by finding cures for today's life threatening diseases.

Is the individual life of each embryo or the population of our world, about one-half with curable diseases, more important? With the aid of stem cell research our world's healthy population would increase due to finding cures to aid patients now, and future patients with diabetes, neuronal tissue damage after strokes, spinal cord injuries, ALS, Alzheimer's, Parkinson's disease, burn victims, damaged arteries and hearts would benefit as well. When I consider that half of our current population would die of curable

diseases or the problems listed above, the pro weight of
stem cell research seems a solid 3. The probability, however, is lower than the top number, that of a 1, due to stem
cell research still being research. Therefore, the probability would be in the mid-spectrum of 0.5. (3 × 0.5 = 1.5)

*Con # 2 By performing stem cell research many embryos are
killed and or destroyed in the process.*

Is the embryo alive, deserving rights and autonomy? Or
is it too young and immature to be considered a human being?
The question also arises about the true connection of death
and disrespect. Death does not necessarily equal disrespect.
Native Americans, for instance, place death within a context
of respectful social practices. Also, the attitudes and actions that demonstrate respect can vary when dealing with
public vs. private interests. And embryos are not fully destroyed, but rather taken for their parts. The DNA is still
intact. Embryos that are used in stem cell research are ones
with no nervous system for feeling, no brain for thinking,
and no muscles for movement.

The life status of an embryo candidate for stem cell research is that of a question and I give the question of the
embryo's life being harmed the probability of a 0.5. The
strength of the embryo's life is problematic also. An embryo
has the potential to be a grown human, but what about all
the embryos sitting in the refrigerators in the fertility
clinics? If we can justify having those have no potential
life then why not use embryos for stem cell research. Therefore, my intuition for strength is 2. (2 × 0.5 = 1)

By numbers alone, the pro of stem cell research wins over that of the con for no stem cell research.

Step 4: Diagnosing Source of Disagreement

Values (strengths)

- The relevant moral values are unclear because of the problematic nature of when life begins.

Probabilities (facts of the context)

- Opponents fail to see the "Big Picture"—the potential social benefits.
- Scientific research may result in unforeseen benefits (AKA the Tang Factor.)

Harms

- Since positive results are not guaranteed, there is always the possibility of harm without offsetting medical justification.
- Perhaps embryos have an ecological importance in the circle of life?
- Potential cures for many present noncurable diseases lead to longer lives for the population and higher costs later.
- Increased government interference in reproduction might foster further attacks on reproductive freedom.

Step 5: Summary and Conclusion

The moral dilemma in question was whether it is morally permissible for the federal government to aid in stem cell research. Many other questions and concerns arise. The questions of an embryo's worth and life status are main concerns. After looking at the strengths and probabilities of a major pro and con for stem cell research—society benefiting from finding cures and the taking of embryo "life"—it was clear that the support for stem cell research was the stronger.

I personally am leary of stem cell research. Organ warehouses would transform human life. But I agree that it is needed to better our world as a whole by finding cures. Tax payers should have a right to choose if their money goes to this cause or not. It is morally impermissible for the government to fund stem cell research without letting people choose for themselves.

14.3   A GROUP PAPER FROM MORAL ISSUES IN PARENTING: SHOULD WE BE RAISING ALTRUISTS?

This final paper is from Moral Issues in Parenting, an upper division general education course in an interdisciplinary cluster titled The Child. Most students taking this course are psychology or child development majors in their junior or senior years. Most students have had only one other philosophy course in critical thinking, so they come to the class with no background in ethical theory or the history of philosophy. As the instructor, I encourage students to make oral class presentations as a means of formulating their perspective and gathering counterarguments. Sometimes, several students make joint presentations that evolve into group papers. Unfortunately, group papers often lack unity. I was pleased to get this paper last semester for the content, the argument, and the unity of expression the four students achieved. The articles the authors refer to are all found in Laurence D. Houlgate, *Morals, Marriage, and Parenthood.* Belmont, Ca.: Wadsworth, 1998.

Should We Be Raising Altruists?

Ronda Roberts

Frank Lavis

Shawn Gillette

Elizabeth Legg

In his article "The Obligation of Parents to Raise Their Children as Altruists," R. Paul Churchill argues that every parent has an obligation to raise a child in such a way that will foster an altruistic character. His argument answers to those people who disagree with the notion that one could in principle raise their child to become an altruist. Churchill bases his views on altruism on his notion of happiness. We will examine different views of happiness (the good life) to situate Churchill's claim that parents should raise their children altruistically.

I. Ruddick: Three Concepts and the LPP

William Ruddick's aim is to show that by moderation between two principles giving parents either too much or too little power over their children, we can raise children in a way that will lead to their flourishing. In "Parenthood: Three Concepts and a Principle," he lays out three concepts associated with what it means to be a competent parent, and then he examines three possible principles for parenthood, settling finally on the Life-Prospect Principle.

The first concept Ruddick lays out is caring for children. What does it mean to care for children? Ruddick explains that caring for children involves the day-to-day tasks of feeding them, tending to them (for example, washing a cut), ensuring the child's good health, and protecting the child from the world outside the family. These features of parenting are generally backed up by law and by cultural practice within a society (children are meant to be cherished, not harmed, children are "God's gift," etc.) Child caring is within a time frame, as Ruddick says, "One striking feature of child-caring is its temporal focus on a child's present needs, especially those that require continuous or frequent satisfaction" (243).

Not only do parents care for their children, but they also raise them. What Ruddick really wants to say here is that the child is a piece of clay, and the parent carefully sculpts and molds that child into an adult. Parents are judged in their child-raising endeavors as being either:

> *Realistic* or *unrealistic* in their hopes for a child; *open-* or *narrow-minded* in the interests they allow to foster, or the lessons they instill; *supportive* or *retarding* of a child's development; *deftly guiding* or *relentlessly pushing* a child in certain directions. (Ruddick, 243)

Child raising, unlike child-caring, involves much more than taking care of basic needs. Rather, child raising involves being attentive to the child's hopes and dreams, and if you are lucky, part of your input will rub off on them to make them successful adults. Every parent has their own notion of what it will mean for their child to lead the good life.

The final concept Ruddick lays out is that of parenthood as "family making." He describes the concept as follows:

> Some children are conceived in order to start, or enlarge a
> family, to commemorate a family member lost through death, or
> to satisfy parents' desire for grandchildren. Likewise, con-
> traceptive or abortive efforts often have familial motives,
> for example, not to shame or burden one's parents, or to post-
> pone one's own family-making or family-enlarging to a better
> time. (Ruddick, 244).

Bringing more children into the world may have motives including the attempt to become immortal for some people. Fam-
ilies provide a means for passing down traditions and
establishing a certain amount of exclusivity.

After Ruddick lays out the three concepts involved with
parenting, he explores three possible principles for parenthood. There is often conflict among parents between which of
the concerns are most important. For example, while growing
up, my brother needed very strong prescription glasses so
that he could see despite his extreme nearsightedness, and I
wanted to play basketball and take after school art classes.
Because my brother's "care" centered need came before my
"raising" centered need, it made sense that my brother received his glasses, and I got to play basketball, but I
didn't get to take art lessons.

The first such principle is what Ruddick brings in from
Joel Fienberg: the Option-Maximizing Principle (OMP). This
principle is derived from the notion that parents have the
duty to provide their children with an open future. "On this
view, it is a principle parental duty to help a child to develop the capacity for autonomy." (Ruddick, 246). The problem with this principle lies in the fact that it doesn't

seem to allow any sort of specialization for a child to have cultivated by his parents. The second principle is the Principle of Parental Self-Perpetuation (PPP). This principle is too coercive by Ruddick's reasoning. The PPP allows for parents to dictate exactly what type of person their child should become.

Since neither of these principles proves satisfying for Ruddick, he must come up with a third principle that respects the child's autonomy while it steers the child in a specialized direction. Thus, Ruddick proposes the Life Prospects Principle (LPP): "It requires that parents provide life-prospects or possibilities for a child: 1. that jointly encompass a range of likely societal changes and 2. each of which would be acceptable sooner or later to both parents and child" (Ruddick, 247). The first condition cancels out any personal parental goal of raising a child to become just like them. The second condition gives allotment for the parent to make sure the child doesn't get into too much trouble roaming the world. The combination provides a basis on which the parents can both allow their child to become autonomous and restrict that child from engaging in possibly harmful activities. This combination will allow for a child to lead a life open to flourishing. This leads into the discussion of happiness and specifically of Aristotelian flourishing.

II. Perspectives on Happiness

Churchill asserts that for a parent to truly fill their parental obligation they must be consistent in the approach that they follow. This approach offers the child tools for happiness. They will be the ones "who love to be free and are truly free to love" (Churchill 255). This consistency is not taught by telling the child how to be, but by showing the child through parental actions. Volunteering shows the child a worthwhile commitment, one that was not forced upon the volunteer. The child should learn to be a selfless doer, not a selfish doer. For the selfless doer the happiness is not the end of helping at the soup kitchen, but it is the moral thing to do. Happiness is eventually found in practicing to be a consistent, selfless, moral agent. . . .

[Here I omit an extended discussion of happiness that utilized the views of Plato, Aristotle, Kant, and Mill.]

III. Churchill and Altruism

Churchill believes that given the necessary resources, people who have chosen to be parents have an obvious moral obligation to raise their children to be extensive persons. Altruistic members benefit society by enhancing social cooperation and other-regarding care and concern and benefit the child by contributing to their development of virtuous character and according to Aristotle experience greater happiness.

Churchill's first challenge was formulating a definition of altruism. For this, he looks to the contributions of Lawrence A. Blum, Samuel P. Oliner and Pearl S. Oliner. He concludes that for an act to be altruistic, it must meet first the following five conditions:

[. . .] (1) it is voluntarily undertaken; (2) it is motivated by concern for others or by conscience or moral principle . . . (3) it is done in the absence of expectation of gain—of receiving 'external' rewards; (4) it manifests an absence of concern for the self, or more accurately, the subjection of concerns for the safety of the self to concerns for the other, and (5) it manifests care marked by a significant degree of 'inclusiveness' that renders irrelevant such characteristics as the gender, race, ethnicity, religion, or nationality of the others toward whom concern is shown. (Churchill, 253)

Churchill believes that by meeting these five conditions, we can begin to understand the nature of altruism.

Next, Churchill explores the two concepts of extensive persons and constricted persons. Extensive persons propel their relationships beyond the normal boundaries of a relationship so other people are experienced as part of ones self. They have two significant personality features: "Attachment, to attach oneself to others in a committed interpersonal relationship and inclusiveness, the propensity towards the 'breadth' of feelings of interpersonal connectedness" (Churchill, 254). Constricted persons exhibit dissociation and detachment, they have a propensity to avoid committed and responsible relationships.

Development of extensive personality is providing a foundation for happiness. Raising children to become extensive persons will be the very best way, and perhaps the only really consistent way of fulfilling our parental obligations to do our best at raising persons who "love to be free and are truly free to love."

IV. Objections to the Altruist

Ruddick would argue with Churchill over the matter of raising children altruistically. He wrote, "it is a principle parental duty to help a child to develop a capacity for autonomy," not for altruism. Raising your children altruistically would violate the "Life Prospects Principle" (LPP), which requires parents to provide life-prospects or possibilities for their children, not to "limit a child's life-prospects that the child will have to lead a life he or she does not want." This principle lies between the liberal "Option-Maximizing Principle" (OMP), which recognizes the "right to an open future," and the principle of parental self-perpetuation (PPP), which gives parents too much power over a child's future. Raising children as altruists violates the LPP by weakening a child's power to choose their path, whether it be altruistic or not, and therefore infringing upon their autonomy.

Another problem Ruddick might have with altruism is the problem of the "real" world. A child raised altruistically would experience many setbacks in life. Attending to others with an "absence of concern for the self" (part of Churchill's definition of altruism) in today's world would lead to the altruist being taken advantage of in many situations. It would also seem that in order for any altruist to be able to extend their help to those in need, they would first need to have taken care of themselves in order to be fit to help another. This, however, is not recognized by Churchill.

Altruism takes on a cult-like flavor when Churchill makes his definition with collected research from the Oliners (publishers of *The Altruistic Personality*), Lawrence A. Blum, and others. The first condition of altruistic behavior is that it is undertaken voluntarily. Right away the LPP is violated assuming that the child was raised to have this tendency without consent. The fourth condition states that "it manifests an absence of concern for the self." This is hugely problematic, especially when survival in today's world is considered. A person with this quality will be "walked all over" in his/her eagerness to help another.

V. Conclusion

Now that we have examined the arguments from both Ruddick and Churchill, and examined notions of happiness, it seems apparent that there is an additional problem with Churchill's paper, namely, that it is impossible to be the sort of altruist he argues for all of the time. Arguments have been given explaining the problem with altruism in our selfish society. Ruddick has said that we should not limit our children in terms of their options, while still making the effort to shape our children into "works of art." Ruddick would be against any set way of raising a child specifically to become something; especially an altruist, or extensive person. Ruddick's arguments seem to much more accurately describe exactly what it is parents should instill. This way we do not violate the autonomy of our children, and we raise them to be virtuous people with their own wishes and dreams.

Glossary of Philosophic Terms

act utilitarianism   The belief that the expected consequences of an action should be weighed in each situation before embracing one option as the moral one (see *rule utilitarianism*)

ad hoc   Latin for "to this" or "to this purpose"; in philosophy, a part of an argument that is fabricated only to serve an immediate purpose and has not been demonstrated to have independent value through added explanatory power or testable predictions

ad hominem   Latin for "to the man"; an informal fallacy committed in an argument by attacking one's opponent personally instead of attacking his or her position

aesthetics   The branch of philosophy that attempts to define, describe, and evaluate art

agnosticism   Conviction that, while a deity may exist, there can be no absolute proof of the deity's existence or nonexistence; an agnostic suspends judgment on the existence or nonexistence of God as opposed to an atheist, who denies God's existence

agape   In Christian philosophy, the term describing the unconditional love that God feels toward humanity; contrasts with other forms of love

akrasia   Greek for "lack of self control"; an inability to do what one knows is right, due to lack of will

altruism   The belief that one should do what is best for others; usually accompanied by the belief that humans may have altruistic motives; holds that unselfish acts are accomplished for unselfish, rather than selfish, reasons

anarchism   The belief that no organized government has the right to coerce its citizens into any action; a rejection of all forms of externally imposed authority

animism   The belief, found in many primitive religions and some philosophical religions, that all things, animate and inanimate, possess a soul

a posteriori   Latin for "from what follows"; arrived at from experience and observation; a method of reaching a conclusion through reasoning from particular facts to general principles; see also *a priori*

a priori   Latin for "from before"; a method of reaching a conclusion independently of experience. Sometimes a priori knowledge is based on the meanings of terms, as when one knows from the meaning of the word triangle—independently of experiencing an actual triangle—that is has three angles and three sides; such tacit knowledge is constitutive of experience; see also *a posteriori*

Aristotle   384–322 BCE; Plato's student, thought by some to be the greatest philosopher; concerned with formalizing the approach to argument begun by Plato and Socrates; a major influence on medieval Christian thought

artificial intelligence   Also commonly known as AI; a field of study which builds or theorizes about machines capable of thought. Some AI advocates believe that intelligent machines must exhibit human thought; others believe that machines are intelligent if they exhibit any kind of problem solving ability

atheism   The belief that there is no deity

begging the question   Another term for "circular reasoning," a type of faulty argument in which a form of the conclusion to be established is used in the premises

behaviorism   An approach to the study of the mind that focuses on the observation of external behavior

best of all possible worlds   A phrase from the German mathematician and philosopher Gottfried Leibniz (1646–1716), who argued that since the world was created by a deity who was perfect and whose works were perfect, then despite all appearances the world is the best of all possible worlds; an idea often treated with derision, as in Voltaire's fantasy novel *Candide*; Leibniz believed that free will was a condition of the best of all possible worlds and explained why the best world contained suffering and evil

bioethics   Ethical positions and arguments concerning biological and medical issues, such as abortion and genetic engineering

Buddha   Siddharta Gautama, the Buddha, 563–483 BCE; founder of the philosophical and religious tradition known as Buddhism, based on the Four Noble Truths; Buddhism seeks to transcend the suffering and contingency of human life through the elimination of the individual self and human desires to attain the state of enlightenment or nirvana

Buridan's ass   The central actor in a story designed to illustrate a problem inherent in the concept that one should do only what seems to be of the greatest good: the hungry ass who, finding itself equidistant from two sources of hay, finds neither source more desirable and so, unable to move in either direction, starves to death

Cartesian doubt   Referring to Descartes' process of assuming that any belief capable of being doubted is false—the first step toward discovering a point of certainty

categorical imperative   Immanuel Kant's phrase for an absolute command, something one must always do regardless of circumstance, since the moral law deserves the highest respect, such as "Tell the truth"

circular reasoning   Reasoning that is faulty because it assumes without reasonable evidence the truth of the statement, in whole or in part, which it is trying to defend; see *begging the question*

civil disobedience   An act contrary to the law, performed in the belief that it is morally acceptable to disobey civil authority in matters where it comes in conflict with one's perceived notions of the moral law, which is generally held to follow from the authority of God or personal conscience

consequentialism   An ethical position which holds that the consequences of an action determine whether that action is morally right or wrong

contemplation   The act of meditating in a manner that reveals ultimate reality and value

cosmology   Theorizing about the origins, the elements, and the structure of the cosmos

creationism   A would-be theory, common to many fundamentalist religions, that the world was created by a deity who intended its elements to be as they are, in opposition to the theory of evolution, which argues for the random beginning and development of life through natural selection

deduction   A form of argument which holds that if the premises of an argument are true, its conclusion must be true, in contrast to inductive arguments where the conclusion is claimed to be only probably true; example of deduction: All bulldogs breathe air; Iris is a bulldog; therefore, Iris breathes air; example of induction: All bulldogs heretofore observed breathe air; Iris is a bulldog; therefore, Iris probably breathes air

deontology   A system of ethical theories which emphasize the importance of duty to making the moral choice

Descartes, René   1596–1650; French philosopher who, by contending that philosophy, independently of revealed religion, could discover the foundations of truth, founded modern philosophy (see *Cartesian doubt*)

determinism   The position that all things (actions, personality traits, natural phenomena) are caused by antecedent factors which are, perhaps, knowable but beyond mediation, so that all things must be as they are

dilemma   A problem in which there is a choice between two or more unacceptable alternatives; a form of argument in which an opponent is offered undesirable alternatives implied by views the opponent advocates

dualism   A belief in the existence of two and only two separate classes of phenomena: spirit and matter, for example; most dualists are really committed to three substances: matter, mind, and abstract objects such as numbers (see also *monism* and *pluralism*)

dystopia   An imagined society in which conditions are as bad as they can be; the reverse of a utopia

Eightfold Path   In Buddhism, the practice of life that aids in the attainment of enlightenment: Right View, Right Aim, Right Speech, Right Action, Right Living, Right Effort, Right Mindfulness, Right Contemplation

empiricism   A belief that experience alone generates all knowledge and that there is no such thing as inherent or innate knowledge; opposed to rationalism

ends versus means   An argument which holds that there are some actions which, as means, are themselves so morally wrong or bad that their consequences, no matter how good, cannot compensate

epistemology   The study of the nature and origins of knowledge

ethics   The collection of beliefs by which a person determines whether an action is right or wrong; a person's set of moral principles; philosophical ethics inquires into the foundation of such principles and seeks to offer rational justification for them

eudaemonia   Greek for "living well"; refers to the Aristotelian belief that the true aim of life is happiness, attained by the proper balance of intellectual and moral virtues

euthanasia   Greek for "a happy death"; the act of killing someone for his or her own good, to relieve suffering due to a fatal illness, for example

existentialism   A modern philosophy which argues for the total freedom of the individual from external or inherited controls on his or her behavior, and, therefore, for the complete responsibility of the individual for his or her own actions; you must figure this philosophy out for yourself; we will not explain it to you

foundationalism   The view that there is a privileged class of belief from which springs the justification of all other beliefs or statements in a particular belief system

Four Noble Truths   From Buddhist teachings: (1) Suffering exists, (2) Suffering has identifiable causes, (3) There is a way to end suffering, (4) The way is to follow the Eightfold Path

freedom   In terms of political freedom, the degree to which the actions of people within a society are allowed by law and sometimes facilitated by government; philosophers generally refer to negative freedom as those areas of human activity allowed by law, and they use the term positive freedom to mark areas in which government facilitates human action by offering assistance—for instance, most people would agree that you have a right to pursue a college degree (negative freedom) without suffering discrimination; fewer people would agree that the government has a right to tax society to provide free college educations (positive freedom)

free will   A characteristic, assumed in certain philosophies, by which people may choose their actions without the influence of internal or external constraints; a troublesome term, since philosophers sometimes redefine free will in a manner that makes it difficult to separate it from the account of choice given in determinism

happiness   In some philosophies, the single basic element necessary for living the good life; usually a pluralistic concept involving a variety of intrinsic goods such as knowledge and pleasure; there are monistic eudaemonists, called hedonists, who argue that happiness is ultimately reducible to pleasure

hedonism   A philosophic position that the pursuit of pleasure is the highest aim in life

historicism   The view that it is impossible to arrive at an understanding of human behavior without understanding its historical context; also, the understanding that one's interpretation of reality is conditioned to an extent by one's historical environment

humanism   Any philosophical position that centers on the innate worthiness of humans and human values

hypothetico-deductive model   A three-step model of scientific justification in which (1) a hypothesis is developed in response to an unexpected observation, (2) statements about reality are deduced from the hypothesis, initial conditions, and other background knowledge, and (3) the hypothesis is confirmed through observation

idealism   The theory that ultimate reality exists only in a nonphysical realm of ideas, and that physical objects in the world are imperfect copies of ideal objects; also, a theory that ultimate reality exists only in the mind

ideal observer theory   A process of ethical reasoning that subjects conclusions to the views of an ideal (and imagined) observer who, possessed of all the facts relating to the conclusion, should be able to make judgments about it that are free of bias

ideology   Any systematic collection of beliefs infected with ethical or religious values, but especially one relating to politics or sociological matters

induction   See *deduction*

infinite regress   A system in which one event is caused by a past event, which in turn was caused by an earlier past event, and so on, backward into eternity; showing that an opponent's position is committed to an infinite regress is generally considered an effective refutation of the position

innateness   The condition of being inherent or inborn, as opposed to originating externally, as through experience or education; an intrinsic quality or object; in philosophy, a term generally referring to questions about the mind, such as whether ways of classifying objects or the ability to learn a language or to reason are innate or learned

intrinsic   Partaking of the essential nature of a thing; also, the quality of having value for itself, rather than for its relationship to something else

introspection   To explore one's own consciousness deeply, looking for self-knowledge; some introspectionists hold that one cannot be mistaken about the contents of one's own mind; you can lie to others about what you think and feel, but not to yourself

intuition   The human faculty of believing something, often suddenly, without subjecting it to argumentation or testing; in philosophy, a general term referring to the having of an experience whether it be sensory, religious, aesthetic, rational, or a combination of these that conveys certainty

mean   A center point between two extremes; in ethics, a term referring to Aristotle's view that a virtue is always the mean between two extremes, as courage is halfway between cowardice and foolhardiness

metaphysics   The branch of philosophy that focuses on the ultimate components of existence, such elements as time, free will, and the nature of matter

Mill, John Stuart   1806–1873; classical liberal English philosopher who defended and popularized utilitarianism; his father, John Mill, and Jeremy Bentham were the major proponents of utilitarianism before him

mind–body problem   The focal point for any attempt to understand the relationship between the physical and the mental substances

monism   A belief in the existence of only one ultimate kind of substance; for example, a belief that existence is comprised of one organic spiritual whole, with no independent elements; a tenet argued in the work of Spinoza (see *dualism* and *pluralism*)

mysticism   Any belief system that relies on direct experience as a means of connecting with ultimate reality, which is usually held to be supernatural truth or God

natural law   In some philosophies, the set of innate constraints that should govern human action; note that unnatural does not mean in violation of the laws of nature in a physical sense: one cannot violate the laws of nature unless, of course, one is God; unnatural means in violation of the proper purposes of nature, as exhibited in nature and apprehendible through reasoning; St. Thomas did not claim that sex outside of marriage was physically impossible, but he did claim that it was unnatural, since it did not attend to the proper function of sex: procreation in a context that provides for the raising of children to adulthood

nihilism   The position that all traditional beliefs and belief systems are unfounded and that life itself is meaningless

nothing   Emptiness, complete void, nonexistence; a philosophical puzzle, since the naming of "nothing" confers upon it an existence. In non-Western philosophy, the term names the unnamable and undifferentiated source of all being and has a positive role to play. The usefulness of the bowl is accounted for by the material out of which it is constructed and the emptiness that provides its shape. Consider the haiku:

> No one spoke.
> Not the host.
> Nor the guest.
> Nor the pink chrysanthemum.

omnipotent   All powerful; capable of any action; a characteristic often assigned to God regardless of such paradoxical facts as that God cannot build a stone so heavy that God cannot pick it up

paternalism   A system in which an authority provides for the needs of its constituents and regulates their conduct, thus, in effect, assuming responsibility for them; even libertarians such as John Stuart Mill argue for instances in which paternalism is justified

personal identity   The combination of personal elements that distinguishes one person from all other people; those characteristics which provide a person with his or her individuality over time

Plato   428?–348 BCE; a student of Socrates and thought by some to be the greatest philosopher of all time; author of the Socratic dialogues and famous for his three theories of forms, which consistently hold that physical reality is composed of imperfect copies of ideal forms of which we can become conscious only through the mystical leap at the penultimate step of the dialectic process of reasoning

pluralism   A belief that there are many equally valid, though incompatible, classes of ultimate ethical or political values; in metaphysics, the belief that there is more than one type of substance, which leads to such questions as the mind–body problem, which questions how the substances interact (see *dualism* and *monism*)

problem of evil   The question of why evil exists in a world built by a benevolent God who has the power to eliminate evil and the knowledge that it will occur

problem of induction   A reference to the difficulty of proving the "principle of reasoning," which holds that it is reasonable to believe that past and present observable properties of nature will continue into the future; inductive proofs of induction are question begging; deductive proofs of induction are lacking

Pyrrhonism   Skeptical philosophy that draws its name from Pyrrho (306–270 BCE) and is preserved in the writings of Sextus Empiricus (second–third centuries CE), who advocates the attainment of happiness through the suspension of judgment; Pyrrhonists engage in philosophical argument to cure others of the sickness of belief

rationalism   A belief that some knowledge is attainable through the processes of reason alone, unaided by experience or education; opposed to empiricism

rule utilitarianism   The belief that general policies should be the focus of our attempt to determine which options will have the best overall consequences; rule utilitarians generally argue against allowing exceptions in contexts where the consequences would be better if we broke the generally beneficial rules (see *act utilitarianism*)

skepticism   The doctrine that knowledge in general or knowledge in certain areas, such as ethics or the question of existence of the external world, cannot be considered certain beyond a doubt; some skeptics deny that humans have knowledge, thus seeming to refute themselves with the knowledge claim; others suspend judgment about whether there is knowledge

sense-data   Those impressions received through the senses and which, according to empirical philosophers, may serve as the bases of all our understanding of external objects; sense data philosophers usually emphasize visual presentations

social contract   The actual or hypothetical agreement between the government or ruler and the governed that outlines the rights of citizens and duties of citizens and the government; social contract theorists differ on the question of whether the governmental authorities are parties to the contract or are constituted as authorities on the basis of a contract between citizens; the concept is often invoked as a way of legitimizing a government

Socrates   470?–399 BCE; teacher of Plato and the principal speaker in the earliest Socratic dialogues; a master of the dialectical method of argument in which opponents are led by a series of questions into revealing the weaknesses in their own positions

solipsism   The theory that the only thing in existence is the self, or the only thing we can know for sure is our self or mind

state of nature   The real or hypothetical condition in which humanity existed before the establishment of government or laws regulating behavior

Tao   Originating in Chinese thought, the name for the unnamable and ineffable unity of all existence and nonexistence

Taoism   Philosophical tradition, originating in China, which believes that humans can find peace and tranquillity through following the Tao; major figures in Taoism are Lao Tzu (sixth century BCE) and Chuang-Tzu (fourth century BCE)

theism   Opposite of atheism; the belief in a deity

utilitarian ethics   A philosophical tradition that places the ultimate moral justification of an action in the overall balance of good consequences over bad ones; utilitarians differ over the nature of the good: some believe that the only good is pleasure; others prefer the more pluralistic term happiness, but they all accept the principle of equality of interests embodied in Jeremy Bentham's statement that each counts for one, and no one counts for more than one

utopia   Greek for "nowhere"; an imagined society of ideal perfection; the reverse of a dystopia

Index

A

Abstract, 107
Ad hominem, 158
Advise for Distance Learners, 100–103
Advise on Writing a Philosophy Paper, 99
Affirming the antecedent, 153
Affirming the consequent, 153
Agassiz, Louis, 24
All I Really Needed to Know I Learned in Kindergarten (Robert Fulghum), 209
Allen, Chris, 219–223
Analogies, 146–147
Analyzing a Professional Code of Ethics, 206–207
Antecedent, 56–57
APME Code of Ethics, Revised and Adopted, 1995, 204–206
Apostrophe, 58–59
Appeal, to loyalty, 161
   to ignorance, 159
   to pity, 161
   to the stick, 161
Appendices, 110
Applications, 149–150
Applying Ethical Theories and Political Philosophy, 202–204
Approaches to Ethics, 188–198
Aquinas, Thomas, 178
Argument
   deductive, 136
   definition of, 135–136
   nondeductive (inductive), 136
   principles of, 133–151
   throws of, 133–135
   two basic types of, 136–137
   valid forms of, 140–141

Aristotle, 178
Asking questions, 35–36

B

Begging the question, 157
Bentham, Jeremy, 74
Books, citing, 114–119
Brainstonning, 34–35

C

Calculating probabilities, 163–164
Capitalization, 59–60
Chapter headings, 109
   primary, 109
   secondary, 109
   tertiary, 109
Chicago Manual of Style (CMS), 113
Chuang Tzu, 7–8, 12–13
Cicero, Marcus Tullius, 176
Clause, independent, 62
Clause, subordinate, 53
Cliches, 41
Cogency, 139
Coherence, 43
College library resources, 87–94
Colon, 61
   in a list, 61
   in a quotation, 61
   in a restatement or description, 61
Comma, 61–63
   in a compound sentence, 62
   with restrictive and nonrestrictive elements, 63
   in a series, 62–63
Comma splice, 61–62

Commonly confused words, 66–67
Commonly misspelled words, 67–69
Communication, writing as, 17–48
Complex question, 157
Composition, 159
Compound sentence, 62
Conclusion, 135, 225
Consequentialism, 188–192
Contents, table of, 107–108
Contents of a History of Philosophy Paper, 183
Contents of a Personal Ethics Statement, 215
Contradictions, 146
Criteria Definition, 225
Critique of brief ethics statement, 223
Cyberspace, philosophy and, 95–103

D

Declaration of Independence, 211
Deductive validity, 137
Denying the antecedent, 152–153
Deontology, Kant, 192–195
Descartes, René, 2–8, 76, 178
Descriptive language, 40
Dilemmas, 145
Directories of Text, 99
Dissertations, 127
Distinction Between Fact and Value, 187
Division, 159
Do Androids Dream of Electric Sheep? (Philip K. Dick), 1
Documentary note system, general format rules, 113–114
  books, 114–119
  endnotes and bibliography, 114
  interviews, 126–127
  multiple notes, 114
  numbered references, 113–129
  numbering system, 113–129
  periodicals, 119–121
  placement of superscript numeral, 114–129
  preliminary decisions, 111–113
  public documents, 121–123
  subsequent or shortened references, 128–129
Double standard, 162
Douglas, Frederick, 19

E

Early Greek Philosophy, Milton C. Nahm, 176
Editing, 44–45
Emerson, Ralph Waldo, 73, 87, 111
Emotive language, 164–166
Encyclopedias, 99
Equivocation, 159
Error Identification, 225
Esenin, Sergey, 22
Euthyphro, 9–11
Evidential certainty, 7

Examples of Famous Statements of Ethics, 209–213
Exclusive fallacy, 153–154
Expository writing, 25

F

Fallacies, 152–166
  ad hominem, 158
  appeal to ignorance, 159
  appeal to loyalty, 161
  appeal to pity, 161
  appeal to the stick, 161
  appeal to unknowable statistics, 158
  avoiding, 152–166
  begging the question, 157
  complex question, 157
  composition, 159
  division, 159
  double standard, 162
  equivocation, 159
  false dilemma, 156–157
  formal, 152–154
  guilt by association, 158
  hasty conclusion, 159–160
  identifying, 162–163
  inconsistency, 156
  informal, 154–162
  invalid appeal to authority, 155–156
  invincible ignorance, 162
  lack of proportion, 158
  popularity, 162
  provincialism, 161–162
  questionable analogy, 160–161
  questionable cause, 160
  straw person, 156
  suppressed evidence, 157
  susceptibility, 154–155
  two wrongs make a right, 158–159
False dilemma, 156–157
Faulty, 55
First Meditation, 4–5
Foreword or introduction, citing, 117
Formality, level of, 40
Formats, 104–110
  abstract, 107
  appendices, 110
  chapter headings, 109
  general page, 105–106
  illustrations and figures, 109–110
  reference page, 110
  table of contents, 107–108
  text, 109
  title page, 106
Forster, E. M., 18
Foucault, Michael, 74
Four Major Directories, 98–99
Freewriting, 33–34

G

Gautama, Siddhartha, 177
General Sources of Information, 98–100
Grammar and style, general rules of, 49–52
    aim for consistency, 51
    competent writing, 49–50
    consider your audience, 50–51
    eliminate chronic errors, 51–52
    have confidence in what you know, 51
Great Philosophers, A Very Short History of, 176–180
Group Paper from Moral Issues in Parenting, Should
    We Be Raising Altruists, 237–245

H

Hasty conclusion, 159–160
Hegel, Georg Wilhelm, 74, 179–180
History of Philosophy Papers, 176–183
    hints on writing, 181–182
Hobbes, Thomas, 76, 178
How to Write a History of Philosophy Paper,
    180–181
How Verses Are Made (Vladimir Mayakovsky), 22
Humanist Manifesto II (American Humanist Associa-
    tion), 211
Hume, David, 179
Hypothetical deductive method, 148–149
Hypothetical syllogisms, 142–144

I

Ibid., use of, 129
Illustrations and figures, 109–110
Inconsistency, 156
Indirect proof, 145–146
Indirect proof or reductio ad adsurdum, 145–146
Induction, 147
    by elimination, 147
    by enumeration, 147
Inference, the best explanation, 148
Information, library, 87–94
Internet Resources for Writing Well, 99–100
Interviews, unpublished, 127
    citing, 126
    published or broadcast, 126
Invention strategies, 33–38
Invincible ignorance, 162

J

James, William, 167
Jargon, 40–41
Journal articles, citing, 119–121
Joy, Bill, 95

K

Kant, Immanuel, 74, 75, 179
Kindergarten wisdom, 209

L

Lack of proportion, 158
Language choices, 39
Lao-Tzu, 177
Laws and statutes, citing, 121–122
Leaves of Grass (Walt Whitman), 17
Legal references, citing, 123
Lower courts, 123

M

Magazine articles, citing, 120
Man of Reason (Genevieve Lloyd), 76
Manuscript in author's possession, 128
Map of How to Arrange a Philosophy Paper,
    150–151
Margins, 105
Mayakovsky Vladimir, 22
Mill, John Stuart, 18–19, 75, 133
Miscues, 45
Mistakes, catching, 45
Modifiers, dangling, 54
Modus ponens, 142
Modus tollens, 144

N

Narrow Sources of Information, 94–98
Newspaper articles, citing, 120
Nondeductive validity, 137–139

O

Organizing, 23–33
Organizing your thoughts, 38
Other Ethical Theories, 196–197
Outlining, 36–37
    for your reader, 37
    for yourself, 36–37

P

Page number, 105
Paper from Biomedical Ethics, Stem Cell Research,
    232–237
Paper from Personal Values, The Matrix, 226–231
Paper presented at meeting, 127
Parallelism, 54–56
Paraphrasing, 85
Pascal, Blaise, 208
Patterns of reasoning, 139–140
Perennial Issues for Political Ethics, Justice and Rights,
    198–202
Periodicals, citing, 119–121
Persuasive writing, 25
Philosopher's Index, The, 80
Philosophical Investigations, 80
Philosophical terms, technical and ordinary usage
    of, 69

Philosophical Works of Descartes, The (Elizabeth S. Haldane and G.R.T. Ross), 4–5
Philosophy, 1–48
  branches of, 17–48
  introduction to, 1–13
Plagiarism, 85–86
Plato, 177
Popper, Karl, 148
Popularity, 162
Position papers, 167–175
  definition, 167
  format of, 175
  steps in writing, 168–175
  writing sound arguments, 167–175
Preamble to the Constitution, 55
Premise, 5, 135
Primary research, 76
Probabilities, calculating, 163–164
Professional Code of Ethics, 204–206
Pronoun, vague references, 56–57
  agreement, 57
  errors, 56–57
  shift in person, 57–58
Proofreading, 46–47
Protagoras, 133
Provincialism, 161–162
Psychological certainty, 6–7
Public documents, citing, 121–123
Punctuation, 58–66
  apostrophe, 58–66
  capitalization, 59–60
  colon, 61
  comma, 61–63
  quotation marks, 63–65
  semicolon, 65–66

Q

Questionable analogy, 160–161
Questionable cause, 160
Questions, asking, 35–36
Quotation marks, 63–65
Quoting, 83–86

R

Reasoning, patterns of, 139–140
Reductio ad adsurdum, 145–146
Reference page, 110
Repetition, 44
Reprints of older works, citing, 118
Research, conducting, 73–129
Research institutes, 94
Research methods, 78–83
  determine usefulness, 80–81
  draft thesis and outline, 82–83
  effective, 77–83
  evaluate sources, 80–82

feedback, 83
first (rough) draft, 83
narrow topic and establish working thesis, 79
note cards, 82
use photocopies, 81
working bibliography, 79–80
Research process, 73–86
  effective methods, 77–83
  ethical use of source material, 83–86
  gaining control, 73–77
  organizing, 73–86
Research schedule, 78
Resources, 87–94
  directories, 87–91
  periodicals, 91–93
  periodical indexes, 93–94
Revising, catching mistakes, 45
  editing, 44–45
  miscues, 45
  proofreading, 46–47
Rorty, Richard, 152
Rough draft, 38–42

S

Sample Student Papers, 226–245
Scientist of Two Worlds, Louis Agassiz, A (Catherine Owens Pearce), 24
Scott, Jeremy, 215–219
Secondary research, 76–77
Semicolon, 65–66
Sentence structure, 52–56
  dangling modifiers, 54
  fused sentences, 52
  sentence fragments, 53–54
Sexist language, 42
Slip laws, 121–122
Socrates, 9–13, 134
Socratic dialectic, 134
Soundness, 137–139
Source material, ethical use of, 83–86
Statistical induction, 147
Statutes at Large, 122
Straw person, 156
Suppressed evidence, 157
Supreme Court, 123
Surface errors, 50
System Definition, 224–225

T

Tables and figures, lists of, 108–109
Tao, 210
Target Statement Analysis, 224
Tautologies, 141–142
Ten Commandments, 209–210
Text, 109
Thesis, 127

Thinking and writing like a philosopher, 131–246
Thoreau, Henry David, 184
Throws of argument, 133–135
Thus Spake Zarathustra (Friedrich Nietzsche), 212
Title page, 106
Two basic types of argument, 136–137
Two Sample Student Ethics Statements, 215–223
Two wrongs make a right, 158–159

U

U.S. Constitution, citing, 122
Unabomber Manifesto, 213
Unity, 43
Unpublished sources, citing, 127–128

V

Valid forms of argument, 140–141
Validity, 137–139
Validity and soundness, 137–139
Verity Identification, 225
Voices of Wisdom (Gary Kessler), 8

W

Walden, or Life in the Woods (Henry David Thoreau), 20
Way of Chuang Tzu, The (Thomas Merton trans.), 12
Weasel words, 41–42
What is Ethics?, 185–187
Wittgenstein, Ludwig, 104
Wright, Chauncey, 148
Writing, 23–33
  defining a purpose, 25–28
  defining your audience, 32–33
  finding a thesis, 28–30
  narrowing your topic, 24–25
  nature of the process, 23
  organizing, 23–33
  selecting a topic, 24
  thesis sentence, 30–32
Writing a Personal Ethics Statement, 208–225
Writing Applied Ethics Papers, 184–207
Writing Your Own Personal Code of Ethics, 213–215

X

Xenophanes of Colphon, 176